From the **Beginning of the End** to the **End of the Beginning**

The Past, Present and Future of Created Life

William S. Hyland

LUCIDBOOKS

From the Beginning of the End to the End of the Beginning
The Past, Present and Future of Created Life

Copyright © 2023 by William S. Hyland

Published by Lucid Books in Houston, TX
www.lucidbookspublishing.com

All Scripture quotations are taken from the (NASB®) New American Standard Bible®, Copyright © 1960, 1971, 1977, 1995, 2020 by The Lockman Foundation. Used by permission. All rights reserved. www.lockman.org

All rights reserved. No part of this publication may be reproduced, stored in a retrieval system, or transmitted in any form by any means, electronic, mechanical, photocopy, recording, or otherwise, without the prior permission of the publisher, except as provided for by USA copyright law.

ISBN: 978-1-63296-601-8
eISBN: 978-1-63296-602-5

Special Sales: Most Lucid Books titles are available in special quantity discounts. Custom imprinting or excerpting can also be done to fit special needs. For standard bulk orders, go to www.lucidbooksbulk.com. For specialty press or large orders, contact Lucid Books at books@lucidbookspublishing.com.

CONTENTS

Introduction	1
Prologue To Life	3
Creation Of Life	41
Yaweh's Sovereign Reign	67
Noah	87
Abraham	113
Isaac	125
Jacob	131
Joseph	147
What Went Wrong	193
Life Today	265
Time Unwinds	375
Time Is Running Out	381
Epilogue	411

INTRODUCTION

The Bible's opening phrase, "In the beginning God," is either fable-oriented or an absolute statement that is "perfect in quality... unqualified by extent or degree... the ultimate basis of all thought and being..." (The American Heritage Dictionary) It introduces the reader to "God" with this distinct contrast: He had existed before "the beginning" while "the heavens and the earth" had not, and the latter's start was made possible by the One Who has no beginning. This verse was inspired by Him (1 Timothy 3:16) through Moses to explain the startup of life in all its forms. God's Word is absolute and eternal, sufficient, clear, authoritative and necessary. (Isaiah 55:6-11) His word "is truth" (John 17:17); it is "living and abiding ...endures forever" (Isaiah 40:7; I Peter 1:23,25), "is alive and active..." (Hebrews 4:12)

It is for these reasons that I have intended all my writings be informed by the universal presupposition that all of Yaweh's inerrant and inspired words have been revealed to His creation as factual history. Many statements in the Scriptures do seem mysterious and elusive for human understanding – but so do the U. S. Navy's 2004 and 2015 confirmed sightings of "unidentified aerial phenomena" (cf. https://www.foxnews.com/tech/ufo-videos-real-navy-acknowledges) which cannot be explained by the sciences currently operative. Much of recorded history provides man a very limited though verifiable understanding of ancient realities.

PROLOGUE TO LIFE

Foundation for Life

"בְּרֵאשִׁית... / Ἐν ἀρχῇ" [In the beginning] opens the sacred writings universally recognized as the Bible. Moses's phrase indicates that God *is* even prior to the commencement of that beginning, that He Himself was not a consequence of His creating activity. I purposefully employ "*is*" because God eternally exists unconstrained by time, a mere aspect in creation. Thus, whatever the context is in the Bible's coverage of Him, even though the past as well as future verb tenses are traditionally used to describe His activities, God only "*does*" because He forever "*is*."

In its Old Testament many אֱלֹהִים are acknowledged (cf. Exodus 34:16), like Baal, Asheroh, Astarte and Anath (cf. Exodus 15:11, 20:3, 23.) The singular of אֱלֹהִים is אֵל, translated as deity or god, and was the title conceived and attributed by man to all four of the above mentioned; yet אֵל also, but infrequently, had been employed by Moses and other prophets when referring to the Creator: יְהוָה, אֵל עוֹלָם {the Lord, the everlasting God.} (Genesis

21:33) But right at the very beginnings of their writings Job and Moses titled the Creator with אֱלֹהִים, the plural of אֵל, which Moses possibly had first learned at the burning bush in Horeb {cf. Exodus 3:6.} And so throughout the Old Testament, whenever אֱלֹהִים is the subject in a sentence, its correlating verb always appears in the third-person singular (not the plural) mode. Interestingly, though, from the theological perspective this grammatical irregularity subtly upholds the unity (John 10:30) of the plurality within אֱלֹהִים:

> וַיֹּאמֶר (singular) אֱלֹהִים (plural), נַעֲשֶׂה (plural)...
>
> and God said, "Let us make..."
> —Genesis 1:26
>
> וַיֹּאמֶר יְהוָה אֱלֹהִים, הֵן הָאָדָם הָיָה כְּאַחַד מִמֶּנּוּ
>
> And Yaweh God said, "The man is becoming as one of us..."
> —Genesis 3:22

There does exist, though, a few exceptions to this general scheme:

- Genesis 20:13 - הִתְעוּ אֹתִי, אֱלֹהִים (plural)
- 2 Samuel 7:23 - אֲשֶׁר הָלְכוּ-אֱלֹהִים (plural)

In verse 2 Moses identifies the Creator as אֱלֹהִים, a formal title of power as well as of prominence. Rather than just being 'gods' { אֱלֹהִים is the plural noun of אֵל }, He is 'god of gods,' 'the true God' [הָאֱלֹהִים – Genesis 22:1,

Exodus 20:20], 'the one and only God.' [Deuteronomy 4:35,6:4] In all of Genesis Moses had designated אֱלֹהִים for God 179 times whereas only 19 times for אֵל. Yet it is interesting to note that in the Book of Job, considered an earlier inspired document than Genesis, Job used אֱלֹהִים only 17 times while אֵל 22 times.

In Genesis 2:4 Moses introduces the Creator as Yaweh [יְהוָה] God's personal name by which the Lord before Moses' time had introduced Himself to Isaac as אֵל אַבְרָהָם אָבִיךָ הֵי {God of your father Abraham} (Genesis 26:24) and to the wandering tribe of Israel as אָנֹכִי יְהוָה אֱלֹהֶיךָ {I am Yaweh your God.} (Exodus 20:2) This biblical combination, the personal name linked to the respective title, is consistent with identifying the Son of God as Jesus the Christ. God's personal name, יְהוָה {Yaweh}, is literally translated as "I am that I am," which indicates the infinite dimensions of His supreme being, power and nature. Jewish tradition, however, cautions man from calling God "Yaweh" because such intimacy offends Him and thus another title of address, אֲדֹנָי {Lord}, should be substituted.

Though all of creation was Yaweh's work, verse 2 mentions the presence only of His third Person, רוּחַ אֱלֹהִים, not of the Father nor of His Son. Both רוּחַ and πνεῦμα, the *LXX* counterpart, are varied and diverse in meaning: spirit, breath, wind, mind and animating force:

> In (the Lord's) hand is the...breath [רוּחַ/πνεῦμά] of all mankind...
>
> —Job 12:10

...life is in me and the Breath [רוּחַ/πνεῦμά] of God is in my nostrils.
—Job 27:3

Elihu:
"The Breath of God [רוּחַ-אֵל/πνεῦμά] has made me and the Breath of the Almighty [נִשְׁמַת שַׁדַּי] gives me life."
—Job 33:4

...If He should gather to Himself His mind [רוּחַ/πνεῦμά] and His breath [נִשְׁמָה]
—Job 34:14

"Thou dost send forth Your Breath [רוּחַ/πνεῦμά], they are created..."
—Psalm 104:30

The grass withers, the flower fades, when the breath [רוּחַ] of Yaweh blows upon it;
—Isaiah 40:7

...(Jesus) ἐνεφύσησεν [blew or breathed upon] (the disciples) and said to them, "Receive the ἅγιον [holy, i.e., set apart by God] Breath."
—John 20:22

And then that lawless one will be revealed whom the Lord (Jesus) will slay τῷ πνεύματι τοῦ στόματος [with the Breath of His words] and bring to an end with the appearance of His coming.
—2 Thessalonians 2:8

And πρὸς μὲν τοὺς ἀγγέλους [for the messengers] He says, "Ὁ ποιῶν τοὺς ἀγγέλους αὐτοῦ πνεύματα [Who {God in prior verse} makes His messengers winds] and His ministers a flame of fire."
—Hebrews 1:7

Human breath sources and conveys words, the process of which is identified as individual speech. I am convinced that Yaweh's רוּחַ is the conveyor of His words in the same way our breath is employed when we speak. He is His Holy Breath, Whom I identify as the Person functioning as the Father's specifically located presence (as opposed to His omnipresence) and executing agent:

> Yaweh:
> "...I will be with your mouth and (Aaron's) mouth, and I will teach you what you are to do ."
> —Exodus 4:15

"It is τὸ πνεῦμά [the Breath] Who gives life; the flesh profits nothing. The declaration I {Jesus} have spoken to you is πνεῦμά [breath] and is ζωή [life]. (John 6:63; cf. Job 33:4) John 4:24 informs us that "God is spirit," that each Person of our Triune God is a Holy Spirit, not just His third Person, and that is why I treat רוּחַ אֱלֹהִים as God's Breath or the Breath.

God's רוּחַ / πνεῦμά proceeds from {indicated by the genitive case} either the Father (Matthew 10:20; Romans 8:10-11; 2 Corinthians 1:21-22 and Ephesians 3:14-16) or His Son (Romans 8:9; Galatians 4:6; Philippians 1:19 and 1 Peter 1:11.) The function of His Breath is to source (Romans 15:19; 1 Corinthians 3:16; Galatians 5:22; Colossians 3:16), convey (Matthew 10:20; John 16:7-8; 1 Corinthians 2:10,13; 1 John 5:7) and execute (Zechariah 4:6; Acts 16:7; Romans 8:11) all that Yaweh desires.

2 Timothy 3:16 affirms that "all Scripture is breathed by God [θεόπνευστος]," the action by which His breath fills a person with the motivation and ability to do something creative for His glory. Whenever God "said," His speech was both caused and borne by His breath; worded anthropomorphically, His 'exhalation' conveyed the content of what God 'said.'

כִּי-כָל-עוֹד נִשְׁמָתִי בִי; וְרוּחַ אֱלוֹהַּ בְּאַפִּי

Job:
"For as long as life is in me and the Breath of God is in my nostrils."
—Job 27:3

One function of God's Breath is to form, convey, teach and remind (John 14:26) what Yaweh wants mankind to know by generating and delivering His "voice" whenever He wishes to "say" and be heard, like as "a voice from heaven." (Matthew 3:17; Mark 1:11; Luke 3:22; John 12:28) The opening and closing phrases of the first chapter in Genesis had been 'breathed out' by God's Breath into Moses' entire being in order to safeguard in written words the complete history of "the heavens and the earth." These God-breathed words are "living and abiding" (1 Peter 1:23), perfect, complete, pure and absolute in truth {cf. Isaiah 40:8.} Breath facilitates the execution and conveyance of speaking {the means} while word represents the content of what is being spoken {the end.} Consequently, this is why I always prefer to name רוּחַ אֱלֹהִים as 'God's Breath,' not His Spirit. After all, John wrote, "God is spirit" (John

4:24), which purports all three of His Persons is "spirit" – not just His third Person.

Now Moses's first sentence asserts that Yaweh had created הַשָּׁמַיִם / τὸν οὐρανὸν and הָאָרֶץ /τὴν γῆν. The Hebrew plural of שָׁמֶּה indicates "heaved up things (or) heights" while the *LXX* Greek singular implies "sky (or) air (and)...refer to the atmosphere just above the earth {cf. Genesis 1:20; Hebrews 1:10-11} in the open expanse of the heavens."[1] In the opening verse, then, "the heavens and the earth" collectively represent not 'an environment with all therein' but a bare foundation {cf. Isaiah 48:13,51:13} conducive for and supportive of what has yet to be created. As verse 2 describes, Yaweh established the earth as barren and empty, far from what we know it as today.

The opening phrase of Genesis is a Hebrew noun prefixed by the preposition בּ, which broadly translates: in, within, among, at, before, by, into, upon or against; its corresponding Koine Greek preposition, ἐν, is translated somewhat similarly: in, on, at, before, among, within. The initial verb is בָּרָא {3 psm *qal* perfect}, indicating a past activity; had verse 2 begun as הָאָרֶץ וְהָיְתָה instead of וְהָאָרֶץ, הָיְתָה, Hebrew scholars would insist the prefixed *vov* [וְ] indicates narrative continuity and because the prior verb in verse 1, בָּרָא, is in the perfect tense, would consequently translation וְהָיְתָה as " and then the earth became empty..." However, וְהָאָרֶץ, הָיְתָה indicates the sense of consequence, a completed result: "and the

---

1. Evangelical Dictionary of Theology, W. A. Elwell, editor, Baker Book House, 2017

earth (was) a waste and emptiness." The *qal* perfect tense of בָּרָא "denotes action that is completed and over with, or a state achieved and complete."[2] Thus the narrative states that the beginning consisted of, not commenced with, God creating what verse 2 describes: water, submerged landmass {cf. v. 10; 2 Peter 3:5} and atmosphere evidently devoid of all gases and particulate matter, all three of which indicate the existence of space.

Completion of "the beginning" also is implied in verses 1 and 4 of chapter 2: "Then the heavens and the earth and the sun, moon and stars] were completed [בָּרָא]...the heavens and the earth ...were created [בָּרָא] ... God made[עָשָׂה] earth and heaven..." Moses's inclusion of צְבָא in Genesis 2:1 indicates expansive and qualitative refinements to what existed in verse 1:2 because the essence of צְבָא was the focus of verses 1:15-17; the *LXX*'s counterpart of צְבָא is κόσμος, which is broader in meaning: world order, universe and mankind – none of which 'existed' in verse 1:2. Note: Moses had not intended any distinction in meaning between בָּרָא and עָשָׂה inasmuch as he treated them as synonymous: "In the day when God בָּרָא man. He עָשָׂה him in the likeness of God." (Genesis 5:1; cf. Genesis 1:26-27,2:3.} בָּרָא is to create and includes to generate, produce, design, make, fabricate, fashion, manufacture, originate, invent, initiate, devise whereas עָשָׂה means to make, fabricate as well as to do. Moses' description, חֹשֶׁךְ עַל־פְּנֵי תְהוֹם [darkness was over a body of water], in verse 2 makes me wonder whether Yaweh's Breath had executed the

---

2. Introduction To Hebrew, Moshe Greenberg, Prentice-Hall Inc., 1965, page 46

creation of "the waters" *ex nihilo* [out of nothing] or had He priorly created it at another spiritual 'project' site. Unfortunately we cannot deduce an answer here because he only tells us His Breath was hovering.

All the water on Earth came from space in exactly the form it's in now, H2O...(It) started out as the finest mist, the smallest ice cubes, drifting around inside an interstellar dust cloud...The hydrogens and oxygens literally mate on the surface of tiny grains of dust that are part of the interstellar clouds...In (an interstellar) cloud, says (Gary) Melnick (Harvard University's Center for Astrophysics), "hydrogen hits the dust grains quite frequently. And every once in a while oxygen will hit the dust grains too, and linger."...Water really is the genesis ingredient for life at all levels – water is so fundamental to everything involved in creating, reproducing, and sustaining life that it's possible to imagine that God created water, and let water do the work to create life.[3]

Then יַעַשׂ אֱלֹהִים, אֶת-הָרָקִיעַ [God made the expanse] to separate "the waters" {v. 7}; in other words, He divided "the waters" in order to create a distance above and below the now separated bodies and called the resulting space "the heavens":

הַשָּׁמַיִם, מְסַפְּרִים כְּבוֹד-אֵל;   וּמַעֲשֵׂה יָדָיו, מַגִּיד הָרָקִיעַ.

> David:
> "The heavens are telling of the glory of God, and their expanse is declaring the work of His hands."
> —Psalm 19:1

---

3. **The Big Thirst**, Charles Fishman, Free Press, NYC, 2011, pages 29-31,44

"The heavens" at that moment apparently had not included what Yaweh would create in verses 11 to 18. To finalize the completion of His foundation for life Yaweh commanded, "let the dry land {possibly the amalgamation of cosmic dust} appear" with "the waters below the heavens" in His designated space; after they had fully materialized, He called the gathering of the waters below salt-free "seas" and the dry land "earth." (vs. 9-10) The status of the waters "above the distance" (v. 7) will be discussed in a later chapter.

"The waters" (v. 2), "the heavens" (v. 8) and "the dry land" (v. 9) comprised "the beginning," a rudimentary foundation upon which God intended to create all of life. The essential purpose of "the beginning" was to serve as the foundation for all that He would then form and create thereafter, outlined by Moses in verses 6 to 31.

> An afflicted man:
> "From ancient times You founded/laid (the) foundation of the earth [לְפָנִים, הָאָרֶץ יָסַדְתָּ]..."
> —Psalm 102:25

> (The Lord) established the earth upon its foundations/bases [מְכוֹנֶיהָ]...
> —Psalm 104:5

> "...Yaweh...created the heavens (He is the God Who formed the earth and made it, He established it and did not create it {to be} a waste place, formed it to be inhabited)...
> —Isaiah 45:18

> For since (the) creation {κτίσις} of the world {κόσμος} His invisible attributes, His eternal power and divine nature, have been clearly seen, being understood through what has been made, so that they are without excuse.
> —Romans 1:20

Nevertheless, the firm foundation {θεμέλιος} of God stands, having this seal,

> "The Lord knows those who are His," and, "Everyone who names the name of the Lord is to abstain from wickedness."
> —2 Timothy 2:19

> "You, Lord, in the beginning laid the foundation {θεμελιόω} of the earth, and the heavens are the works of your hands;
> —Hebrews 1:10

Life had yet to exist before or during Yaweh's creation of "the heavens and the earth" and as described in verse 2 neither was life a consequence of "the beginning"; the foundation for life was the rock on which all of life would come into being.

Now the start of verse 3, וַיֹּאמֶר אֱלֹהִים, appears nine times in Genesis 1 and has been traditionally translated "God said," but without ever indicating to whom. Was He addressing a spiritual audience like heavenly hosts? Or was He talking reflexively, i.e., communicating within Themselves? The opening verses of Genesis offer no solution to this quandary inasmuch as they do not specify the presence of Yaweh's two other Persons Who comprise His indivisible unity {cf. John 10:30,15:26.} Thus it seems reasonable to deduce that in verse 2 the Father and His Son, though unmentioned, were indeed present with רוּחַ אֱלֹהִים and that in verse 3 God's audience was the unified 'Themselves,' the Father, His Son and His Breath. Therefore, God was decreeing [אָמַר] mutually agreeable deeds to and among Themselves {cf. Genesis 3:22.} It's interesting to note that preceding Moses's recording of His creating "the heavens and the earth" no such decree had been recorded, nor was there any "and the heavens and the earth became" mentioned by Moses.

The three spiritual Persons unified as Yaweh serially expressed Their decisive intentions of what was to become and thereby automatically triggered the accomplishment of what They had in mind. Each of Yaweh's addressing Themselves in effect serves as a decree, a unanimous agreement of all three Persons, of what sequentially was to become 'reality' in and on the then created land mass. These nine declarations possess a causative power, the nature of which was attributed later in the Scriptures as out-workings of God's Breath. Whatever Yaweh had decreed with the words "there is to be" automatically comes to pass by the agency of His רוּחַ.

So then, what is "the light?" Jesus indeed was the light in and of the world but is He "the light that became" for which we are searching? The answer is found in the melding of the following verses the apostle John had been inspired to write:

Ἐν ἀρχῇ ἦν ὁ λόγος, καὶ ὁ λόγος ἦν πρὸς τὸν θεόν, καὶ θεὸς ἦν ὁ λόγος. [In the beginning ἦν

[was {imperfect tense}] the Word and the Word ἦν [was] πρὸς [in company with] God and God ἦν [was] The Word.
—John 1:1

He was in the beginning with God. All things came into being through Him...
—John 1:2-3

...the world was made through Him and the world did not know {cf. Revelation 19:12} Him... And The Word became flesh..."
—John 1:10,14

And I {the apostle John} saw heaven opened and behold, a white horse and He who sat upon it is called Faithful and True and in righteousness He judges and wages war...and is clothed with a robe dipped in blood and His name is called ὁ λόγος τοῦ θεοῦ [The Word of God {which no one knows except Himself}]
—Revelation 19:11-13

Essentially John 1:1 [Ἐν ἀρχῇ ἦν ὁ λόγος...πρὸς τὸν θεόν, καὶ θεὸς ἦν ὁ λόγος] serves as the heart of my reasoning, with Revelation 19:13 providing this key: His name is called ὁ λόγος τοῦ θεοῦ. Then follow these reasonable deductions: aided by Genesis 1:2:
  1. **His Breath was also in company with God and God was the Breath (Genesis 1:2);**
  2. **The Word of God and His Breath were in company with God {cf. John 1:2-3} and God was The Father;**

3. Jesus: "I and the Father are one." (John 10:30);
4. Jesus: "He who believes in Me does not believe in Me but in Him who sent Me." (John 12:44)

Therefore, the unity of אֱלֹהִים, the Father, the Son and His Breath, was present בְּרֵאשִׁית /'Ἐν ἀρχῇ [in the beginning (Genesis 1:1)] and thus Jesus Christ was indeed present for "by the Word of God heavens existed long ago and earth was formed out of water and by water." (2 Peter 3:5) As the direct consequence, Jesus was not the light that יְהִי [became (Genesis 1:3)] inasmuch as He ἦν [was {note: the imperfect tense, which describes event(s) ongoing or without a specific time period in the past}] eternally in the company of God and thus ἦν present בְּרֵאשִׁית /'Ἐν ἀρχῇ. Mankind's comprehension of human life created in Genesis 1 makes it difficult for it to understand as well as to relate to Yaweh's eternal existence, expressed as "I am that I am." (Exodus 3:14) A cause for this predicament is that all the actions His Breath conveys by means of verbal inspiration contain no verb tenses, like, for instance, Yaweh is always: He was, is and will be, "having neither beginning of days nor end of life…(and) abides…perpetually." (Hebrews 7:3) Mankind's ζωή [life], on the other hand, is a created state and environment and is subject to termination; but for a "few" (Matthew 7:14,20:16), the "many" (Matthew 20:28; Mark 10:45 ;Romans 5:19,12:5; Hebrews 2:10,9:28), their disembodied souls will become resurrected to a state with an everlasting duration. Ἡ ζωή had not existed prior to Genesis 1:1-3 because it was the focus as well as the byproduct of Yaweh's creating process which started at "the beginning." Yaweh's utterance by His Breath, "light יְהִי" [becomes], excluding both בָּרָא and עָשָׂה and thus inferring an action that is neither creative nor sculpting in essence. The verb at the end of verse 3, יְהִי is not synonymous with either בָּרָא or עָשָׂה, for it indicates that "the light" was neither" created (or) made" (Genesis 2:3.); rather it was in the state/action of not-yet-accomplished.[4]

From the human perspective believers of Yaweh respect Him as three omnipresent spiritual Persons yet of just 'one substance,' infinitely present everywhere simultaneously. The Scriptures inform us that "the light" is His glory, His discernable, radiant presence; φῶς is the light of God's presence {cf. 2 Corinthians 11:14; 1 Timothy 6:16}:

> ...Yaweh was "in a pillar of fire by night to give them light, that they might travel by day and by night. He did not take away...the pillar of fire... from before the people...
> —Exodus 13:21-22

> For throughout all their journeys...there was fire in (the tabernacle) by night, in the sight of all the house of Israel.
> —Exodus 40:34,36-38

> "...the light of (the Lord's) countenance...
> —Psalm 4:6, 44:3, 89:15; Isaiah 2:5

---

4. Introduction to Hebrew, Moshe Greenberg, Prentice-Hall Inc., 1965, page 49

Now God says in Genesis 1:14, יְהִי מְאֹרֹת / *LXX*: γενηθήτωσαν φωστῆρες, and the respective translations give the sense that what had become is markedly different than what has been traditionally rendered: מְאֹרֹת is the plural of מָאוֹר and translates: lights, luminaries like the sun, the moon; and φωστῆρες is the plural of φωστήρ and translates: lights, luminaries {cf. Philippians 2:15.} Moses explains the purpose for creating these lights / luminaries is to "give light on the earth and to govern the day and the night and to separate and to govern the day and the night, and to separate the light from the darkness; and God saw that it was good." (Genesis 1: 17-18) What He deemed כִּי טוֹב verse 18 was the universe He had just completed creating. Therefore, the essence of "the light" in verses 4-5 is not part of the luminaries in verse 14. Light is the symbol for goodness and righteousness; this metaphor represents as well Yaweh's special presence but does not appear in verses 1-2. Though Jesus, too, is not "the light," He indeed was "the light" while He was in this world; His life while on the earth reflected and beamed "the light" of the spiritual realm Genesis 1:3-5 mentions. The divinely written Book of Life provides a convincing understanding as to what it really might be:

> David:
> "...in (the Lord's) book were all written the days that were ordained for me, when as yet there was not one of them.
> —Psalm 139:16

...grace...granted us in Christ Jesus πρό χρόνων αἰωνίων (from the beginning of time)... now has been revealed by the appearing of our Savior Christ Jesus, who abolished death and φωτίσαντος (brought to light) life and ἀφθαρσίαν (immortality) through the gospel.
—2 Timothy 1:9-10

...(God) chose us in Him πρό (before) καταβολῆς (beginning) κόσμου (of universe)...
—Ephesians 1:4

...God has chosen you from the beginning for salvation...
—2 Thessalonians 2:13

...who are chosen according to πρόγνωσις (foreknowledge) of God, by the sanctifying work of the Breath...may obey Jesus Christ and be sprinkled with His blood...For {Christ} προγινώσκω [was foreknown] πρό [before καταβολῆς [beginning] κόσμου [of universe]... but has appeared in these last times for the sake of {the chosen.}
—1 Peter 1:1-2,20

All who dwell on the earth will worship (the Beast), everyone whose name has not been written ἀπὸ [since] καταβολῆς [beginning] {κόσμου [of universe] in the book of life of the Lamb {cf. 21:27} who has been slain.
—Revelation 13:8

...those who dwell on the earth, whose name has not been written in the book of life ἀπὸ [since] καταβολῆς [beginning] {κόσμου [of universe]...
—Revelation 17:8

> Anyone whose name was not found written in
> the book of life was thrown into the lake of fire.
> —**Revelation 20:15**

That no light nor reflection of it had existed in "the beginning" is verified when by His Breath God announced יְהִי אוֹר . (verse 3) The Hebrew verb, יְהִי, is in the jussive 3psm mood and translates, "is to be" whereas the *LXX* reads γενηθήτω {3ps aorist 1 passive imperative)}, "is to become." Moses responds with the same verb but as 3 וַיְהִי, psm *wow* consecutive, translated in the past tense, "was so;" the *LXX* was similar: ἐγένετο (3ps aorist 2), "became." His Breath causes הָאוֹר to become, not be created. The *jussive* mood expresses the speaker's desire, wish or command and Moses confirms what God's Breath has caused to become, not be created: הָאוֹר. (verse 4) While Moses's account implicitly attributes full authorship of the book of life to the triune God אֱלֹהִים, Jesus inferred that His Father is its major author {cf. Matthew 20:23,24.36.}

The next eight decrees by Yaweh possess the same causative power, the nature of which is described later in the Scriptures as out-workings of His Breath. Each of His nine decrees, authorized by unanimous agreement of all three Persons, becomes automatically part of the expanding reality in and on the 'infant' earth, even though mankind will never know how long that took.

What God saw in verse 4 was הָאוֹר whereas what He had decreed to become in the prior verse is אוֹר. Addition of the definite article highlights the distinction of general light versus specific light. God regards "the light" [הָאוֹר / *LXX*: τὸ φῶς] as pleasant / good [כִּי-טוֹב] in its completed state and then, in verse 5, distinguishes [בָּדַל] it from "the" darkness, the definite article's specificity referring darkness here to that "over the surface of the deep" in verse 2, by naming "the light" day [יוֹם] and "the darkness" night [עֶרֶב]. To me the appropriate translation here for יוֹם, however, should be "aura," defined as a distinctive quality that seems to surround and be generated by something. My reasoning is based on this translation of verse 4: God regarded the light as agreeable / pleasant [טוֹב] and God perceived/ became aware of the difference [וַיַּבְדֵּל-3 psm *hifil* future] between the light and the darkness. There is no moral sense for darkness here; the distinguishing factor attributed to darkness is its essence is totally devoid of any light.

Light of "day" today is the natural agent stimulating sight and making objects visible but "the light" God saw in verse 4 is definitely not the lights He formed in the fourth יוֹם {cf. verses 14-17.}

In no way is man enabled to appreciate the essence of "I am that I am," i.e., Yaweh's 'personal' name which reflects His eternal existence: God is always; He was, is and will be, "having neither beginning of days nor end of life...abides...perpetually."(Hebrews 7:3) But to mankind life [ζωή] is a created state within a created environment; it is subject to a start followed by a termination, though for a "few" (Matthew 7:14,20:16), the "many" (Matthew 20:28;Mark 10:45; Romans 5:19,12:5;Hebrews 2:10,9:28), it becomes resurrected to an everlasting domain. Ἡ ζωὴ, however, had yet to come into existence in the first five verses of Genesis 1 but from verse 6 it becomes the focal theme of Yaweh's creating prowess and accomplishments.

His Breath's utterance in Genesis 1:3 used the verb יְהִי, not בָּרָא nor עָשָׂה, nor was Moses's וַיְהִי at the end of the verse synonymous with either בָּרָא or עָשָׂה. This signifies not that "the light" had been the result of having been created out of nothing but that it merely 'became'; it just came into existence inasmuch as וַיְהִי, a wow consecutive, 3 psm verb form, connotes completion. While darkness had reigned over "the surface of the deep" God had ordered light and it inexplicably just "became" (verse 2), like as Paul had written:

> "Light shall shine out of darkness."
> —2 Corinthians 4:6

> The light shines in the darkness, and the darkness did not overpower it.
> —John 1:5

To perpetuate "the light's" difference/distinction with the deep's "darkness" He called [וַיִּקְרָא] the former 'day' and the latter 'night' as moral/ethical symbols; in 'divine parlance,' day is to symbolize goodness as night is to symbolizes evil for when time becomes created {cf. Psalm 139:16.}

While at this point the identity and essence of "the light" still remains elusive, 1 John 1:1 provides a very fruitful clue:
1. What was from the beginning [Ὃ ἦν ἀπ' ἀρχῆς] ...what we beheld and our hands handled

[ὃ ἐθεασάμεθα καὶ αἱ χεῖρες ἡμῶν ἐψηλάφησαν], **concerning the word of life** [περὶ τοῦ λόγου τῆς ζωῆς -]

The relevancy here is that λόγος, usually translated as "word," has been rendered "book" {cf. Acts 1:1}, though rarely. Thus "λόγος τῆς ζωῆς" could be translated as a synonym for βίβλος τῆς ζωῆς but with this distinction: the former refers to eternal life with Christ Jesus while the latter's focus is on earthly, temporal life during which the former is spread. In other words, the λόγος τῆς ζωῆς is the 'spine' of, the continous theme throughout, the βίβλος τῆς ζωῆς, to which, later on apparently when speaking to John, an angel had referred. The βίβλος τῆς ζωῆς contains the λόγος τῆς ζωῆς whereas the λόγος τῆς ζωῆς is the developing subject of the βίβλος τῆς ζωῆς.

While in a state of mind with God's Breath, John was informed that "all who dwell on the earth will worship (the beast) {every one} whose name has not been written ἀπὸ καταβολῆς κόσμου [from the foundation of the world in the book of life of the Lamb who has been slain."(Revelation 13:8) Then in Revelation 17:8 the angel affirmed to him that "the book (and thus the word) of life" had been written ἀπὸ καταβολῆς κόσμου [from the foundation of the world.]" In both verses ἀπὸ, a preposition, purports the sense of 'when': forth from {out from a starting point and forward}, derivation from. Thus Revelation 17:8 can be read: the book (and thus word) of life had been written from completion of the world's founding. Paul employs the preposition πρὸ to posit a physical position - in front, before (of place - cf.

Matthew 11:10): ...just as He chose us in Him in front of the completed foundation of the world [πρὸ καταβολῆς κόσμου]... (Ephesians 1:4) And other verses as well allude to the timing of the writing of the book of life:

> David:
> "...in (the Lord's) book [סֵפֶר / βίβλος] were all written the days that were ordained for me, when as yet there was not one of them.
> —Psalm 139:16

> ...the Lord has a day of vengeance...seek from the book [מֵעַל-סֵפֶר / -] of the Lord...
> —Isaiah 34:8,16)

> ...grace...granted us in Christ Jesus before the beginning of time [πρό χρόνων αἰωνίων]
> —2 Timothy 1:9

> ...God has chosen you derived from the beginning [ἀπαρχὴν] for salvation...
> —2 Thessalonians 2:13

> For (Christ) was foreknown before beginning of universe [προγινώσκω πρό καταβολῆς κόσμου]...
> —1 Peter 1:20

> ...everyone whose name has not been written since beginning of world [ἀπὸ καταβολῆς κόσμου] in the book of life of the Lamb {cf. 21:27}...
> —Revelation 13:8

Ὁ λόγος / βίβλος τῆς ζωῆς is "Your book which You have written" (Exodus 32:32), "the book of the Lord" (Isaiah 34:16), "the book of life" (Psalm 69:28; Philippians 4:3), "the Lamb's book of life." (Revelation 13:3) The Book of Life (Philippians 4:3) includes the complete census of those who are enrolled [ἀπογράφω] in heaven (Hebrews 12:23), the heirs of Christ's kingdom. (James 2:5)

> Jesus:
> "...rejoice that your names are recorded [ἐγγράφω] in heaven."
> —Luke 10:20

"...the light of life" (John 8:12) is eternal life and the word of life (Philippians 2:16) is the Gospel of Jesus Christ. Life's light, word and book comprise the Scriptures, which have been heard and seen (Acts 4:20), beheld (John 1:14), handled (Luke 24:30) and manifested (John 1:4; 1 John 1:4) since after creation.

1 John 1:1 declares: Ὁ λόγος τῆς ζωῆς ἦν ἀπ' ἀρχῆς [the word of life was before the beginning] with ἀπὸ translating as 'since, at a subsequent time, after some point in the past,' thus signifying that the Lamb's (Revelation 21:27) Book of Life had been divinely completed before Yaweh had separated the waters from the waters. [Genesis 1:6] Yet it's the following three words which 'zero in' on what "the light's" essence and identity are:

1. προγινώσκω/πρόγνωσις [know before/ foreknowledge.] Πρόγνωσις sounds like

'prognosis' but does not mean a forecast, prediction or prophecy; rather it indicates that Yaweh had foreknown the "few" and "many" sinners He had chosen for His Son's heavenly kingdom. Collectively considered, these three words point to a 'master plan' in which the book of life plausibly comes into being as part of a divine strategy, as a stipulation of a divine pact among the three Persons of the Godhead. Also, the book of life presupposes a termination of what He will create: a 'new life' for His chosen many. John 1:8 informs us that "Jesus μαρτυρήσ) ῃmight testify/ declare) about "the light." Jesus's mission on earth was twofold: to testify as a witness about "the light of life" [John 8:12] and to mediate (cf. Hebrews 12:24) and fulfill the pact He had made with His Father and His Breath, the same pact which Christians all revere as the Covenant of Grace. πρόγνωσις is God's foreknowledge [πρόγνωσις], His infinite ability to know beforehand [προγινώσκω] all that happens in life:

For those whom He foreknew [προγινώσκω], He also predestined to become conformed to the image of His Son...
—Romans 8:29

God has not rejected His people whom He foreknew [προγινώσκω].
—Romans 11:2

> ...who are chosen according to the foreknowledge [πρόγνωσις] of God, by the sanctifying work of the Breath...
> —1 Peter 1:1-2

> For He was foreknown [προγινώσκω] before [προ – of place] the foundation of the world, but has appeared in these last times for the sake of you (1 Peter 1:20) ...those who were long beforehand marked out [προγράφω] for this condemnation, ungodly persons who turn the grace of our God into licentiousness and deny our only Master and Lord, Jesus Christ.
> —Jude 4

2. ὁρίζω = determine

> "For indeed, the Son Of Man is going as it has been determined [ὁρίζω];
> —Luke 22:22

> Peter:
> "this is the One who has been appointed [ὁρίζω] by God as Judge of the living and the dead."
> —Acts 10:42

> Paul:
> "and he made from one man every nation of mankind to live on all the face of the earth, having determined [ὁρίζω] their appointed times and the boundaries of their habitation..."
> —Acts 17:2)

> Paul:
> "He will judge the world in righteousness through a Man whom He has appointed [ὁρίζω]..."
> —Acts 17:31

3. βουλή = plan

> **Paul:**
> "...David, after he had served the plan [βουλή] of God in his own generation, fell asleep..."
> —Acts 13:36

> ...we have obtained an inheritance, having been predestined according to His plan [βουλή] who works all things after the counsel of His will...
> —Ephesians 1:11

> God, desiring even more to show to the heirs of the promise the unchangeableness of His purpose [βουλή]...
> —Hebrews 6:17

The amalgamation of the notion provided by these three words, 'foreknowledge emanating from a predetermined plan,' has been well expressed by Peter:

> "this Man, delivered over by the predetermined plan [τῇ ὡρισμένῃ βουλῇ] and foreknowledge [πρόγνωσις] of God, you nailed to a cross by the hands of godless men and put Him to death.
> —Acts 2:23

Collectively considered, then, these three words point to the notion that the book of life is the perfect spiritual plan for the creation of life on the earth, the foundation for which was to be the start of Yaweh's creating activity. This reminds me of Jesus' wisdom regarding the planning of a project:

"For which one of you, when he wants to build a tower, does not first sit down and calculate the cost to see if he has enough to complete it?...Or what king, when he sets out to meet another king in battle, will not first sit down and take counsel whether he is strong enough with ten thousand to encounter the one coming against him with twenty thousand?"
—Luke 14:28,31

That God was guided by the book of life became evident to various godly authors:

Moses: "...Your book which You have written."
—Exodus 32:32

"You have taken account of my wanderings; put my tears in Your bottle. Are they not in Your book [סֵפֶר]?"
—Psalm 56{55}:8

David: ἐ / אִמְסֵפֶר חַיִּים βίβλου ζώντων [a book of life]
—Psalm 69(8):28

"Your eyes have seen my unformed substance and in Your book [סֵפֶר / βίβλος] were all written the days that were ordained for me, when as yet there was not one of them.
—Psalm 139:16

It will come about that he who is left in Zion and remains in Jerusalem will be called holy -everyone who is recorded [כָּתַב / γραφή] for life in Jerusalem.
—Isaiah 4:3

...seek from the book [סֵפֶר / -] of the Lord...
—Isaiah 34:16

Vision to Daniel:
"...at that time your people, everyone who is found written in the book [/ סֵפֶרβίβλος], will be rescued."
—Daniel 12:1

...whose names are in the book [βίβλος] of life [ζωή].
—Philippians 4:3

All who dwell on the earth will worship him, everyone whose name has not been written from the foundation of the world in the book [βίβλος] of life [ζωή] of the Lamb who has been slain.
—Revelation 13:8

... those who dwell on the earth, whose name has not been written in the book [βίβλος] of life [ζωή], from the foundation of the world...
—Revelation 17:8

And if anyone's name was not found written in the book [βίβλος] of life [ζωή], he was thrown into the lake of fire.
—Revelation 20:15

...and nothing unclean, and no one who practices abomination and lying, shall ever come into it, but only those whose names are written in the Lamb's book [βίβλος] of life [ζωή].
—Revelation 21:27

Its synonyms include "the book of the Lord" (Psalm 139:16; Isaiah 34:16); "the Lamb's book of life"(Revelation 13:3, 21:27); Ὁ λόγος τῆς ζωῆς [the written narrative of life] (Philippians 4:3), which is the complete 'census' of the heirs of Christ's kingdom (James 2:5); "...the light of life" (John 8:12) is life in its 'eternalness' and the λόγον ζωῆς [word of life] (Philippians 2:16) is the revelation and teachings of Jesus Christ. These three synonyms, the book, the light and the word, comprise the entire Scriptures, which have been heard and seen (Acts 4:20), beheld (John 1:14), handled (Luke 24:30) and manifested (cf. John 1:4; 1 John 1:4) ever since the founding {cf. Psalm 102:25;104:5; Hebrews 1:10} of life's foundation, "the beginning [ἀρχή] of creation [κτίσις.]"(II Peter 3:4).

While pondering what the "light" in Genesis 1:3-5 is, a wise inquiry by Jesus 'came to mind': "For which one of you, when he wants to build a tower, does not first sit down and calculate the cost to see if he has enough to complete it?" (Luke 14:28) Today a wise person wishing to build a 'dream' home depends on a myriad of specialists for guidance: architect, interior designer, lighting designer; structural engineer, zoning lawyer, development regulation expert, environmental scientist, landscape architect, accountant, etc. Building the 'ideal' house is a major human task that requires a team of professionals for guidance toward a desired accomplishment. Genesis 1:2 generally describes the spiritual 'location' Yaweh had chosen for His intended project. But יְהִי, the qal future, 3psm of היה, implies Yaweh had not yet completed but was still in the process of finalizing the 'ultra' meticulous details of Their plans for this site. There is absolutely no way we humans are able to know whether the accomplishments of Genesis 1 and 2 were the Trinity's first such venture or merely one of Their many, and consequently we cannot speculate on whether Yaweh had any prior involvement with the semblance of 'life' in physical space and time. His involvement with the formation of "the light" included the complete compilation of the book of life, which back then would have had to include even the many who have yet to been born today.

The phrase "the heavens and the earth" in the opening verse signifies the fulfillment of life's creation, all of which is to be accomplished between the dawning of the second "day" (v. 6) and the end of the fourth "day." (v. 19) In saying this I realize I've lumped vegetation in with water and minerals as ingredients of the earth but I consider all three elements of the earth merely as sustenance for the life yet to be created. In other words, I consider flora part of the earth, an element for the support of life {cf. v. 29}, not life itself, which is the next focus of Yaweh's creating activities in verses 20-27.

The completeness and integrity of the book of life are protected by God forever, even though He made this threat: "Whoever has sinned against Me, I will blot out [מָחָה] of My book [סֵפֶר / βίβλος]" (Exodus 32:33), which was offered inversely by the angel to John: "He who overcomes will thus be clothed in white garments; and I will not erase his name from the book [βίβλος] of life [ζωή]..." (Revelation 3:5) David echoed His sentiment: "May they be blotted out [מָחָה] of the book [סֵפֶר / γραφή] of life [חַיִּים / ζώντων] and not be listed with the righteous."(Psalm 69:28{29}) But these 'threat-like' statements were outgrowths of the speakers' serious concerns about, and possible veiled threats against, mankind:

> The Lord mourned [נָחַם / -] that He had made man on the earth, and He suffered pain [עָצַב / -] in His heart. The Lord said, "I will destroy [מָחָה] man whom I have created from the face of the land, from man to animals to things and to birds of the sky; for I grieve [[נָחַם that I have made them."
>
> —Genesis 6:6-7

The book of life [βίβλος τῆς ζωῆς] is "the light" of Genesis 1:3 because it "became" God's perfectly comprehensive, guiding plan for creating all life as well as the environments for its sustenance. The word of life [λόγος τῆς ζωῆς], His gift of eternal life to all the world's inhabitants (John 3:16-17), is the theme woven throughout this book, up to and including the complete destruction of earthly life itself.

Though the book of life determines the ultimate termination of all that He was to create (cf. verses 6 to 31), it focuses on a spiritual 'new life' for God's chosen many proclaimed and procured in Jesus's earthly ministry: to testify/ declare [μαρτυρήσῃ] about the light." (John 1:8) The basic function of the book of life is to enable fulfillment of "the eternal purpose which (God would carry) out in Christ Jesus." (Ephesians 3:11) Jesus's mission in earthly life was twofold: to testify as a witness about "the light of life" (John 8:12) and to mediate {cf. Hebrews 12:24} and fulfill the pact, woven throughout the book of life, He had made with His Father and His Breath, the same pact which the Christian faith reveres as the Covenant of Grace.

The divine forming and creating activity of Genesis 1:6-31 over and under the foundation of verse 2 was to be guided by "the light," His book of life, His perfect plan for the creation of life and the environment to nurture and sustain it. The book of life is the Trinity's infinitely detailed 'master plan' for the creation of life, including its design, architecture, blue prints, development, construction, code of ethics {rules to godliness}, jurisprudence { all the covenants culminating in the New Testament}, sovereign governance as well as its cataclysmic termination. In addition, it incorporates the complete the "word of (eternal) life" {cf. John 8:12} as well as retains the full record of those who are enrolled [ἀπογράφω] in heaven. (Hebrews 12:23) Before the start of life, its outcome had been determined; though fraught with symbols, hints and mysteries leading up to it, the final phase of Yaweh's plan for life is the book of Revelation itself. The essence of His πρόγνωσις (foreknowledge) had been established before life began. The governance dynamic He administered in His relationships with every human being is expressed well by Genesis 50:20: what man means for evil Yaweh means for good. And today's status of creation is precisely as He has intended and planned: Yaweh's providence (His completely holy, wise and powerful preserving and governing every creature and every action, ordering them all to His own glory) and sovereignty (supreme power & authority) includes His foreknowledge of all that happens in life inasmuch as He originally planned and created it. To boggle your mind about that, just ponder how your own birth had worked its way onto the stage of life through one of the first couple's children!

Though the 'author' of the book of life is the Triune God, Jesus purports there is something only the Father knows concerning the concluding part of this book {cf. Matthew 24:36; Mark 13:32.} Jesus had pledged the earthly sacrifice of His human form in exchange for the Father's forgiveness of all sins committed by those humans named in the book, yet He apparently had not been privileged to know the exact time, i.e., "the day and hour," when He would join the heirs {cf. Matthew 25:34; James 2:5} of His kingdom. A hierarchical authority structure within Yaweh's divine unity is made apparent:

> Jesus:
> "All things have been handed over to Me by My Father..."
> —Matthew 11:27

> And Jesus came up and spoke to them, saying, "All authority has been given to Me in heaven and on earth."
> —Matthew 28:18

> Jesus, knowing that the Father had given all things into His hands, and that He had come forth from God and was going back to God,
> —John 13:3

Jesus:
"...even as You gave (Me) authority over all flesh...
—John 17:2

Jesus received such authority from His Father to enable Him to fulfill the covenant He had "cut," i.e., formally made, with Him. After the covenant's fulfillment the Son returned to "the right hand of the Father" to prepare for His welcoming all the saints into His heavenly kingdom:

Daniel to Darius:
"I kept looking in the night visions, and behold, with the clouds of heaven One like a Son of Man was coming, and He came up to the Ancient of Days and was presented before Him. And to Him was given dominion, glory and a kingdom, that all the peoples, nations and men of every language might serve Him. His dominion is an everlasting dominion which will not pass away; and His kingdom is one which will not be destroyed.
—Daniel 7:13-14

David:
The Lord says to my Lord: "Sit at My right hand until [עַד / ἕως] I make Your enemies a footstool for Your feet."
—Psalm 110:1-2; {cf Matthew 22:44-45; Mark 12:36; Luke 20:42-43; Acts 2:34-36}

He, having offered one sacrifice for sins for all time, sat down at the right hand of God, waiting from that time onward until [ἕως] His enemies be made a footstool for His feet.
—Hebrews 10:12-13

The Hebrew word עַד and the Koine Greek word ἕως both translate as the preposition 'until,' 'up to the time of,' thus affording me the insight to be able to dispel the possibility the Son had not been privileged to know the "the day and hour" when God will terminate the heavens and the earth. Simply stated, עַד / ἕως indicate that Jesus the Christ knows when He will welcome all the saints to the New Jerusalem: after His Father first "makes the Son's enemies a footstool for His feet." Thus to the Son of God that future event is 'time-certain' only at the discretion of His Father and until that time, then, Jesus is to remain seated by His Father's "right hand." That is the divine Father-to-Son hierarchical paradigm: the Father reigns while His Son waits patiently:

> Be patient...brethren, until the coming of the Lord...be patient ...for the coming of the Lord is at hand.
> —James 5:7-8

> The Lord is not slow about His promise, as some count slowness, but is patient {cf. Romans2:4,9:22} toward you, not wishing for any to perish but for all to come to repentance.
> —2 Peter 3:9

> ...regard the patience of our Lord...
> —2 Peter 3:15

The light of Genesis 1:3, יְהִי, [became] the divinely approved master plan for God's creation, development and administration of life after the completion of "the beginning." It is the Creator's 'blue prints' to guide

Him both in the creating and in administering life in the world. This "light" is the book of life, which focuses on the creation of earthly life and climaxes with eternal spiritual life in Yaweh's kingdom for the "many" who had been created in His image. Earthly life is a physical organism's earthly state which exists from its conception to its death whereas eternal life, eligible apparently for humans only, will be bestowed on God's chosen "many" at the end of time, when Jesus Christ returns to embrace them. This book lists individually every inheritor of eternal life chosen by Yaweh {cf. 1 Peter 2:9} "from the foundation of the world," i.e., at the foot of the formless, empty earth (v. 2 {cf. 2 Peter 3:5}.) "The light's" unifying theme is "God so loved the world, i.e., mankind." (John 3:16)

> **David:**
> "Your eyes have seen my unformed substance and in Your book they were all written, the days that were ordained {for me}, when as yet there was not one of them."
> —Psalm 139:10

> ...as many as had been appointed to eternal life believed.
> —Acts 13:48

> ...{God} chose us in Him πρὸ [before {in time or place}] the foundation of the world that we should be holy and blameless κατενώπιον [in His presence.] In love He predestined us to adoption as sons through Jesus Christ to Himself, according to the kind intention of His

will...{God} made known to us the mystery of His will, according to His kind intention which He purposed in Him with a view to an administration suitable to the fullness of the times, the summing up of all things in Christ, things in the heavens and things upon the earth.
—Ephesians 1:4-5,19-20

...we are His workmanship, created in Christ Jesus for good works which God had prepared beforehand...
—Ephesians 2:10

For {Christ} was foreknown before the foundation of the world, but has appeared in these last times for the sake of you.
—1 Peter 1:20

The foundation God בָּרָא [created] for life was comprised of the heavens and the earth.

CREATION OF LIFE

The book of Genesis is devoted to the historic development of life prior to Moses' birth, circa mid-1450's B.C. Endowed with an inspiration sourced in and by Yaweh's Breath, the prophet's {cf. Deuteronomy 34:10} knowledge seems to have been drawn from various personal relationships: 1) his natural mother and sister, 2) his adopted royal family, 3) the priest of Midian and his family, 4) the Hebrew people whom he led through the wilderness for forty years and 5) the various tribes he met during the house of Israel's wandering.

The "beginning" implicitly commenced in darkness, during a first 'evening,' and was completed on the first 'morning':

....וַיְהִי־עֶרֶב וַיְהִי־בֹקֶר, יוֹם אֶחָד

... καὶ ἐγένετο ἑσπέρα καὶ ἐγένετο πρωί, ἡμέρα μία.
And there was evening and there was morning, one day.

—Genesis 1:5

Both "morning" and "evening" infer the presence of physical light which God had yet to create. The total darkness appearing in verse 2, the absence of all light, He "called night" when juxtaposing it in verses 4 and 5, to the book of life. This contrast was divinely moral in essence, thereby establishing 'night' as a metaphor for evil:

> Jesus:
> "And his master praised the unrighteous manager because he had acted shrewdly; for the sons of this age are more shrewd in relation to their own kind than the sons of light."
> —Luke 16:8

> Jesus:
> "We must work the works of Him who sent Me as long as it is day; night is coming when no one can work."
> —John 9:4

> So Jesus said to them, "For a little while longer the light is among you. Walk while you have the Light, so that darkness will not overtake you; he who walks in the darkness does not know where he goes. While you have the light, believe in the light, so that you may become sons of light."
> —John 12:35-36

> Paul:
> "...to open their eyes so that they may turn from darkness to light and from the dominion of Satan to God..."
> —Acts 26:18

> **for you were formerly darkness, but now you are light in the Lord; walk as the children of light**
> —Ephesians 5:8

> **you are all sons of light and sons of day. We are not of night nor of darkness;**
> —1 Thessalonians 5:5

Although I am fully devoted to the Scriptures' inerrancy and infallibility, I believe it theologically 'healthy' to inquire whether we must accept as historically factual Moses's sequential format for the account of life's creation in Genesis 1:6-31. If so, how can "the day that the Lord God made earth and heaven {cf. 2:1}" in Genesis 2:4 be reconciled to the six-day creation activities in chapter 1? The activities of 2:4 all seem to have occurred concurrently whereas those of chapter 1 seem to have consecutively happened. These options also are presented by the phrase, "God saw that it was good," the occurrence of which in Genesis 1:4,10,12,18,21,25 argues for a series of consecutiveness while in 1:31 כָּל [all] indicates simultaneity. Could Genesis 2:4 be a 'macro' version of the 'micro' presentation in Genesis 1:6-31? As Job positivized (23:7) "the upright would reason with" God, Who through the prophet Isaiah (1:18) declared, "Come now and let us reason together"; and in Acts 17:17 we learn Jesus had reasoned with the Jews in their synagogue. I include these citations merely to point out that reasoning with divine words is not necessarily a blasphemy nor offensive to Yaweh and thus I respectfully offer two

reasons why I think the chronological format of Genesis 1 cannot be linearly historical:

1. Without the sun earthly life could not exist though Moses had dictated through his scribes that in the third day Yaweh had created all forms of flora even though the sun had yet to come into existence. Seed-bearing vegetation, dependent on the sun, would not receive the nourishment necessary for survival as well as its perpetuation;
2. Without the sun there could not have been earthly "morning(s) and evening(s)" for days one to three. In other words, man could not have discovered and employed 'time' until day four.

Contextually (cf. 2:3-4) as well as logically (1:3-13), יוֹם [*yohm* {day}] cannot represent the earth's complete rotation from one sun rise to the next for God had not formed "the greater light to govern the day and the lesser light to govern the night" until the fourth *yohm*. It was only then that man had been enabled to discover and employ our sense of 'time'.

No human had been present to witness "the beginning"; only Yaweh God had participated in it and thereby sourced the Genesis 1 narrative. Chapter 1 is a description of what They had done but without any mention of the temporal span of time it took Them to do so. Until the existence of our solar system {"for days and years" (verse 14)}, no measurement of chronological progression can be provided for the first three yohms; though each is introduced by the phrase וַיְהִי־עֶרֶב וַיְהִי־בֹקֶר they actually are anachronistic because of the fourth yohm. From another perspective, the content of verses 5 to 25 in chapter 2 offers descriptions of events not mentioned though implicitly subsumed within chapter 1. These verses serve as a complimentary expansion of the prior chapter, but with this distinction: 6 *yohms* have become collapsed into 1 *yohm*. In order to harmonize this reduction, *yohm* in Genesis 1 (except in the start of verse 5 and the middle of verse 14) and 2 must be translated as an era or a phase and I specifically prefer to render each of these *yohms* as a 'phase of creative activity,' the duration of each Yaweh has chosen not to divulge. This means, then, that all of creation had been completed either in a trillionth, or less, of a 'solar second' or in billions of celestial years {cf. Psalm 90:4 and II Peter 3:8.}

A conceivable explanation for the first three *yohms* being anachronistic is the liberal nature of 'poetic license' in mnemonic devices used to perpetuate folk lore; mnemonic serves as a didactic tool for improving and assisting the memory capacities of listeners, singers and speakers through the millennia of mankind's existence. Moses's understanding of life's commencement most likely came to him as oral Hebrew tradition preserved by Yaweh's Breath and he in turn dictated it *verbatim* to his scribe(s) to serve as the structural essence and format of Genesis 1. This structure is like an ancestral prototype of the contemporary meme, a communication device that spreads a theme from person to person within a culture. The employment of the 'refrain' concept in ancient Hebrew folklore could well have prompted this present observation: "Reiterated lines sometimes beget music; and much of Jewish musicality grew from the resonance of repeated words."[5]

> **VERSE 1**: After creating the foundation for life, God acknowledges light, which He calls day and darkness He calls night:
> **REFRAIN**: "And there was evening and there was morning, one יוֹם."
> —Genesis. 1:3–5

> **VERSE 2**: God first proposes and then creates an all-encompassing sky by "separat(ing) the waters from the waters":
> **REFRAIN**: "And there was evening and there was morning, a second יוֹם."
> —Genesis 1:6–8

> **VERSE 3**: God first proposes and then creates dry land (earth) and gathers the waters below the created sky, thereby forming seas. He then speaks again and creates all forms of flora with their seed:
> **REFRAIN**: "And there was evening and there was morning, a third יוֹם."
> —Genesis 1:9–13

> **VERSE 4**: God first proposes and then creates celestial bodies "to separate (i.e., to change, not to distinguish {verse 4}) the day from the night (evening/ twilight and morning/sun rise)... for signs, and for seasons, and for days and years... to give light on the earth...":

---

5. Jews and Words, Amos and Fania Oz, Yale University Press, 2012, page 28

REFRAIN: "And there was evening and there was morning, a fourth יוֹם."

—Genesis 1:14 – 19

VERSE 5: **God first proposes and then creates water creatures and birds**
REFRAIN: "And there was evening and there was morning, a fifth יוֹם."

—Genesis. 1:20 – 23

VERSE 6: **God first proposes and then creates land creatures; He then speaks and creates man "in His own image...":**
REFRAIN: "And there was evening and there was morning, the sixth יוֹם."

—Genesis. 1:24 – 31

It is reasonable to accept that the "evening" and "morning" in verses 1:5,8 and 13 above were employed figuratively as a foreshadowing of the temporal "evening" and "morning" later created in verse 16.

Serialized by six "*yohms*," [יוֹם] Genesis 1:2-31 scans an immeasurable amount of temporal time in describing the full development of life. The measurability of this span, unfortunately, is complicated by the varying Hebrew meanings for *yohm* when comparing verses 5,8,13, 19,23 and 31 to Genesis 2:4:

- This is the account of the heavens and the earth when they were created, in the יוֹם that Yaweh God made earth and heaven.

Translation of the Hebrew word יוֹם varies and thus depends on the context in which Moses applied it. In its 'debut' (v. 5) he employed it twice: first as Yaweh's title for His book of life and then as commencement of segmenting the varying aspects of His creation activity described in the rest of Genesis 1. After the book of life was completed, He "called" it יוֹם, possibly intending its translation as "daylight" (Genesis 18:1, 29:7,30:32,31:39 {cf. John 9:4 and I Thessalonians 5:5}) to designate figuratively His complete creation plan as the 'guiding light' for all of His life-creating events. "The light" was not Yaweh's divine aura {Moses had not mentioned its accompanying Him in verse 3} nor the sun {it would not come into existence until the plan's fourth phase (verse 19)}, nor Jesus Christ {"the light of the world" (John 8:12) when He became divinely conceived within Mary.} The *LXX* scribes translated יוֹם as ἡμέρα, which like *yohm*, is defined as either:

1. the interval from sunrise to sunset {cf. Genesis 1:5,8:22; Numbers 11:32; Judges 19:9; I Kings 8:29; Esther 4:16; Psalm 74:16; Isaiah 38:12&13; Amos 5:8};
2. the interval of 24 hours {cf. Zechariah 14:7};
3. an era, period, span of time {cf. Genesis 4:3, 18:11, 24:1, 47:29; Exodus 20:11, 31:17; Leviticus 14:46; Deuteronomy 4:32; Joshua 3:15; Judges 15:1; Job 14:6; Psalm 27:5, 41:1(2), 50:15; Proverbs 25:13, 19; Jeremiah17:16-18, 51:2; Nahum 1:7.}

The clincher for 'phase' to be *yohm*'s translation during all of God's creating activity is verse 7 of Moses's folklore format: "by the seventh יוֹם God completed His work...and He rested [שָׁבַת] from/ceased His labor..." (Genesis 2:2) The tense for שָׁבַת is the perfect, which denotes an action in its completed state. The absence of the anticipated refrain, "there was evening and there was morning, the seventh יוֹם," indicates not only that the seventh day had not come to an end but that we today are within that seventh day. Also ...שָׁבַת מִכָּל... בָּרָא לַעֲשׂוֹת (Genesis 2:3) clearly indicates that God had only "ceased from all creat(ing) and forming," not from any other activity. He completed [יְכַל] and refrained [יִשְׁבֹּת] from His creating labors but, as His Breath informs us, He is still very active today:

> The psalmist:
> "He will not allow your foot to slip; He who keeps you will not slumber. Behold, He who keeps Israel will neither slumber nor sleep."
> —Psalm 121:3-4

> Jesus:
> "My Father is working until now, and I Myself am working."
> —John 5:17

> But when the fulness of time came, God sent forth His Son, born of a woman, born under the law.
> —Galatians 4:4

Based on Genesis 1:8 time becomes identified as a repetitively sequential measurement of the earth's motion, i.e., of its rotation.

Yaweh is not constrained by the confinements of His Creation, including time; He is not subjected to a past or a future and now is and remains 'occupied' with managing and administering life's labyrinthine activities strictly in accordance with His book of life.

As David and Peter alluded to in their similes of exaggeration:

> "...a thousand years in Your sight are like yesterday when it passes by..."
> —Psalm 90:4

> "...with the Lord one day is as a thousand years and a thousand years as one day."
> —2 Peter 3:8

A finite human mind would dare to describe it this way: God does not create, administer, judge and terminate all lives linearly over time; rather He creates, administers, judges and terminates all lives simultaneously in no time, literally speaking.

Mankind continue to exist as will Yaweh continue to sovereignly administer His creation until "the last day." (John 6:39) The morning of this seventh *yohm*, then, started at the completion of the creating activities and will last until Jesus Christ returns to earth in the clouds. Consequently, Genesis 2:4 requires 'phase,' a span of time, as the translation for *Yohm* and its *LXX* counterpart from Genesis 1:5 to 2:3. Reason dictates this rendering must prevail even in verses 1:5,8,13 even though the sun and moon would not begin to exist until later in verse 16. Masorete scholars during the 7th to 10th centuries AD, in pursuing restoration of the lost 4th to 2nd century BC Hebrew Bible with considerable reliance on " ἦ ἡμέρᾳ " in the *Septuagint* (circa the 3rd century AD), affirmed that Moses, inspired by Yaweh's Breath, had indeed intended יוֹם, not יָמִים, its plural, in Genesis 2:4.

Thus the singular of *yohm* persuades one to conclude that the six creation *yohm*s in Genesis 1 collectively represent the span of time, i.e., one *yohm*, during which Yaweh created what is summarized in 2:4. The six *yohm*s in Chapter 1, the seventh *yohm* in 2:2–3 as well as one *yohm* of 2:4 all make sense when translating each as either an indefinite span of time, an era or a phase. After all, the Lord is not subject to what He creates:

> ...with the Lord one day is as a thousand years
> and a thousand years as one day {cf. Psalm 90:4}
> —2 Peter 3:8

My motive for focusing on *yohm* is to caution the reader that there is very little, if any, biblical support that God had created the heavens and the earth and all its dwellers in six 24-hour periods or that Genesis 2:4 supports the notion of the 'big bang' creation theory, the cause for which the field of science is unable to identify. Another mystery, though, is the chronology, the order and arrangement of events, in chapter 1: flora's creation (verses 11-13) appears to have happened prior to that of its sustainer, the sun (verses 16-18.) Without altering any Scriptural content from chapter 2 but just repositioning and slightly expanding portions of it, I believe this reasonably represents the book of life's chronological order of life's development:

1. Preparation for Life's coming into existence:

God made the expanse, and separated the waters which were below the expanse from the waters which were above the expanse;
—Genesis 1:7

God manipulated the waters so that dry land, earth, appeared {cf. Psalm 9:2};
—Genesis 1:9-10

2. Life appears on the heavens and the earth:

Now no shrub of the field was yet in the earth, and no plant of the field had yet sprouted, for the Lord God had not sent rain upon the earth, and there was no man to cultivate the ground but a mist used to rise from the earth and water the whole surface of the ground.
—Genesis 2:5-6

The earth brought forth vegetation, plants yielding seed after their kind, and trees bearing fruit with seed in them, after their kind,
—Genesis 1:12

God made the two great lights, the greater light to govern the day, and the lesser light to govern the night; He made the stars also God placed them in the expanse of the heavens to give light on the earth.
—Genesis 1:16-17

God created the great sea monsters and every living creature that moves, with which the waters swarmed after their kind, and every winged bird after its kind;
—Genesis 1:21

God made the beasts of the earth after their kind, and the cattle after their kind, and everything that creeps on the ground after its kind;

—Genesis 1:25

So the Lord God caused a deep sleep to fall upon the man, and he slept; then He took one of his ribs and closed up the flesh at that place. The Lord God fashioned into a woman the rib which He had taken from the man, and brought her to the man.

—Genesis 2:21-22

God created man in His own image, in the image of God He created him; male and female He created them. God blessed them; and God said to them, "Be fruitful and multiply, and fill the earth, and subdue it; and rule over the fish of the sea and over the birds of the sky and over every living thing that moves on the earth." Then God said, "Behold, I have given you every plant yielding seed that is on the surface of all the earth, and every tree which has fruit yielding seed; it shall be food for you; and to every beast of the earth and to every bird of the sky and to every thing that moves on the earth which has life, I have given every green plant for food";

—Genesis 1: 27-30

Thus the heavens and the earth were completed, and כָּל־צְבָאָם [all their multitude {of living creatures}.]

—Genesis 2:1

I next question the chronological continuity and thought process of Moses's narrative in verses 2:18-21. To me verse 18 seems more appropriate to follow verse 20:

> 19 Out of the ground the Lord God formed every beast of bird of the sky, and brought them to the man to see what he would call them; and whatever the man called a living creature, that was its name.
>
> 20 The man gave names to all the cattle, and to the birds of the sky, and to every to every beast of the field, but for Adam there was not found a helper suitable for him.
>
> 18 Then the Lord God said, "It is not good for the man to be alone; I will make him a helper suitable for him."
>
> 21 So the Lord God caused a deep sleep to fall upon the man, and he slept; then He took one of his ribs and closed up the flesh at that place.
>
> 22 The Lord God fashioned into a woman the rib which He had taken from the man, and brought her to the man.

After first man is placed in the garden at Eden to cultivate it, the narrative then needs to mention his introduction to and naming of beasts and birds in order to acquaint himself with their complementing cultivating relevance before switching to a different subject: Yaweh's fabrication [בָּנָה] of a mate suitable for him.

CREATION OF LIFE

Now Genesis 2:1 appears to be Moses's concise summation of his recollection of the ancient Hebrew folklore and tradition he had secretly received {cf. Romans 10:17} as a heritage from his birth mother and sister while growing up apart from them in the care of Pharaoh's daughter. In that case, then, verses 2 and 3 would serve as Yaweh's Breath's inspiration to Moses as the 'coda' to all of chapter 1. But is that really true? Am I getting persuaded that way because of the chapter change? After all, Moses had not dictated chapters and verses; they had been devised by Nathan, a Jewish rabbi in 1448. Thus it's just as conceivable that the first three verses of chapter 2 form the ending of the ancient Hebrew folklore. There is another argument for this interpretation: from Genesis 1:1 to 2:3 אֱלֹהִים appears 32 times but then is replaced by יְהוָה אֱלֹהִים until the start of chapter 4.

My primary reason, then, for including Genesis 2:1 to 3 in Moses's recounting of ancient Hebrew creation folklore is the fact that אֱלֹהִים, the Creator's title, is the divine source for all the creating activities mentioned. The shift to יְהוָה אֱלֹהִים [Yaweh God] does not necessarily prove a change in authorship for to me it's more likely to be due to another scribe {#2} replacing the one {#1} who had transcribed Moses's dictation of Genesis 1 to 2:3.

Either Moses and/or his scribe #2 chose to personalize God to acknowledge His 'post Creation' status with life: His complete power and reign over the earth's vibrant nature, the collective interrelationships of plants, animals, the landscape, and other features and products of the earth. The one quirk to this 'theory' is that #2 scribe included 4 times אֱלֹהִים {Genesis 3:1-5}, all of which were included in Eve's conversation with the serpent. But why "God" here when in Genesis 4:1 she attributes her first son's birth אֶת־יְהוָה [by the Lord]? Because from verses 1 to 24 Moses and/or another of his scribes employed "the Lord" 8 times. Even more confusing, though, is while in verse 25 Eve had attributed the birth of Seth to אֱלֹהִים, Moses narrates in verse 26 after Enosh had become Seth's offspring, אָז הוּחַל, לִקְרֹא בְּשֵׁם יְהוָה [then man began to invoke the name Yaweh.] Then אֱלֹהִים returns 4 times in chapter 5, but I was struck by the fact that God, His title and not His personal name, had a uniquely close relationship with Enoch. In general, from chapter 6 there on, Lord and God were interchangeable employed by Moses and/or his scribes, but with this exception: in Genesis 15:2,8 Abram reverently addressed the Creator as אֲדֹנָי יְהוִה [Lord Yaweh.] I point out the varying addresses early man had developed over time to identify and address God merely for the reader's interest. I am not a literary scholar and have no desire to open up debate with 'higher criticism,' the secular 'theology' which denies the Scriptures' divine inspiration.

אֵלֶּה תוֹלְדוֹת הַשָּׁמַיִם וְהָאָרֶץ,

—Genesis 2:4

אֵלֶּה is the plural common demonstrative pronoun and refers back to the entire content of the preceding chapter;

תּוֹלְדוֹת is a noun, in the plural state, with varying meanings: birth (Exodus 28:10), generations, families; family history, origin. None of these translations seemed to make any sense to me until I discovered this definition for 'generation' in the American Heritage Dictionary: "A period of sequential technological development and innovation";[6] הַשָּׁמַיִם can be translated either 'the heavens,' the space or sky surrounding all of the earth or 'heaven', the spiritual dwelling for *omnipresent* Yaweh. Only the specific content in which it appears can determine which one is appropriate:

> **SPACE:** Genesis 1:89,14,15,17; 2:1,4; 14:19,22;
>
> **ATMOSPHERE / SKY:** Genesis 1:26,28,30; 2:19,20; 6:7,17; 15:5; Psalm 19:1; 103:11;
>
> **SPIRITUAL HEAVEN:** Genesis 21:17; 22:11,17; 24:3,7; 28:17; Isaiah 65:17; Malachi 3:10.

The narrative of Genesis 1:1 to 2:4 is dominated by two verbs, בָּרָא and עָשָׂה, both of which the *LXX* renders ποιέω. A termination is both the opposite as well as result of a beginning and what begins replaces what is terminated. Thus by deduction it is reasonable to state that the essence of "the beginning" of verse 1:1, described in verse 2, succeeds the termination of something, which was the state of nothingness. Nothing had existed prior to what verse 2 portrays, attributing the trait of *ex nihilo* to בָּרָא and עָשָׂה: created out of nothing:

> In the beginning God created [בָּרָא] the heavens [הַשָּׁמַיִם] and the earth.
> —Genesis 1:1

---

6. https://ahdictionary.com/word/search.html?q=generation Viewed: 3/2023

God made [עָשָׂה] the two great lights, the greater light to govern the day, and the lesser light to govern the night, the stars also.
—Genesis 1:16

I wish to stress that הַשָּׁמַיִם in Genesis 1:1 included not the sun and the moon, not our galaxy and not the universe.

The translation of הַשָּׁמַיִם depends on the context in which it appears:

1. Space:
   - Genesis 1:7–8 - God formed and called the space [הָרָקִיעַ] heavens
   - Genesis 1:9 - Then God said, "Let the waters below the heavens be gathered into one place..."
   - Genesis 1:14,15,17 - lights in the expanse of the heavens
   - Genesis 2:1 - the heavens and the earth
   - Genesis 2:4 the heavens and the earth when they were created [בָּרָא]...the Lord God made [עָשָׂה] earth and the heavens
   - Genesis 14:19, 22 - God Most High (is) possessor of heavens and earth

2. Sky:
   - Genesis 1:26,28,30; 2:19,20; 6:7 - עוֹף הַשָּׁמַיִם [birds of the sky]
   - Genesis 6:17 - destroy all flesh in which is the breath of life from under the sky
   - Genesis 15:5 - Lord to Abram: "Look toward the sky and count the stars"

- Genesis 22:17 - the stars of the sky
- Psalm 19:1 - David: "the skies are telling the glory of God and the expanse proclaims work of His hand."

3. God's spiritual abode:
   - Genesis 21:17; 22:11 - Angel of God called from heaven
   - Genesis 24:3,7 - the Lord, God of heaven
   - Genesis 28:17 - Jacob: "this is...the house of God and this is the gate of heaven
   - Psalm 103:11 - David: "For high as heaven [שָׁמַיִם] is above the earth so great is His lovingkindness"
   - Isaiah 65:17 - The Lord: I create [בָּרָא] heaven [שָׁמַיִם]
   - Malachi 3:10 - The Lord of hosts: "open for you the window of heaven [הַשָּׁמַיִם]

Genesis 2:3-4 clearly shows that בָּרָא and עָשָׂה are synonyms:

> Then God blessed the seventh day and sanctified it, because in it He rested from all His work which (God created to fabricate (בָּרָא אֱלֹהִים לַעֲשׂוֹת). This is the generations of the heavens and the earth when they were created [בָּרָא], in the day that the Lord God made [עָשָׂה] earth and the heavens.

All the other creating works performed by Yaweh involved His forming and fabricating composites from

the water and landmass He had created *ex nihilo* "in the beginning":

- Genesis 1:7 - God 'expanded' [עָשָׂה] the heavens by separating the water below it from the water above it;
- Genesis 1:9 - God gathered the water below the heavens, permitting the land to dry;
- Genesis 1:12 - God enabled the earth to bring forth vegetation, plants and trees, all bearing their seeds;
- Genesis 1:14-15,17 - God placed lights in the expanse of the heavens;
- Genesis 1:21 - God formed [בָּרָא] from the earth {cf. 2:19} marine monsters, swarming creatures and bird;
- Genesis 1:25 - God formed [עָשָׂה] from the earth beasts, cattle and everything that creeps on the ground;
- Genesis 1:26-27 - God made [עָשָׂה/בָּרָא] man {from the earth (v. 2:7).}

Although I am no literary scholar, I consider Genesis 2:4 to 25, except verse 24, to be Moses's inspired explanatory complement of Genesis 1 to 2:3. Isolating together the various germane verses I get a much fuller understanding of the sequence involved when first man and woman entered life:

> וַיִּבְרָא אֱלֹהִים אֶת-הָאָדָם [and God created the human being {representing both genders}] in His image (1:27)

He breathed into the nostrils of (the human being) the breath of life and the human being became נֶפֶשׁ חַיָּה [a living being] (2:7)

הָאָדָם is both [בָּרָא אֹתוֹ] male [זָכָר] and female [נְקֵבָה] (1:27)

He fabricated [בָּנָה] a woman from the rib of הָאָדָם [the human being] (2:22)

אִשָּׁה [woman] is לוֹ עֵזֶר, כְּנֶגְדּוֹ [an aid/helper as over against him; i.e., his counterpart] and becomes wife of אִישׁ [man], whom God calls אָדָם [Adam.] (2:18,25, 3:17)

I stated above that I consider all of chapter 2 "to be Moses's inspired explanatory complement of the first chapter" and thus wish to explain what I mean by 'inspired.' It's the special relationship Moses had been chosen by God to have with Him through His Breath whereby the divine thoughts and words the prophet received were not dictated to him and his processing into human words this divine communication was in keeping with his character and personality; "Dictation is not involved; there is no violation of the of the personality of the writer."[7]

My reason for excepting 2:24 is because it seems to be a later thought Moses had been inspired to insert, particularly since the first couple had not yet (4:1) experienced the additional role as either אָב [father – cf. 4:20] or אֵם [mother – cf. 3:20.] In addition, עַל־כֵּן [for

---

7. Evangelical Dictionary of Theology, Walter Elwell, editor, Baker Book House, pg. 1139

a pedestal {i.e., something to look up to}] introduces the marital principle of leave/ cleave/weave derived from the intimate originating relationship (2:21-22) the first wife in history had with her 'counterpart,' the first husband (3:6). Please be assured that in no way am I wanting to alter or deny any factual material appearing in all of Genesis. Whatever I raise critically here is intended not to challenge any facts of God's work; rather I seek to challenge the physical location, not content, of certain citations so to enhance the integrity and continuity of Moses's narrative. For instance, regarding the content of Genesis 1 and 2, here are my interpretive observations and suggestions:

1. The quoted phrases God spoke (verses 3, 6, 9, 1114, 20, 24, 26) are spiritual communications strictly within the eternal triune union {cf. "us" (3:22)};
2. All the works of creating/forming, while physical in nature, is performed by one or more of the triune's three spiritual Persons;
3. God's statement to every "living creature that moves" (verse 22) was a verbal blessing;
4. God's quoted instructions (1:28-30 and 2:16-17), spiritual in origin, were received and comprehended by first man and first woman; it has to be assumed that they understood 'from the start' His language and messages;
5. Verse 1:27 that both "His own image" as well as the life God breathed into first man (2:7) were included in His fabrication (2:22) of the woman;

6. God's instruction, "Be fruitful and multiply," (1:28) is such that it's difficult to discern whether 'fruitful' focuses on productive usefulness, inferred in verse 22, or is a synonym for 'multiply,' as seems the case in verse 11. It's awesome just to realize the multi-trillions (!) of human souls (all those designated for earthly life by the book of life, not just the 'many chosen ones') that had been stored pyramid-wise in Eve's eggs and first man's semen at the moment of her being formed;

7. Reverses 2:8,10,15-17, it's assumed that wherever God put first man, his wife was his constant companion;

8. The first appearances of אָדָם [Adam] are in verses 20 and 23 of chapter 2 though Moses continues to use הָאָדָם [the man] frequently through chapter 4, after which the name Adam prevails;

9. Verse 3:6 infers that Adam knew how to identify the forbidden tree (2:17);

10. Initial glance at verse 2:3 infers a cause-and-effect statement due to כִּי being translated 'because', but כִּי is a relative pronoun, not the causative conjunction, Thus the more appropriate rendering of this verse could be: God יְבָרֶךְ [adored] and יְקַדֵּשׁ [appointed a feast on the] seventh day כִּי [which] in it He rested. This then would satisfy my quandary as to why He had not treated any of the other six days in the same manner;

11. Verses 3:22-24 in Moses's narrative imply that God was unable to anticipate what first man was going to do after his first deed of disobedience and thus had to take precautions to prevent him from obtaining eternal life on his own. But while these verses seem unscripted in His book of life, the sacrifice of His Son is eternally the focal theme throughout that book;
12. It's interesting to note Job's claim of his kinship {cf. 2:7} to first man: רוּחַ־אֵל עָשָׂתְנִי; וְנִשְׁמַת שַׁדַּי תְּחַיֵּנִי [Breath of God has made me; the Almighty breathes me life] (Job 33:4);
13. Based on assumption 4.), Eve in verse 3:3 misquoted what she had heard directly from Yaweh {cf. 2:17} by deleting "to die" and then by 'fencing' it (a tendency by Hebrew priests and scholars to protect and impress theological laws and rules) with this addition: "or touch (the forbidden fruit)";
14. Comparison of Exodus 20:8-11 to Genesis 2:2-3 poses a mystery: did Moses dictate the latter earlier than when Yaweh had spoken to the people of Israel at the foot of Mount Sinai or was the latter Moses's addendum to Genesis 2 after God's address on Mount Sinai? I query this due to the similarity in wording between them:

Genesis 2:3 - וַיְבָרֶךְ אֱלֹהִים אֶת־יוֹם הַשְּׁבִיעִי,

Exodus 20:10 - בֵּרַךְ יְהוָה אֶת־יוֹם הַשַּׁבָּת

Even though the second phrase expands the significance:

> Genesis 2:3 - and God praised [exalted (raised in rank/status)] the seventh day
> Exodus 20:10 - Yaweh praised [exalted (raised in rank/status)] a day (as) the day of rest

When pondering the immense totality of what God created/ formed in chapter 1, I keep wondering for what or whose benefit He had created the heavens? In other words, are some or all of life's participants benefiting from the existence of the planet Saturn and if so, how? From another perspective, what had He purposed for that planets existence? And, at 'the end times' will all the universe be destroyed together with this world? I like the way David addresses my quandary: "The heavens are telling of the glory of God; and their expanse is declaring the work of His hands." (Psalm 19:1)

Moses's summation, "These (are) generations (of) the heavens and the earth" (2:4), parallels Genesis 1:1. His 'coda,' the seventh *yohm*, introduces the final 'chapter' of Yaweh's book of life; there will be no 8th *yohm*. From the human perspective I deem it sad that this life, which came into being out of nothingness, will again become nothingness but I am comforted knowing that all this God had been pleased to plan from "the beginning" in "the light," His book of life.

> "All things come of Thee"
> —1 Chronicles 29:14

> The Lord by wisdom founded the earth; by understanding He established the heavens; by His knowledge the deeps were broken up and the skies drip with dew.
> —Proverbs 3:19-20

> ...all things originate from God.
> —1 Corinthians 11:12

At the completion of Genesis 2, the works of Yaweh's creating/ forming settled into place and verse 25 depicts the first (and only, unfortunately) moment first man and his counterpart/woman/wife enjoyed absolute peace on earth because they were sinless, free from any disobedience to their Creator.

Life has come into physical existence over all of creation's foundation specifically in the universal form of blood (Genesis 9:4; Deuteronomy 12:23) because life itself is בַּדָּם [in the blood.] (Leviticus 17:11)

God's book of life remains effective, though, to guide the operation, maintenance and governance of the life in this world.

YAWEH'S SOVEREIGN REIGN

Yaweh Most High is...a great King over all the earth...God reigns over all the nations.
—Psalm 47:2,8

Yaweh has established His throne in the heavens and His sovereignty rules from Shiloh {cf. Genesis 49:10}.
—Psalm 103:19

...God causes all things to work together for good to those who love God, to those who are called according to {His} purpose.
—Romans 8:28

And on the seventh [הַשְּׁבִיעִי] day God finished [וַיְכַל] His work which He had made [עָשָׂה]; and He rested [וַיִּשְׁבֹּת] on the seventh [הַשְּׁבִיעִי] day from all His work which He had made [עָשָׂה]. And God praised [וַיְבָרֶךְ] the seventh [הַשְּׁבִיעִי] day, and dedicated [וַיְקַדֵּשׁ] it formally to His purpose; because in it He rested [שָׁבַת] from all His work which God [בָּרָא] created to make [לַעֲשׂוֹת].
—Genesis 2:2-3

Verses delineate Yaweh's transitional activities:

- God finished / completed / ended [יְכַל] (His creating work [לַאכְתּוֹ]);
- God rested /ceased or refrained [יִשְׁבֹּת] (from His creating work [מְלַאכְתּוֹ]);
- God praised / conferred or invoked divine favor upon [יְבָרֶךְ] the seventh day;
- God יְקַדֵּשׁ [sanctified / formally dedicated to His purpose / בֵּרַךְ [praised / exalted / raised in rank/ status {cf. Exodus 20:10} the seventh day. [Note: there is no mention of an evening in v. 3 because the 7th day will not end until Revelation 21:1.]

Yes, He did complete [יְכַל] and refrain [יִשְׁבֹּת] from His creating labors, but not from any of the necessary tasks, efforts and activities for plying His sovereignty and administrative duties delineated by His book of life. His first attention focused on nature, the 'engine' of life, becoming 'primed and running' for the sustenance of all life. And His Breath informs us He is still active today by His personal interacting with all mankind:

> The psalmist:
> "He will not allow your foot to slip; He who keeps you will not slumber. Behold, He who keeps Israel will neither slumber nor sleep."
> —Psalm 121:3-4

> Jesus:
> "My Father is working until now, and I Myself am working."
> —John 5:17

> But when the fulness of time came, God sent forth
> His Son, born of a woman, born under the law.
> —Galatians 4:4

> ...God...is at work in you, both to will and to
> work for {His} good pleasure.
> —Philippians 2:13

Though not constrained by the confinement of time, i.e., by the aspects of past, present or future, Yaweh remains 'occupied' with managing and administrating life's labyrinthine activities in accordance with His book of life. By inference as well we today are living in the historic seventh day of Genesis 2:2:

- **the seventh day incorporates the six prior days**
- **there is no mention of the seventh day's evening**
- **creating work stopped at end of the sixth day, when God rested**
- **the seventh day apparently ends in Revelation 20.**

The stage (landmass and sea) has been set and the cast (all the creatures) have been formed so that all earthly life can commence under control of the forces of nature, a physical phenomenon the Lord's book of life had designed. In Eden's garden plot He has "caused to grow every tree that is pleasing to the sight and good for food" (Genesis 2:9), including the tree of the life [עֵץ הַחַיִּים], whose fruit when eaten would bestow life "forever" (Genesis 3:22), and the tree of the knowledge of good and evil [עֵץ הַדַּעַת טוֹב וָרָע], whose fruit when eaten would bestow the ability to know good and evil. These

two trees have been placed in the garden together with all the other trees for Adam and his helpmeet to "eat in order to enjoy" [אָכֹל תֹּאכֵל]. (Genesis 2:16) "Enjoy" is the III meaning for אָכַל (The Analytical Hebrew and Chaldee Lexicon, Benjamin Davidson; Zondervan, page 24) and consequentially I am reminded of an early-21st-century political astuteness: you have to taste it in order to know if you like it. And yet, in verse 17 Yaweh has specifically forbidden them from eating the fruit of the tree of the knowledge of good and evil along with an existential threat to them if they do so. Soon thereafter (Genesis 3:6) Moses dictated תֹּאכַל and יֹּאכַל, signifying that both Eve and Adam had 'eaten and enjoyed' the forbidden fruit in defiance of their Creator's warning.

Curiosity concerning this account arrests my thinking:

- how were they able to distinguish the tree with the forbidden fruit from all the other trees?
- did the forbidden fruit possess eye-appeal?
- of all the trees available in the garden, had first man and his helpmeet randomly or purposefully chosen the tree's forbidden fruit?
- did they have a propensity or a penchant to 'spec out' what was forbidden as well as to understand why it was?
- did they see the tree of life and know what their eating of its fruit would offer them?
- could they comprehend what 'live eternally' mean?
- if so, why had they not eaten its fruit?
- why was that fruit unappealing?

- **had they originally eaten all the other fruits before having to choose between that of the tree of life and that of the knowledge of good and evil?**
- **why did Eve decide to eat the forbidden fruit without first consulting with her helpmate?**
- **did the timing of Yaweh's reactions (Genesis 3:22-23) imply that God had lacked all foreknowledge about the first couple eating the forbidden fruit?**
- **Also, why had He not protected in advance the tree of life, since He had already 'cut the covenant' for men's salvation with His Son {cf. Revelation 5:7}?**

All of life's past, present and future plans, specifications and activities had equipped its Author with the divine ability of 'foreknowing' and thus He had been prepared for Adam's and his wife's initial disobedience to Him. He knew that was going to happen inasmuch as He had already recorded in the book the many names of the couple's future offspring whom His grace would bless with eternal life through His Son's covenantal sacrifice. Because the focus of the 'divine plan' was and remains the Son's selfless sacrifice out of love both vertically (for His Father) as well as horizontally (for the many offspring of Adam and Eve.) But it must be asserted here that the first couple had not been entrapped or programmed to disobey their Creator; rather, they had been created with unencumbered wills which afforded them the freedom to choose actions completely on their own. The apparent dichotomy between preordained will and free will is a mystery to mankind which only Yaweh can resolutely reconcile: His grace.

Moses to the Israelites:
"...the word {of the Lord your God} is very near you, in your mouth and in your heart, that you may observe it."

—Deuteronomy 30:14

David:
"I delight to do Your will. O my God. Your law is within my heart."

—Psalm 40:8

Genesis 2:25 portrays Adam and his helpmeet as having clean consciences because they originally had felt no shame in being naked to one another. Though only creatures and thus not divine, they were initially created with a Christ-like character: "in (them) there (was) no sin" (1 John 3:5); they "knew no sin" (2 Corinthians 5:21) and had "committed no sin." (1 Peter 2:22) But that changed, though, when Eve engaged in a conversation with the craftiest creature God had made, a serpent. Orally challenged by this lowly creature, she repeated His warning but with the amendment "or touch it"(Genesis 3:3), which simulates the Jewish traditional practice of חומרה [khumra], 'fencing a law,' an amended prohibition or obligation exceeding a law's bare requirements. As the consequence of this 'chat,' Eve was emboldened by the serpent, as was Adam by her, to disobey Yaweh and eat the 'forbidden fruit' (v. 2:17), which would enable them לָדַעַת טוֹב וָרָע [to know/ discern /recognize good and evil, Godliness and non-Godliness.] (Genesis 3:22) It's reasonable to posit that it was the serpent's lie-based dare (v. 4) and not the visual enticement of the tree's fruit that moved the first couple to eat it. After all, prior to the first swallow of that fruit the couple had no righteous awareness that what they were pondering would have not affected their relationship with their Creator. As the result of their disobedient action, the first couple immediately noticed a change in each's unclothed body, particularly in their loins (v. 7); their nakedness had exposed indelibly to them the sinfulness of their physical beings, a sudden alteration that none of the first couple's seed can appreciate because none of us know what they physically looked like prior to succumbing to the serpent's dare. Consequently they experienced shame for the first time, having sensed guilt for what they had done. Their nakedness showed them that their soul/self had become tainted with what God called חַטָּאת [sin] to them, a deliberate disobedience of His known will: "חַטָּאת crouches at the door {like an animal} and its desire is for" all mankind. (Genesis 4:7) After rightfully expelling them from the garden "the Lord God made garments of skin...and clothed them" (Genesis 3:21), a foreshadowing of the sin-covering ritual He later established with the wandering tribe of Israel.

Though serpents had been created in Genesis 1:21, a talking one had not. Satan, an angelic creature who prior to 'the beginning' rebelled against its Creator and in the guise of the talking serpent "caused the fall of the human race..." (Evangelical Dictionary of Theology; Walter Elwell, editor; Baker; page 972) It is reasonable to assume that Satan had overheard the precise wording of God's command to the first man (Genesis 2:17) because of his denial to Eve: "You will not die to die." (Genesis 3:4) This negation of the precise warning Yaweh gave first man contrasts with her imprecise understanding of it. (v. 3) In Adam's presence (v. 6) she related imprecisely to the serpent the essence of God's warning to her husband: פֶּן-תְּמֻתוּן [lest you die.] But Satan, recalling the exact wording God had spoken in Genesis 2:17, tried to woo Eve with His exact wording, לֹא-מוֹת, תְּמֻתוּן [you will not die to die] by inserting "not" in it. Did Adam forget Yaweh's exact wording of the prohibition he had conveyed to her [מוֹת תְּמֻתוּן]? This exact and rare verb combination was millennia later passed by His Breath through Moses's mouth into his scribe's ear and transcription. Yaweh protected this phrase because of its future theological significance.[8]

Moses's Old Testament narratives are neither fable nor fiction. Intrusive spiritual engagements in the reality of life are to be expected inasmuch as its Maker and Possessor is also its Regent and Administrator. Though all His image-bearers are accountable to Him, for His glory He simultaneously permits Satan and his minions free reign to interact with His image-bearers.

Each reader of Genesis is confronted with the challenge to accept as absolute truth the initial recorded conversation (Genesis 2:17) God had with first man. The medium He employed, i.e., the language, to relate directions, instructions, etc. to first man and his helpmeet most likely was not Ancient Hebrew, which

---

8. Biblical Concept of Hell, William Hyland (author), Newman Springs Publishing, Inc., 2020

would not come into social existence for many millennia to come. The precise meaning of verse 17's content He safeguarded through His Breath to Moses's cognition in appropriate Hebrew words. Also incredibility arises over another truth: Satan, disguised as a serpent, spoke to Eve, who in turn replied to 'it' in a mutually intelligible language which His breath likewise 'inspired' the prophet to translate precisely into his own language the accuracy of these first (as well as of all future) quoted conversations.

Adam "was with her, and he ate" the forbidden fruit just after she had. (Genesis 3:6) Sadly it seems he did not object to either what the serpent asserted or to her taking the first bite without conferring with him. "Adam passively and cowardly st(ood) by"[9] To defend himself from being disobedient to his Creator Adam blame-shifted: "she gave me from the tree and I ate," (v. 12) but without any expression of remorse. In like manner Eve responded to God's inquiry, "The serpent deceived me, and I ate," but not remorsefully. (v.13) Then God indicted Adam of hearkening/ obeying [שמע] his wife (v.17) by eating the forbidden fruit. Adam had disobeyed the voice of Yaweh by neglecting to discern, assess and judge his wife's words and deed. Their insensitivity to His warning has permanently stained the first couple's 'vertical' relationship to Him because they were now like Him in that they knew good from evil. That knowledge enabled them to see their nakedness before Yaweh,

---

9. Politics & Evangelical Theology, Brian Mattson, CreateSpace Independent Publishing Platform, 2012, page 33

the metaphor for accountability to Him. Sensitivity to the realization of that accountability made them feel extremely vulnerable and uncomfortable in "the presence of the Lord God." (v.8) Having first deceived themselves with the attempt to 'cover' their nakedness before their Creator, they started the temporal routine of blame-shifting in the hope of dodging their answerability to Him: Adam blamed Eve with the reminder that she was His gift to him, and his wife in turn blamed the serpent for lying to her.

This act of disobedience, apparently with no forethought of responsibility and thereby followed by their complete lack of remorse, indicated their lack of respect towards Him as well as a strain within their evolving 'marital' relationship. Marriage's hierarchy either had yet to exist or was being ignored by both participants. But Yaweh had anticipated {cf. Psalm 139:15-16; Isaiah 49:5; Jeremiah 1:4-5} this and customized their justified punishment to address it. To Eve He decreed an increase in her (and her female descendants') child-birthing {cf. John 16:21} and אֶל-אִישֵׁךְ, תְּשׁוּקָתֵךְ, וְהוּא, יִמְשָׁל-בָּךְ [your longing/desire (will be) towards your husband, he will rule over you.] (v.16) Because the landmass [הָאֲדָמָה] has been cursed by his disobedience, first man from then on had to toil hard in preparing the ground to grow all the food for both his family as well as his livestock. And finally, Yaweh sentenced him to death: "you are dust and to dust you shall return," the תָּמוּת of מוֹת תָּמוּת. (Genesis 2:17) In verse 21 we learn that God's love provided them the covering of their nakedness, which had exposed their disobedience of Him. In so doing He had reconciled them with Him, thereby restoring their personal relationship with Him, foreshadowing the reconciliation to Yaweh His Son's death on the cross would later accomplish for all the saints. This disobedience is life's first חַטָּאת [sin], though Moses delayed using that word until Genesis 4:7, in which God likened it to an aggressive beast crouching at the door of one's heart, waiting for just even a crack in the door to appear because its desire is to fully rule that heart. Interestingly, the vibrancy of its longing is the same as what He had incorporated in Eve's punishment in Genesis 3:16: תְּשׁוּקָה .

There are three mysteries for me regarding the content of His punishment:

1. The lack of a *vov* consecutive verb commencing Genesis 4 infers Eve had experienced no prior pregnancy, thereby making me wonder how the increase of something she had yet to experience could make her feel punished;
2. God's death sentence was addressed only to Adam yet his wife had justly deserved it as well. Was that because He had treated him as her "ruler" (v.16) and thereby subjected Eve as well as "all (the) living" (v.20), to her husband's destiny?

> ...through one man sin entered into the world, and death through sin, and so death spread to all men, ἐφ' ᾧ all sinned;
> —Romans 5:12

The interrogative ἐφ' ᾧ is comprised of ἐπί and the dative of ὅς, which Zondervan's The Analytical Greek Lexicon {1975} translates "wherefore, why." Thus "through the one man's disobedience the many were made sinners" (Romans 5:19), in Adam "all had sinned" {cf. 1 Corinthians 15:22}, both statements of effect, not of causation. The entire future of mankind was present in Adam's loins and Eve's ovary, collectively considered, when the first couple had disobeyed Yaweh and thus "all had sinned" {cf. 1 Corinthians 15:22.} Every human was, is and will be conceived with sin in his/her body and thereby viewed justly by Yaweh as a sinner:

הֵן-בְּעָווֹן חוֹלָלְתִּי; וּבְחֵטְא, יֶחֱמַתְנִי אִמִּי: דָוִד

David:
"Behold, with sin I was born, and my mother conceived me with sin."
—Psalm 51:5{7}

The first couple's sin has stained all mankind because each individual conception was, is or will be formed by Adam's future sperms fertilizing Eve's 'exponentially pyramiding egg chain':

"...mitochondrial DNA, snippets of DNA that reside outside the nuclei of living cells, are passed down by mothers from generation to generation."[10] Each human

---

10. Why should mitochondria define species?, "Human Evolution", Mark Stoeckle at Rockefeller University and David Thaler at the University of Basel, 2018, Vol. 33 - n. 1-2 page 1-30

being has been, is or will be conceived as a sinner {cf. Genesis 3:20}, but not because he/she at birth had sinned. In effect the sperm and eggs necessary for the conceptions of all mankind existed in Eve's ovary at the precise moment of disobedience and thus became mortally stained by that sinful act. The natural effect of this immoral stain is that at conception man is predisposed to sinning and thus is born in order to die.

And 3] אֶל־אִישֵׁךְ, תְּשׁוּקָתֵךְ, וְהוּא, יִמְשָׁל־בָּךְ [your desire (will be) towards your husband, he will rule over you.] (Genesis 3:16)

This part of Eve's penalty for disobeying God must be analyzed in the context of Genesis 2:23-24 because it addresses how the "one flesh" is to operate structurally as well as harmoniously. While they "cleave" she is to experience "greatly" magnified pain when birthing and he is to brave all the earth's elements in hunting and gathering edibles for his hungry family. Yet the next two phrases seem uncomplimentary: the wife is to desire the one who rules over her. In other words, it can be taken as she is to take whatever he gives and he does not have to desire the woman whose life he rules. This to me sounds like the gateway to polygamy and/or wife abuse. As they say today, there is no 'equal justice' in Eve's sentence! The word for desire [תְּשׁוּקָתֵךְ] is derived from שׁוּף, which means to run after, hence desire and longing. If I had read this in Moses's time I would have thought Eve's punishment turned her into a second-class human, no longer one of God's image-bearers, subjecting her to the whims of a tyrant. I am relieved, however, that I can rely on Paul's words in the 5th chapter of Ephesians for clarification of what I might have thought had I lived over three millennia ago.

Sinning started to take a 'hold' on life when the couple's first son, Cain, in a fit of jealous rage murdered Abel, his brother:

> Yaweh to Cain:
> "Why are you angry? And why has your countenance fallen? If you will יָטַב will not {your countenance} be lifted up? And if you will not יָטַב, sin is crouching at the door; and its desire {cf. 3:16} is for you, but you must master it."
> —Genesis 4:6-7

The *Hiphil* of יָטַב translates 'to do well/good,' which better reads 'to do a good thing well.' What Yaweh had explained to Cain was that anger had a threshold which when exceeded would lead to sin and sinning. Rage can be easily discerned in the human face, making the bearer unattractive socially. God gave Cain the 'key' to "mastering" anger: do a good deed well. This means that a chosen action is both content-wise {good} and completion-wise {well} acceptable to Him for resisting sin's allurement, the power of which is directly proportionable to rage's strength. In a broad sense this applies favorably when dealing with any 'horizontal' {social} relationship whereas for the 'vertical' {divine} one Jesus instructs:

> "If...you are presenting your offering at the altar and there remember that your brother has something against you, leave your offering

> there before the altar and go your way; first be reconciled to your brother and then come and present your offering."
>
> —Matthew 5:23-24

Then there is Paul's admonition relevant to both the vertical as well as horizontal relationships:

> Be angry and [yet] do not sin; do not let the sun go down on your anger and do not give the devil an opportunity.
>
> —Ephesians 4:26-27

From then on murder plagued all future families, tribes and cultures and spawned relational distrust, envy and hatred down through the ages in the human race. Recognizing the shame of being hidden from Yaweh's face while still in His presence (cf. Genesis 4:14,16), Cain fled to Nod, which was east of Eden, but before departing expressed to his Evictor, "whoever finds me will kill me." (v. 15) Heedful of that concern, the Lord "appointed a sign" (v. 15) to warn away all potential assassins. But for me His solution begs this quandary: of whom was Cain thinking – his own siblings or wandering strangers? If the latter, how did they come into? In order to sort this out, we need to understand what social relationships came into being when He made the first אָדָם [human being] in His image, particularly אִישׁ [a man].

Yaweh formed a אִשָּׁה [woman] out of a rib of אָדָם (Genesis 2:23) to be his עֵזֶר [helper (v. 20)] as well as his אִשָּׁה [wife (v. 24).] She was named חַוָּה [Keh-vah (life)]

by him to acknowledge her becoming "the mother of all living {beings}" (Genesis 3:20) {Note: the LXX translation for the first woman is Ζωή [Zo-ay (life)] which Latin scribes later translated as Eva and English tradition promoted as Eve.} Cain had a אִשָּׁה [woman, wife (4:17)] as did Seth (4:26), which for me immediately raises the question: "From whom and where?" Moses's silence on this question permits mankind only to speculate as to how the earth became humanly populated by the first couple's children. According to various Abrahamic traditions as well as the Book of Jubilees, Awan was the wife and sister of Cain as well as the daughter of Adam and Eve while in other Abrahamic texts, like the Cave of Treasures, she is called Qelima. Similarly, her sister Azura was the wife of Cain's two brothers, Abel and Seth (the Book of Jubilees, chapter 4.) In one Hebrew chronological work, she is called Balbira. (Wikipedia)

Well now, a few questions come to me which pertain to how the first couple exponentially expanded a third and following generations:

1. Did the first man have relations with his daughters as did Lot supposedly with his two daughters (Genesis 19:30-36)?
2. How many children did Eve bear successfully for not only first man but for her son(s) as well?
3. Who assisted Cain in building a city (Genesis 4:17) out of Yaweh's presence?

Yaweh's Breath had conveyed to Moses that first man had not been conceived and carried in a woman's womb prior to being born, but rather had been formed by Yaweh out of the earth's dust. (Genesis 2:7) Nor was his helpmeet, whom He had "fashioned" (v. 21-22) from one of Adam's ribs. This couple was the first mentioned to procreate children, thereby establishing mankind's initial generation. Today's human practices of biological couplings are strictly forbidden by law today: either a mother sleeping with her son or a daughter sleeping with either her father or a brother. My faith guides me to believe the 'genesis of humanity' was divinely permitted and protected health-wise by nature's setting for a few generations in order for the earth to become populated.

There is another perspective I wish to share that is germane to my three questions. It is offered by a personal friend of mine, Tremper Longman III:

> ...the past twenty years have brought powerful new evidence in favor of evolution, primarily in the field of genetics...with the growing evidence that human beings go back to an original population of some thousands of individuals, not an original couple named Adam and Eve." (p.xvi)[11]
>
> "Science has proposed a theory {cf. p. 76}, evolution, that has been supported by abundant evidence provided by the fossil record and, more recently and pointedly, by genetic evidence. The evidence is so consistent with the theory that only outlier scientists doubt that humanity was created through an evolutionary that involves common descent...these scientists...believe {the Bible} teaches that God created human beings

---

11. Confronting Old Testament Controversies, Tremper Longman III, Baker Books, Grand Rapids, MI, 2019, page 64

> by a special act of creation and not through the providence-guided means of evolution {i.e., "evolutionary creationism"

Here I consider Tremper's 'Acihilles heel' to be: what was the foundational origin for the evolutionary process of 'common descent'? Was it the creation of marine creatures, or of birds, or of cattle, or of creeping things, or of cattle?

> Evolution does not work by producing a single couple out of a previous population; rather, a certain group of the previous population becomes isolated from the larger group, and their distinctive gene pool leads to the new species. This process is complex...but the bottom line is that the genetic evidence is clear that humanity does not go back to a single couple from which all later *Homo sapiens* descended...we can have *Homo sapiens* who were not endowed with th(e) status {of divine image bearers}...the image of God is not a quality or an attribute of human beings but rather a status that comes with responsibility. (*ibid*, p. 62)

Does the Bible recognize any existence of a human being who does not bear God's image?

> It is my conclusion that evolution and all its entailments are no threat to the biblical account of creation, which has no interest in telling us about God's method, the 'how,' of creation...to argue against evolution...brings embarrassment to the gospel (in the sense that Augustine

> describes those who try to argue that the Bible differs from the conclusions derived from the honest research of even non-Christian thinkers).
> (*ibid*, p. 76)

Not all research is honest due to many investigators' dependence on needed funding. Also, the 'take-away' I garnered from the Covid-19 pandemic is that not all of science is 'settled', including climate change as well as genetics.

NOAH

From the original gene pool of only two, life's human population over centuries swelled exponentially. According to the book of Adam's generations in Genesis 5, Noah reached the age of 500 approximately 6,650 years after God had created the first couple. Just imagine what the world's human population had become over that time span! The conventional metric (a society doubles in population every 25 years) I've heard would make it in the billions, though severe diseases and war should make it lower substantially.

When I first came to accept Yaweh's Son as my Lord, I studied with interest the extension of years Moses literally narrated between the first man and the life of Noah. Unfortunately, the one memorable result of my computation was that Methuselah had drowned in the same flood that ark had survived. The one assumption my calculations took into account was that יָלַד [to beget; to father/sire; to generate; to produce; to cause to exist] Moses employed 33 times in three forms from Genesis 4:18 to 5:32 was that "begat"/ "became the father of" inferred 'immediately generated', thereby ignoring the possibility that 'multi-generationally skipping' could have occurred. But such might not be the case. My first thought questioned how Moses described the generations of Abraham's two sons: for Ishmael, Abraham "יָבֹא [went into] Hagar and she conceived" (Genesis 16:4) whereas for Isaac, "Yaweh יַעַשׂ [accomplished] what He had promised to Sarah...she conceived and תֵּלֶד [begat] a son לְ [for] Abraham." (Genesis 21:1-2) In other words, Isaac's conception by 'divine interruption' occurred within Sarah during Abraham's "old age." (v. 2) The only relevance I can wean from these two clippings of Abraham's life is that Ishmael was his first born, not Isaac, but Yaweh's book of life had intended that the Patriarch's grandson, Jacob {Israel}, was to come to life via Isaac's seed, which He had "accomplished" in his grandmother.

Another potential argument for 'multi-generationally skipping' is the first entry itself in first man's book of generations:

> When Adam had lived one hundred and thirty years he יָלַד [begot] in his own likeness, according to His image...Seth."
> —Genesis 5:3

Neither Cain, the first couple's first born son (Genesis 4:1), nor Abel, his brother he murdered, are named in this entry. Thus, the book commences with the mention of a third {at least} son – not the first born. But though the 'multi-generationally skipping' aspect is feasible in יָלַד, I prefer not to pursue that because it might convey erroneously my bias toward 'science' when interpreting Genesis 5. The presupposition of my belief in and of Jesus Christ is that God's Breath has inspired the preserved writings of all the Bible's content and, thus, my faith must not rely on what is empirically sourced to solve divinely sourced mysteries defying comprehension for all of us created in His image.

It's interesting, however, to wonder: does this 'firstborn' theme dominate all of Genesis 5: the oldest son תֵּלֶד [begat] by his father and his אִשָּׁה [wife] alive when the father dies becomes entitled to the family's בְּכֹרָה [birthright {cf. Genesis 25:31-34}]? I included "and his אִשָּׁה [wife]" in order to exclude, based on Ishmael's origin {Genesis 16:4}, any father's son who had been 'extramaritally' born. Is it possible Yaweh's Breath through Moses inspired the book of Adam's generations to serve as the paradigm for primogeniture {the state of being the firstborn child; the right of succession belonging to the firstborn child, especially the rule by which the whole real estate of an intestate passed to the eldest son} to provide a smooth succession of future family governance? Considering Moses's childhood royal upbringing in Egypt, when three female pharaohs {Merneith (3200-2900 BC), Sobekneferu (1806–1802 BC) and Hatshepsut (1578-1478 BC) had already reigned, the notion of primogeniture must have been unknown to him. But it's worth noting that in ancient China up to the 20th century "the eldest son...was the rightful heir" of his dead father's estate.[12]

---

12. **Life and Death in Shanghai**, Nien Cheng, Grove Press, NY, 1986, page 88

Now by the time of Noah the world had become exponentially populated by two 'classes' Moses distinguished as sons of God and daughters of man. (6:2) My quandary is whether this is a moral or generational difference. If the latter, then we fall into the grips of 'science', for it believes that up to nine (and counting?) distinct species of humans [הָאָדָם of Genesis 6:1] had roamed the earth in early history. Included in this belief was the absorption of Neanderthals (an extinct human species that roamed ice-age Europe between 120,000 and 35,000 years ago and was physically distinguished by a receding forehead and prominent brow ridges) into the Homo sapiens species, a similar group of individuals capable of exchanging genes through interbreeding. Were the Neanderthals Moses's הַנְּפִלִים [the Nephilim / giants {cf. Numbers 13:33, 1 Chronicles 20:6}]? Science provides no explanation for either species' origin while Paul challenges the foundational belief of science:

> (God) made from one (some manuscripts add "blood") every nation of mankind to live on all the face of the earth, having determined their appointed times and the boundaries of their habitation.
> —Acts 17:26

So what, then, would the moral distinction be? My guess is that "the sons of God" (v. 2) is a traditional metaphor alluding to both males and females seeking and obeying Yaweh (influenced by Job 1:6, Isaiah 63:16, Hosea 1:10) whereas "the daughters of man," another traditional metaphor, refers to males and females who

subscribe to humanist/paganistic practices. Erosion of the former cultural community becomes apparent from verse 2: "the sons of God ...took wives for themselves" solely because of their beauty; discernment of character had no influence on the sons of God for they took as wives "whomever they chose." The families seeking Yaweh slowly disappeared, compelling Him to say to Themselves, "My Breath shall not judge/punish [דין - IV: to judge, punish with accusative בְּ]¹³ man [בָאָדָם] forever when he errs, he is flesh; his days shall be one hundred and twenty years."(v.3) Now first man had lived to the age of 930 (Genesis 5:4), Seth to 912 (v. 8), Enosh to 905 (v. 11), Kenan to 910 (v. 14), Mahalalel to 895 (v. 17), Jared to 962 (v. 20), Enoch only to 365 (v. 24), Methuselah to 969 (v. 27), Lamach to 777 (v. 31) and Noah was 500 (v. 32) when he "found favor in the eyes of the Lord." (Genesis 6:8) Yet the life-span drop to the age of 125, though severe, had no effect for the Lord determined that "every intent of the thoughts of (man's) heart was only evil continually" (v. 5), that "all" mankind's moral discerning and choosing had turned from Him:

> David:
> Yaweh has looked down from heaven upon the sons of men, to see if there are any who understand, who seek after God. They all have turned aside; together they have become corrupt. There is no one who does good, not even one.
> —Psalm 14:2-3

---

13. The Analytical Hebrew and Chaldee Lexicon, Benjamin Davidson, Hendrickson Academic, New edition, 1981, page 147

And the grave consequence is Genesis 6:6-7:

... וַיִּנָּחֶם יְהוָה, כִּי־עָשָׂה אֶת־הָאָדָם בָּאָרֶץ; וַיִּתְעַצֵּב, אֶל־לִבּוֹ
וַיֹּאמֶר יְהוָה,.... כִּי נִחַמְתִּי, כִּי עֲשִׂיתִם

<u>**LXX**</u>: καὶ ἐνεθυμήθη ὁ θεὸς ὅτι ἐποίησεν τὸν ἄνθρωπον ἐπὶ τῆς γῆς, κα ἰδιενοήθη. κα ἰεπῖεν ὁθεός...ὅ 'τι ἐθυμώθην ὅτι πέοίησα αὐτούς.'

[And Yaweh was sorry that He had made man on the earth and He was grieved in His Heart....And Yaweh said...I am sorry that I have made them.]

The two words here, "sorry" and "grieved," raise difficult questions concerning the attributes of God, which are enshrouded in the realm of incomprehensibility:

> Yaweh:
> "...My thoughts are not your thoughts, neither are your ways My ways."
> —Isaiah 55:8
>
> Job:
> "...these are the fringes of His ways, and how faint a word we hear of Him but His mighty thunder – who can understand?"
> —Job 26:14
>
> David:
> "Great is Yaweh and highly to be praised, and His greatness is unsearchable.
> —Psalm 145:3

His complete 'personhood' can only be understood in the metaphysical way inasmuch throughout the history of His image bearers His attributes have been based

solely on speculative, abstract reasoning. Reformed theologians today recognize His divine nature in two distinct nuances:

1. His absolute attributes seek to describe God before creation and include immutable, omniscient, infallible, self-sufficient, incomprehensible, omnipresent, impassible, invisible and eternal;
2. His relative {those which apply to Him in relation to His creation} attributes comprise blessed (1 Timothy 6:15), perfect (Matthew 5:48), most wise (Romans 16:27), just and right (Deuteronomy 32:4), "most merciful and gracious, long-suffering, and abundant in goodness and truth." (Westminster Confession of Faith's Larger Catechism, Q. 7)

The two Genesis 6 verses above compel me to wonder whether God's reactions of sorrow and upset had been the result of His being surprised or had He foreknown this. Was His response of regret a surprise or had He expected this? Can Yaweh ever be surprised? No, because his omniscient attribute encompasses both foreknowledge within His creation as well as His all-knowing of the life He had created. His book of life did not allow for such a possibility inasmuch as Yaweh had authored its entirety, thus enabling Him to foreknow the disposition of every man's heart toward Him precisely as Moses by His Breath had dictated in Genesis 6.

But then there also is this question: does God's impassable nature, the inability to suffer or feel pain, indicate He is apathetic and unaffected by all emotions and thereby prohibited from being loving and compassionate with His image bearers? In other words, how can Yaweh have a passible nature when His absolute attribute of immutability accompanies Him wherever and whenever He sovereignly engages His creation {cf. Westminster Confession of Faith 5.1-3 and Larger Catechism, Q. 18,20}? There is no answer here because of Yaweh's incomprehensibility. The impossibility for any answer reminds me of the prosecuting lawyer who had asked the defense witness, a husband, in court: "When did you stop beating your wife?"

> Yaweh:
> "I am God...and there is no one like Me, declaring the end from the beginning and from ancient times things which have not been done, saying, 'My purpose will be established and I will accomplish all My good pleasure.'"
> —Isaiah 46:9-10

In summary, then, with this rhetorical question I wish to move on: In Genesis 6:6-7, was God reacting in a divine way while His Breath had inspired Moses to 'anthropomorphize' it as sorrow and grief for man's appreciation? His remorse is later put into a 'balance':

> "Do I have any pleasure in the death of God, "rather than that he should turn from his ways and live?...For I have no pleasure in the death of anyone who dies," declares the Lord God. "Therefore. Repent and live"
> —Ezekiel 18:23,32

> For the word of the cross is foolishness to those who are perishing.
> —1 Corinthians 1:18

> The Lord is...patient toward you, not wishing for any to perish but for all {of you} to come to repentance.
> —2 Peter 3:9

While God bears no responsibility for people turning away from Him, their second death {cf. Revelation 2:11} in no way contradicts His loving nature. For the eternal consequence of every sin a person commits Yaweh presents him/her with a safety net: repent and sin no more. Politicians today have developed an insincere, self-contradictory form of apology, "If I have offended anyone, I am sorry," but then go forth acting as if they hadn't done anything wrong. Judas's social regret (Matthew 27:3) exemplifies what a true social repentance would yield. Being honestly 'sorry' is not an expression of repentance but of regret. His regret for giving life to that magnitude of humanity established over multi millennia was merely an emotional sadness about the impending demise of the earth's total or partial population {cf. vs. 7,13.}

Here is a sketchy perspective of mankind's history prior to Noah's era as theorized by science:

- The paleolithic phase of the Stone Age lasted about 2.5 million years, when primitive stone implements were made and used[14]

---

14. Who Discovered America?, Gavin Menzies, Harper Collins Publishers, 2013, page 48

- **Double-bladed stone hand axes were made in Africa 800,000 years ago**[15]
- **Circa 300,000 B.C. Indo-Europeans settled in central Anatolia {Asia Minor}**[16]
- **Paleolithic man dwelt in Anatolia 200,000 years ago**[17]
- **Neolithic (denoting the later part of the Stone Age, when ground or polished stone weapons and implements prevailed) man settled southern Crete 100,000 years ago**[18]
- **Florida and Brazil were settled circa 40,000 B.C.**[19];
- **The environs of Ephesus date back to 8,200 B.C.**[20];
- **People began worshipping at Stonehenge circa 7,200 B.C.**[21]
- **The Minoan civilization began circa 7,000 B.C.**[22];
- **The book of Genesis was dictated by Moses circa1445-1405 B.C.**

---

15. The Lost Empire of Atlantis, Gavin Menzies, Harper Collins Publishers, 2012, page 91
16. Who Discovered America?, Gavin Menzies, Harper Collins Publishers, 2013, page 330
17. Who Discovered America?, Gavin Menzies, Harper Collins Publishers, 2013, page 48
18. Who Discovered America?, Gavin Menzies, Harper Collins Publishers, 2013, page 42
19. Who Discovered America?, Gavin Menzies, Harper Collins Publishers, 2013, page 246
20. Who Discovered America?, Gavin Menzies, Harper Collins Publishers, 2013, page 48
21. The Lost Empire of Atlantis, Gavin Menzies, Harper Collins Publishers, 2012, page 229
22. Who Discovered America?, Gavin Menzies, Harper Collins Publishers, 2013, page 42

I offer this smattering of historic trivia merely to position science's notion of when Adam was created: over 800,000 years ago in Mesopotamia, the region of Western Asia situated within the Tigris–Euphrates river system. Though the Scriptures are silent about when mankind's history commenced, science's theory of dating in no way disputes that Noah was 500 years old after some 6,650 years had already transpired since his ancestors, the first couple, were made.

What the heavens continued to declare, God's glory, the great multitude of His image-bearers had ceased doing when Noah was 500 years old. Because His book of life had called for destruction of all humans alive at that time, Yaweh had retained Noah, "a righteous man, blameless in his time {who} walked with {Him}" (v. 9; 7:1), his wife, their three sons and daughters-in-law for the care of the animals onboard, to keep the ark afloat and to source the gene pool for future generations, just as did Adam, Eve and their first procreated children. Noah's days had been significantly designed as a foreshadowing of His Son's later coming {cf. Matthew 24:37.} To him the Lord confided: "The end of all flesh has come before Me...I am about to destroy them with the earth."(v. 13) While God's sorrow over this extraordinary annihilation was strong, His sense of justice prevented Him from altering the book of life's 'directions':

> Balaam to Balak:
> "God is not a man that he should lie, nor a son of man that he should repent."
> —Numbers 23:19

> "...(the Glory of Israel) is not a man that He should change His mind."
> —1 Samuel 15:29

David:
> "Yaweh has sworn and will not change His mind [נחם]."
> —Psalm 110:4

Observable and sense-experienced situations bring into question whether God's means, i.e., "with the earth," to drown the entire (Genesis 7:21-22,8:13; 2 Peter 3:6) world's population was plausible considering the quantity of water needed to substantially cover all the earth's landmass {cf. Genesis 7:19-20; 8:5; 2 Peter 3:5} One theory focuses on the Black Sea's metamorphosis as the explanation for the flood occurring only on a portion of the earth:

> "At one time, the Black Sea was a freshwater lake (with) a water level (formerly) much lower (than) during (contemporary) quest(s) for ancient shorelines, drowned river valleys and human-built structures that all suggest a once-shallower Black Sea (resulting from) the last glaciation — but when, and especially how rapidly, it became a sea is still hotly debated.
> In 1997, Walter Pitman and Bill Ryan of Columbia University proposed a controversial hypothesis: that the sea level abruptly rose about 7,200 years ago, due to salty Mediterranean water breaking through a natural dam across the Bosporus Strait and flooding the freshwater Black Sea—timing that they note coincides roughly with the biblical story of Noah's Flood (see Geotimes, February 2004). The hypothesis

is still disputed, and archaeologists, historians and oceanographers continue to search for evidence of Neolithic sites that might have been inundated by the rising sea."[23,24]

"Four years ago, scientists thought they had found the perfect place to settle the Noah flood debate: A farmer's house on a bluff overlooking the Black Sea, built about 7,500 years ago — just before tidal waves inundated the homestead, submerged miles of coastline and turned the freshwater lake into a salty sea. Scholars agree the Black Sea flooded when rising world sea levels caused the Mediterranean to burst over land and fill the then-freshwater lake. The flood was so monstrous it raised water levels by 509 feet (155 meters) and submerged up to 58,000 square miles (150,000 square kilometers) of land, an area roughly the size of the state of Georgia. But scholars are divided on when the flood occurred, and how rapidly. Most believed it took place about 9,000 years ago and was gradual. But Columbia University marine geologists Walter Pitman and William Ryan wrote in 1997 that the flood was sudden and took place about 7,150 years ago. The scientists' conclusions reinvigorated the Noah flood debate."[25]

---

23. Buried Beneath the Black Sea: Cities and Ships Submerged by Carolyn Gramling, http://www.geotimes.org/jan07/feature_BlackSea.html Viewed: 3/20023
24. cf. "Evidence for a Flood" by James Trefil, April 1, 2000: smithsonianmag.com
25. (Ocean archaeologists hunt Noah's flood under Black Sea, Richard C. Lewis, Associated Press, https://www.chron.com/news/nation-world/article/Ocean-archaeologists-hunt-Noah-s-flood-under-1642816.php, Viewed 3/2023

Dr. (Robert) Ballard's ongoing Black Sea project seeks evidence of a great flood that may have struck the region thousands of years ago[26]:

"Originally a land-locked fresh water lake, the Black Sea was flooded with salt water from the Mediterranean Sea during the Holocene {cf. paragraph below.} The influx of salt water essentially smothered the fresh water below it because a lack of internal motion and mixing meant that no fresh oxygen reached the deep waters, creating a meromictic body of water. The anoxic environment, which is hostile to many biological organisms that destroy wood in the oxygenated waters, provides an excellent testing site for deep water archaeological survey.

In a series of expeditions, a team of marine archaeologists led by Ballard identified what appeared to be ancient shorelines, freshwater snail shells, and drowned river valleys in roughly 300 feet (100 m) of water off the Black Sea coast of modern Turkey... Radiocarbon dating of freshwater mollusk remains indicated an age of about 7,000 years.

In 2000, the team conducted an expedition that focused on the exploration of the sea bed about 15–30 km west of Sinop, and an additional deep-water survey east and north of the peninsula. Their project had several goals. They sought to discover whether human habitation sites could be identified on the ancient submerged landscape...

According to a report in New Scientist magazine (May 4, 2002, p. 13), the researchers

---

26. https://www.oceanexplorationtrust.org/our-founder Viewed: 3/2023

found an underwater delta south of the Bosporus. There was evidence for a strong flow of fresh water out of the Black Sea in the 8th millennium BC. Ballard's research has contributed to the debate over the Black Sea deluge theory."[27]

∙∙

[Note: the Holocene Epoch is the current period of geologic time...The Holocene Epoch began 12,000 to 11,500 years ago at the close of the Paleolithic Ice Age and continues through today. As Earth entered a warming trend, the glaciers of the late Paleolithic retreated.]

∙∙

A good friend of mine, a backer of Dr. Ballard's expeditions, a decade ago confirmed to me that He had captured on video various ancient structures resting on the old freshwater shoreline but his busy schedule had prevented him and his crew from doing any of the submerged exploring he and his crew had done on the Titanic.

But there exists an interesting argument to counter science's concern about the lack of water to cover the entire earth, including the tops of the Himalayan mountains: existence of "the waters... above the distance" (Genesis 1:6-7) formed by Yaweh to separate the waters below that distance. The waters above this expanse could well have been a physically invisible

---

27. https://en.wikipedia.org/wiki/Robert_Ballard#Black_Sea Viewed 3/2023

water reservoir on reserve for His intended and foreknown need:

> ...by the Word of God {the} heavens existed long ago and {the} earth was formed out of water and by water through which the world was destroyed, being flooded with water.
> —2 Peter 3:5-6

> "At any one instant, the Earth's atmosphere contains 37.5 million-billion gallons of water vapor – enough to cover the entire surface of the planet with 1 inch of rain if condensed. This amount is recycled, through evaporation powered by the Sun, 40 times each year in what is known as the hydrologic cycle." (Posted on February 5, 2018 by "WeatherGuys" Editor)

After all, nothing is impossible with God. (Luke 1:37)

Now Native American archaeology today asserts that Indian migrations some 30,000 years ago had spawned small villages in coastal parts of Central America. This has come to light by carbon-dating organic residues surrounding man-made rock implements, mostly arrowheads and spear points. But because carbon-dating rock is futile, science cannot discount that these implements could have been humanly discarded at a much later date:

> At its most basic level, carbon dating is the method of determining the age of organic material by measuring the levels of carbon found in it. Specifically, there are two types of carbon found in organic materials: carbon 12 (C-12) and

carbon 14 (C-14). It is imperative to remember that the material must have been alive at one point to absorb the carbon, meaning that carbon dating of rocks or other inorganic objects is nothing more than inaccurate guesswork.[28]

Even the histories of Chinese and Egyptian civilizations postdate Noah's flood and thus, whether that flood had universal or only local presence, its effect was indeed universal because all {cf. Matthew 24:39} human flesh was "blotted out" (6:7) except for Noah and his family afloat in their ark.

Moses had not been inspired to note the location of where nor the date of when the ark started to float but he did dictate when the ark had rested on Mt. Ararat (in Turkey)[29]: on the seventeenth day of the seventh חֹדֶשׁ [month.] (Genesis 8:5) This is Moses's first use of חֹדֶשׁ, indicating either that Noah was trained in astronomy and had kept a log on the ark that folklore later adopted or that His Breath had inspired Moses to be somewhat precise in dating an event. It's important to note that many contemporary archaeologists and anthropologists are convinced many civilizations from 4,500 BC to 1500 BC were well versed in marine navigation, erecting calendar monuments and telling time: Egyptian, Minoan, Sumerian, to name some of the major ones. However, what was the year the ark landed on Mt. Ararat remains a mystery, even though the above scholars theorizing a local flood surmise around 7,000 years ago.

---

28. Labmate-online.com, May 20 2014
29. cf. this youtube video: https://www.youtube.com/watch?v=oQwfU7DvUyE

The pious ritual of Genesis 8 mirrors the offerings Cain and Abel had made to Yaweh in Genesis 4:3-4: God had regard for Abel's "fat portions," implying a burnt offering, whereas Noah's clean animals and birds burnt on an altar was a "soothing aroma" (Genesis 8:21) to Yaweh. The altar's form then "of no prescribed shape (was) constructed of earth and stone...Noah's sacrifices on the alter were an expression of thanksgiving for deliverance from the flood."[30] Since the ark had been closed up for some 200 days, many of the animal pairs began procreating so that by the time Noah built the altar, he had an ample choice of "clean" ones to offer to the Lord without diminishing the respective gene pools that had originally entered the ark.

Then some 2½ months after the ark had settled on Mount Ararat, "the tops of the mountains became visible." (Genesis 8:5) After an additional 47 plus days a released dove brought "a freshly picked olive leaf" (v.11) in its beak back to Noah. From Google online I learned:

> The olive tree is a hardened fighter. It can withstand conditions of stress that in other trees would be unimaginable. It withstands low temperatures and high ones also. It puts up with a shortage of water and can be productive from sea level up to an altitude of 1,200 meters.

Inasmuch as Mount Ararat's peak (5,137 meters) appeared many days before the soil at the 1,200 meter elevation had dried out, was it possible for the olive

---

30. Evangelical Dictionary of Theology, Walter Elwell, editor; Baker; pages 35-36

leaf's tree to mature in Ararat's base within a forty-day period? Now as for the Black Sea's changes in water content and depth, the case for the flood having been a merely a local event is unconvincing, particularly since those changes could just as well have been the result of a flood over all the earth. What is useful, though, is that the above archeologist and maritime explorer both peg the era to be roughly 5,000 BC. While the answer to this enigma could influence the debate over the flood's scope, the compelling case for universality is that God's covenant with Noah and his family had addressed it:

> The Lord:
> "I will never again destroy every living thing as I have done."
> —Genesis 8:21

> The Lord:
> "...neither shall there again be a flood to destroy the earth...never again shall the water become a flood to destroy all flesh."
> —Genesis 9:11,15

The 'divine/human' covenant He graciously offered to Noah, his family "and every living creature that (was) with (him), for all successive generations."(v. 12) The covenant beneficiaries included every creature which had disembarked from the ark (9:10). It was from Noah, his wife, his three sons and one grandson that "the whole earth was populated" (v.19) again.

The Lord went ahead with the formalization of His pledge to "never again curse the ground...and I will never again destroy every living thing," regardless of His full knowledge that "the intent of man's heart is evil from his youth..." (Genesis 8:21), which included the ninth and tenth generations of the original sinners, Adam and Eve.

Noah died at the age of 950, not 120 (Genesis 6:3), implicitly because he had performed "all that God had commanded him..." (Genesis 6:22) Chapter 10 focuses on the growth and separations from one another of the eleventh and beyond generations, resulting in the elimination of the language unifying Noah and his immediate family: "everyone according to his language (v.5), "according to their languages, by their lands, by their nations," (v. 20) "according to languages, by their lands, according to their nations." (v.31) Yet for a reason I cannot explain, chapter 11 commences as if the time has reverted back to when Noah's family had disembarked from the ark: "Now the whole earth used the same language and the same words." But Genesis 11:10 to 19 appears to reasonably bridge verse 10:24 with verse 25, thereby using 11:1-9 as explanation why distinct languages had come into existence. Among the vastly expanding Noahic generations.

The inescapable tension of using scientifically derived dates for the history of God's image-bearers up to Noah's era to provide a sense of 'factual accuracy' to Moses's inspired narrative is irreconcilable to my mind; discoveries for instance like double bladed stones found in Africa pointing to human life some 800,000 years ago and traces of the flood which indicates its occurrence to be circa 5000 BC. If these became superimposed onto

Moses's first nine chapters of Genesis one conceivably could assert that Adam and Eve had roamed the earth roughly 800,000 years ago, inferring a time span 795,000 years between chapters 1 and 9. The only way this could possibly be true is the interpretation (without any Biblical merit) that the lineage from Adam to Noah (Genesis 5:4-32) was not direct but interspersed with thousands upon thousands of unlisted individuals.

Now what had become the moral system guiding mankind from Adam to Genesis 11:24? In other words, by what rules had the generations of the first couple been guided in order to avoid offending Yaweh? Moses had provided very little evidence:

- The first couple gained the knowledge of distinguishing good from evil (Genesis 3:6,22);
- The Lord posed the sanction on Eve to long/desire towards her husband and to abide with his rule over her (Genesis 3:16);
- Every man was responsible to God for all things he/she did (Genesis 3:12-13);
- Yaweh told Cain he had to rule/have power over sin. (Genesis 4:7)

As the perfect 'Father', it has to be assumed that He would not have mentioned "sin" to Cain without explaining to him exactly what it entailed. It's most likely as well that His foreknowledge of Cain's future slaying of Abel had prompted this warning, thus implying He had included the murder of a fellow human being as a sin {cf. I John 3:12.}

After Cain's banishment by Yaweh for his murdering Abel in a fit of rage, over a period of time Eve gave birth to another son, Seth, to replace Abel's absence. Sometime later she must have also birthed a daughter to enable Seth to father his own son, Enosh, the first couple's first grandchild:

אָז הוּחַל, לִקְרֹא בְּשֵׁם יְהוָה [then they {Adam, Eve, Seth} began {cf. Genesis 9:20} to invoke Yaweh's name.]
—Genesis 4:26

Here is the first family, paradigm of the extended family, invoking their Creator's personal name {cf. Exodus 3:14} in prayerful gratitude for a new generation's life. Moses' use of the Hophal preterite impersonal for חָלַל gives this sentence the lack of a determinate subject and thus infers all mankind as well, establishing the first nuclear family's invocation as the standard for future reverential prayers to the Creator:

...Abram built an alter to Yaweh וַיִּקְרָא בְּשֵׁם יְהוָה [and invoked Yaweh's name.]
—Genesis 12:8

וַיִּקְרָא שָׁם אַבְרָם, בְּשֵׁם יְהוָה [and there Abram invoked Yaweh's name.]
—Genesis 13:4

וַתִּקְרָא שֵׁם-יְהוָה [and she {Hagar} invoked Yaweh's name...]
—Genesis 16:13

וַיִּקְרָא-שָׁם--בְּשֵׁם יְהוָה, אֵל עוֹלָם [and there Abraham invoked {the} name of Yaweh, {the} everlasting God.]

—Genesis 21:33

So Isaac built an alter there וַיִּקְרָא בְּשֵׁם יְהוָה [and invoked Yaweh's name.]

—Genesis 26:25

The burnt offering [עֹלָה] appears initially in Genesis 8:20 when after the flood had disappeared Noah had sought to appease Yaweh with the varying aromas of charred meats. (Genesis 8:20-21) From then on the burnt offering became reverentially instituted as mankind's humble and loving worship of Him.

Now merely as a note of interest I wish to delineate how the Scriptures variously call, name and identify the Creator, eventhough I disagree with the hypotheses of biblical higher criticism and detest providing any 'false fodder' for it:

- From the blazing bush He told Moses, "אֶהְיֶה אֲשֶׁר אֶהְיֶה [I AM WHO I AM]... and say to the sons of Israel, 'אֶהְיֶה [I AM] has sent me to you.'" (Exodus :14)
- Up to Noah's era Moses had employed אֱלֹהִים, which signifies His title. (Genesis 1:1 to 2:3{2x}; 4:25)
- Moses very rarely used its modification: הָאֱלֹהִים. (Genesis 5:22; 6:2,4,9)
- Then Moses's narrative began to employ יְהוָה, an apparent derivative of אֶהְיֶה from Exodus 3:14. (Genesis 4:3,4,6,9, 13, 15{2x})

- **The Creator's formal name was the combination of His personal name preceded by His title:** יְהוָה אֱלֹהִים. (Genesis 2:4,5,7,8,9,15,16,18,19,21,22; 3:1,8,9,13,14,21,22,23)
- **And the regal salutation to Yaweh [יְהוָה] became** אֲדֹנָי יְהוִה [Lord Yaweh.] (Genesis 15:2,8)

Now Genesis 5:22,24 says, "Enoch walked with God... and he was not, for God received him {cf. 2 Kings 2:11.}" At the beginning of Noah's life Yaweh ruefully {cf. 6:6} reminded Themselves that His "Breath לֹא־יָדוֹן [will not judge] man forever" (6:3), inasmuch as "the wickedness of man was great" (v. 5), immense in the quantity of sins associated with each person's behavior, possibly implying extreme depths and breadths of varying sinful actions; Satan had influenced man's mind to commit to all degrees every form and manner of disobedience to Him {cf. v. 11.} Yet Noah "found favor in the eyes of Yaweh...Noah was a righteous man, blameless in his time; Noah walked with הָאֱלֹהִים"(vs. 8-9) {cf. Genesis 5:22,24.} This means that while Noah had not lived the Christ-like, sinless life, he stood out to Him as relatively blameless when compared to his contemporaries, because he had sought to walk with הָאֱלֹהִים [The God], i.e., to emulate divine perfection. "Noah did...all that אֱלֹהִים had commanded him..." (v. 22) Though in Noah's time whatever earthy moral guidance may have existed for mankind's benefit and guidance, "all flesh" (v. 12) refused to "walk with" what Noah walked.

The specifics of God's first covenant with "all flesh" (vs. 11,17) included:

- His rescinding of the curse He had placed on the ground (Genesis 8: 21 {cf. 3:17});
- expansion of the cultural mandate, whereby all non-human flesh were to regard and treat mankind with suspicion because they would now {cf. Genesis 1:29} become acceptable prey for man {cf. vs. 3,9-11};
- the restriction of any human consumption of blood-filled flesh (v. 4);
- the establishment of the death sentence for any human murder, upholding the dignity of all Yaweh's image bearers (vs. 5-6);
- its termination: "while the earth remains" (v. 8:22), referring to the last chapter in His book of life.

Years after the ark had settled on Ararat and Noah had raised a productive vineyard, the father had fallen asleep, drunk and naked. His youngest son had inadvertently seen his nakedness and was later cursed by Noah. That response could well have been to a pre-flood observance of Yaweh's dignifying His first image-bearers by covering their nakedness (Genesis 3:21), the foreshadowing of sin covering necessary for forgiveness by and reconciliation with God.

Noah's cursing of Ham thus was punishment for simply seeing a man's nakedness, a convention that today has 'gone by the wayside' in western cultures.

It's interesting to note that years later Abraham honor Noah's curse on Canaan (Genesis 24:3.)

The moral system after Noah's death remained understandable to all survivors of the flood because "the whole earth used the same language and the same words."(Genesis 11:1) That solo language contributed to maintaining unification of the flourishing population returning to reclaim all sections of the earth inhabited before the flood; misinterpretations or misunderstandings could not exist as a threat to that unity.

The grandson of Noah's youngest son, the one he had cursed, was Nimrod, "a mighty one on the earth...a mighty hunter לִפְנֵי [in front of] Yaweh. And the beginning of his kingdom was Babel..." (Genesis 10:8-10), located on "a plain in the land of shinar..." (Genesis 11:2) In this town the citizens united to build a tower all the way to heaven, which concerned Him enough to "confuse" the common language so that the tower was abandoned and the resulting array of tongues spread through out the world; one common language no longer prevailed.

ABRAHAM

Now the fourteenth {possibly higher} generation of Noah's oldest son, Shem, was Abram (Genesis 11:27), known as the Hebrew (Genesis 14:13) because he was recognized as a descendant of Eber, Shem's great-grandson (Genesis 11:16-17.) {Note: later Yaweh changed his name to Abraham (v. 17:4.)} Milcah, the wife of Nahor, Abram's brother, was the daughter of Abram's other brother, Haran. (Genesis 11:29) Worded differently, Milcah's husband had been fathered by her grandfather, Terah. Just as interesting, Abram's wife, Sarai, was a daughter of his father, Terah, but by a different mother (Genesis 20:12.) The only child of Abraham and Sarah, Isaac, continued the practice by marrying Rebekah who was a granddaughter of Nahor, Abraham's brother, and of Milcah, the daughter of Abraham's other brother, Haran. (Genesis 24:24) But this incestuous marriage had been willfully orchestrated by Yaweh, as experienced by Abraham's trusted servant:

> "Blessed be the Lord, the God of my master Abraham, who has not forsaken His lovingkindness and His truth toward my master;

> as for me, the Lord has guided me in the way to the house of my master's brothers... And I bowed low and worshiped the Lord, and blessed the Lord, the God of my master Abraham, who had, guided me in the right way to take the daughter of my master's kinsman for his son."... Then (the daughter's father and brother) replied: "The matter comes from the Lord; so we cannot speak to you bad or good. Here is Rebekah before you, take her and go, and let her be the wife of your master's son, as the Lord has spoken."
> —Genesis 24:27,48,50-51

Yaweh's book of life had planned this incestuous marriage, just as it had for Cain, Seth and their wives {had to be their sisters} (Genesis 4:17,26), for the children of Shem, Ham, Japheth and their wives (Genesis 7:7; 8:18) as well as for Abram and Sarai and Nahor and Milcah as well as for Lot (Genesis 19:36.) Incest followed by inbreeding started and later ensured the postdiluvian continuity of Eve's gene pool of life tainted with sin {cf. Genesis 3:20.} It's seems probable, though, that then such an arrangement would have been driven by ever-expanding, herding/ farming tribal families' need for peace, security and trust when fulfilling God's mandate to "multiply." (Genesis 1:28; 9:1) For how much longer, though, inbreeding had been practiced Moses provided no answer but I would like to learn some day what became civilization's rationale for outlawing incestual marriages.

The practice of an immoral deviation of Genesis 2:23-24 emerges with the in-house woman identified as a פִּלֶגֶשׁ [concubine] (Genesis 22:24; 25:6; 35:22; 36:12 {the only times Moses mentioned this word}),

a woman who cohabited with a man but bore a lower status than did his wife or wives. And Hagar was Sarah's Egyptian maid, a servant fully accountable to her mistress. When Sarah encouraged her husband to sleep with Hagar, her motive was "to obtain children through her" (Genesis 16:2); in other words, she was forcing her maid to become a surrogate mother for her, a legal relationship today but immoral since it in no way resembles the adoption process. Another grievous marital sin occurred when "Reuben went and lay with Bilbah, his father's {concubine}..." (Genesis 35:22) More will discussed in the next chapter, which deals with God's assessment of His creation when time began.

After his father's death Yaweh spoke to Abram, "...I will make you a great nation... and make your name great...in you all the families of the earth shall be blessed." (Genesis 12:2-3) Then when Abram was 75 years old God "appeared to him" (v. 7), promising to give the land of Canaan to his descendants, in gratitude for which Abram erected an altar for thank offerings; shortly thereafter in Bethel he built another altar and "called upon the name (of) Yaweh" (v. 8); he invoked God's intimate, personal name to prayerfully express his gratitude for all He had promised.

Abram with his wife and nephew, Lot, briefly visited Egypt but returned to Bethel and settled down with all their possessions. While the land was prime for farming and livestock, Abram's herds and those belonging to Lot "were so great that they were not able to remain together." (Genesis 13:6) Consequently, Abram without

Lot settled in Canaan, where the Lord enlarged His earlier promise to him:

> "I will make your descendants as the dust of the earth, so that if anyone can number the dust of the earth, then your descendants can also be numbered."
> —Genesis 13:16

> Later the word of Yaweh told Abram, "...look toward the heavens and count the stars if you are able...(s)o shall your descendants be."
> —Genesis 15:5

> When Abram was ninety-nine years old Yaweh personally said to him, "I am אֵלָיו אֵל שַׁדַּי [God Almighty]...and I will multiply you exceedingly... you shall be the father of a multitude of nations... your name shall be Abraham for I will make you the father of a multitude of nations."
> —Genesis 17:1-5

Lot chose to relocate his own family and livestock to Sodom, because the terrain their seemed to him to be "like the garden of Yaweh" (Genesis 13:10) but was not aware that "the men of Sodom were wicked exceedingly and sinners against Yaweh" (v.13); and Yaweh concurred: Sodom's and Gomorrah's "sin is exceedingly grave." (Genesis 18:20) Abram's nephew learned this evidently {"he urged [the two angels] strongly" (Genesis 19:3)} after settling down in Sodom. After the two angels had entered Lot's home, "the men of the city, the men of Sodom, surrounded the house,"

(v. 4) demanding Lot to "bring [the two men] out to us that we may יָדַע [know {i.e., have relations with} them.]" (v.5) Lot's dissuading these immoral men from acting "wickedly" (v. 7) followed by their response that he was "acting like a judge" (v. 9) strongly indicates he knew they were homosexuals and thus his offer of his two daughters in the place of the two overnight guests was intended as a ploy. Then warned by his guests of Sodom's impending destruction by Yaweh and guided the next day by the two angels to a safe refuge, Lot and his two daughters escaped the "brimstone and fire from Yaweh out of heaven" (v. 24) - but not his wife, for she had not followed the angel's warning and was consequently transformed into "a pillar of salt." (v. 26)

At about the same period of time Abram had voiced to God his concern about having no heir and He repeated the promise that he would become the father of a multitude of descendants as well as possess a large tract of land. At this, Abram "believed in Yaweh and He reckoned it to him as righteousness {cf. Romans 4:5,18.}" (Genesis 15:6) To seal this promise God 'cut' a covenant:

> Abram gathered "a three year old heifer and a three year old female goat and a three year old ram and a turtledove and a young pigeon...and cut them in two and laid each half opposite the other; but he did not cut the birds...when the sun had set...a smoking oven and a flaming torch passed between these pieces."
> —Genesis 15:9-10,17

God's physical presence, appearing as an oven and a torch, formally authenticated and guaranteed His promise. But within this promise came a view of the future that would impact the narrator who had been inspired by Yaweh's Breath to dictate the book of Genesis:

> And God said to Abram, "Know for certain that your descendants will be strangers in a land that is not theirs, where they will be enslaved and oppressed four hundred years. But I will also judge the nation whom they will serve, and afterward they will come out with many possessions."
> —Genesis 15:13-14

In spite of this Abraham did exactly the same thing for which Adam had been convicted by God {cf. 3:17}: he "listened to the voice of Sarai" (16:2), his wife and "went in to Hagar" (v.4), her Egyptian maid, so that Sarai could "obtain children through her."(v.2) Because Hagar conceived, his wife (possibly realizing that her husband was not at fault for her womb being barren) became enraged at him because her maid "despised [the sight of her.]" (v.5.) In retaliation Sarai's harshness toward her led the maid to flee to the wilderness. There the angel of Yaweh told her to return to Sarai and submit to the latter's authority. Also the angel promised: "I will greatly multiply your descendants so that they shall be too many to...you shall bear a son and you shall call his name יִשְׁמָעֵאל [Ishmael, translated "God hears"]...and he will be a wild donkey of a man, his hand against everyone, and everyone's hand against him. And he will settle to the face {i.e., freely[31]} of his countrymen." (Genesis 16:12). "Hagar bore Abram a son when he was eighty-six years old" (Genesis 16:15-16), although fourteen years later God proclaimed to Abraham that his son by Sarah, Isaac, was his "only son." (Genesis 22:2) While Ishmael was circumcised along with Abraham as their sign of an expanded covenant {cf. Genesis 17:2-16} with God, the father professed to Him: "Oh that Ishmael might live before You." (v. 18) In response He said, "I will bless him and will make him fruitful and will multiply him exceedingly. He shall become the father of twelve princes, and I will make him a great nation {cf. 21:13,18}. But My covenant I will establish, with Isaac," the son Sarah would bear to him a year later. (vs. 20-21) When Sarah finally gave birth to Abraham's heir, verified by God to him (Genesis 21:12), Ishmael's father, now a surrogate, humanely evicted his mother and him into the wilderness and "his mother took a wife for him from the land of Egypt." (v.21) When Abraham died Ishmael and Isaac, "his sons"(-Genesis 25:9), both attended his burial. It's interesting to note that the Islamic faith reveres Ishmael as a prophet, a patriarch, an apostle to Arabia and father of Arabians. The Arab world today includes Muslims, Christians and Jews. Any person who adopts the Arabic language, the official and the original language of the Qur'an, is typically called an Arab. Although it

---

31. The Analytical Hebrew and Chaldee Lexicon, Benjamin Davidson, editor, page 627

is believed that the origin of Islam dates back only to the 7th century in Mecca, Saudi Arabia, it very well could be "the nation" (v. 18) Yaweh had promised to make out of Ishmael's lineage.

After Abraham and his wife had parented their son into a strong {cf. v. 6} youth, God sought to test [נִסָּה] him, i.e., to determine the quality of his faith: He instructed him to take his "only son,...Isaac, and go to the land of Moriah and offer him there as a burnt offering..." (Genesis 22:2) Now the burnt offering, the burning of any flesh with blood, is considered a "sacrifice"[32], the resulting smoke of which creates "a soothing aroma to Yaweh." (Leviticus 1:9 {cf. Psalm 66:15}) Silence in Moses's narrative prevents us from learning what happens to the burnt meat but in Leviticus two options are inferred: burn the meat to ashes or serve the cooked meat to the participating suppliants {cf. Genesis 31:54.}

Along the way the patriarch informed his servants, "I and the lad... will worship [שָׁחָה] and return to you." (Genesis 22:5) When Isaac asked him where they would be able to capture a lamb for this form of worship, his father calmed him {and possibly himself as well} verbally with the assurance that "God will provide." (v. 8) Abraham trusted God as well as had faith in Him. So when the altar had been built, Abraham bound his bound son on it and drew out his knife with the intention of sacrificing his only heir as Yaweh's intended offering

---

32. Evangelical Dictionary of Theology, Walter A. Elwell, editor, Baker Book House, Grand Rapids, MI, page 788

to Himself. This he did in faithful obedience to his God, but most likely with great distress for he had not only believed God, i.e., trusted the promises of future heirs He had covenanted with him (Genesis 15:6 {cf. Hebrews 11:17-19}) but also he believed in {cf. Romans 4:5} God, i.e., that Yaweh was capable of delivering that promise. And then Yaweh's angel from heaven (v. 15) abruptly stopped him, declaring, "עַתָּה [now, at this time] I know you fear God." (v. 12) Here עַתָּה infers not that God had doubted Abraham's fear of Him; rather He was proving the outworking of his faith. In other words God was testing the enduring strength, not just the existence, of Abraham's faith.

A physical gesture of worship became expressed in Abraham's time:

> He "bowed [שָׁחָה] to the earth" in Yaweh's presence;
> —Genesis 18:2

> Lot "bowed [שָׁחָה] face to the earth" to His two angels;
> —Genesis 19:1

> Abraham's envoy bowed [קָדַד] the head and bowed down [שָׁחָה] to Yaweh;
> —Genesis 24:26,48

> Abraham's envoy שָׁחָה [bowed down] to Yaweh.
> —Genesis 24:52

> Israel שָׁחָה [bowed down] upon {the} head of the couch.
> —Genesis 47:31

Bow down [שָׁחָה] is both an expressive gesture of fealty, i.e., a formal acknowledgement of loyalty to a human {cf. Genesis 33:3, 42:6}, as well as a ceremonial mode of worshipping God, i.e., of professing complete subservience to Him. Now another profession I enjoy is what Abraham's envoy had acknowledged to Laban: "The Lord in front of whom I הָלַךְ [have lived.[33]] (Genesis 24:40) Abraham's servant in effect was saying that he lived his life daily in full accountability to Yaweh, knowing with confidence He also 'had his back', i.e., protected him from all harm. The exact opposite 'profession' had been expressed when the first couple experienced the fear of the Lord: they "hid themselves from the presence of יְהוָה אֱלֹהִים..." (Genesis 3:8)

While assessing Sodom before destroying it, Yaweh had said to the two angels posing as travelers:

> "Abraham {cf. 17:4} will surely become a great and mighty nation and in him all the nations of the earth will be blessed.., Because I am able to recognize [יָדַע] that he will command his children and his household after him to keep the way of Yaweh by doing righteousness and justice, Yaweh will bring upon Abraham what He has spoken about him."
> —Genesis 18:18-19

Here we discover a major attribute possessed by God: His ability to know [יָדַע] everything infinitely and eternally. The fullness of every human being's life is

---

33. The Analytical Hebrew and Chaldee Lexicon, Benjamin Davidson, editor, page 189

fully covered in the book of life He authored after He had created the foundation for life. Moreover, because Yaweh exists eternally; to Him there is no past nor future, only the present. God "is" forever. What to me is so mind-boggling is the effort and knowledge He temporally expends simultaneously with life's entire human population in one way or another.

ISAAC

Moses was inspired to skip pretty much over Isaac's early life as the Patriarch's 'only' son in a landed estate of much wealth. He first met his wife-to-be, Rebekah, when he was 40 (Genesis 25:20), recently after Sarah had died. (Genesis 24:67) Through divine providence she became the focus of his father's search for a suitable {not from Canaan (v. 3)} bride for him. It was 'love at first sight' and the couple first 'knew' each other in "his mother Sarah's tent."(v. 67) After a period of barrenness Rebekah conceived but her pregnancy was rather painful because twins "struggled together within her." (Genesis 25:22) She learned directly from Yaweh why that was occurring:

> "Two nations are in your womb; and two peoples shall be separated from your body and one people shall be stronger than the other and the older shall serve the younger."
> —Genesis 25:23

When she delivered the first baby, she named him Esau but, as Yaweh had sovereignly ordained, his twin brother exited her birth canal holding fast on to Esau's heel, earning the name Jacob, which translates 'one who takes by the heel or takes the place of.' (v. 26) The twins' physical similarity was immediately challenged, as Jacob later explained to his mother: "...Esau my brother is a hairy man and I am a smooth man."(Genesis 27:11) From surfing through Google on the internet I have been able to learn that monozygotic {identical} twins result from the fertilization of a single egg which has split in two. As a result, identical twins share all of their genes and are always of the same sex. In contrast, dizygotic {fraternal} twins result from the fertilization of two separate eggs during conception. Though fraternal twins (two separate eggs and two separate sperm) are always surrounded in their own sacs and have their own individual placenta, 70% of identical twins could end up sharing a single placenta. Consequently, although identical twins usually share the same genetic material, they may actually grow up looking different.

Now Esau, favored by Isaac, was the 'outdoorsman', an adroit hunter, while his younger brother, favored by his mother, "was a peaceful man, living in tents" (v. 27) as well as cooked. Pressed by perceived hunger, Esau demanded a taste of the bread and red lentil stew that Jacob was cooking; the latter did so only after Esau had capitulated to his demand by swearing and selling his birthright to Jacob. Here was partial fulfillment of Yaweh's prediction: the older shall serve the younger.

Due to a famine, Isaac had intended to move his family to Egypt but on the way toward Gerar, Yaweh spoke to him:

> Sojourn in this land and I will be with you and bless you, for to you and to your descendants I will give all these lands, and I will establish the oath which I swore to your father Abraham."
> —Genesis 26:3

So Abraham's son settled in Gerar, where reigned Abimelech, king of Philistia, the boundaries of which today lie within modern Israel. This monarch was the same Abraham had confronted amicably {cf. Genesis 20:2-18} concerning Sarah's alluring beauty but now Isaac was concerned for his personal safety because Rebekah was beautiful as well. He too claimed his wife was his sister but in defense before Abimelech Isaac professed he had lied because he thought some Philistine men would kill him if they believed she was his wife. Though Isaac's ruse was unethical, Abimelech appreciated Isaac's reasoning. It's interesting to note that Isaac's father had experienced a second episode that paralleled these two with Abimelech: when Abram had journeyed to Egypt, he feared for his life due to Sarai's beauty and thus asked his wife to tell any inquiring Egyptian that she was her husband's sister {cf. Genesis 12:11-20}, a half-truth purposed for deception, just as Abraham had done with Abimelech.

Over time Yaweh had blessed Isaac's estate so well that the Philistines became so envious of him that their monarch asked him to depart. Obligingly he moved to

Beersheba, where God appeared to him and blessed him. In response, Isaac "built an altar there and invoked the name of Yaweh..." (Genesis 26:25) An invocation is a formal prayer to God for Isaac's inspiration, i.e., for the mental process that will stimulate and enable the supplicant to please Him. The fruit of this prayer later becomes evident to Abimelech and his advisers in their acknowledgement to Isaac, "We see plainly that Yaweh has been with you..." (Genesis 26:28) And yet, to Isaac and Rebekah the two wives of Esau had developed into the source of "bitterness of spirit." (Genesis 26:35) I am not persuaded that Esau's polygamy, his breaching the standard of Genesis 2:24, is what had troubled his parents; it rather seems more to have been their prejudice against "daughters of Canaan" {cf. Genesis 27:46 - 28:1,8-9.}

When old age began to blind Isaac, he realized it was time to pronounce and bless his older twin son's birthright. So he asked the son to catch, prepare and serve him fresh game, his favorite meal. Rebekah overheard her husband's request and immediately devised with Jacob a plan to override by deception the intended inheritance so that the younger twin would gain it. She clothed him in Esau's finest garment, prepared a meal of two slaughtered kids and applied portions of the kids' skins to his hairless hands and neck so that when he took the meal to his father, Isaac would think Esau was serving him game. But because the father was first doubtful and questioned Jacob whether he was Esau, the younger twin son twice lied to him (Genesis 27:19,24). When the father asked how the meal had been so quickly prepared, Jacob attributed it to the will of Isaac's, not their (Genesis 27:20), Yaweh, indicating the Lord was not Jacob's God {cf. Genesis 28:20-21.} Just in 'the nick of time' Jacob obtained his twin brother's birthright, which Esau years earlier had sold to his twin brother merely for bread and lentil stew to satisfy his pressing hunger {cf. Genesis 25:34.}

JACOB

The success of Rebekah's devious plan had enraged Esau to the point of threatening the life of his twin brother (Genesis 27:42) and consequently she urged Jacob to flee to the land of her brother, Laban. Isaac did also, even encouraging his son to take as a wife one of Laban's daughters. In his farewell blessing the father called on Yaweh, still not Jacob's Lord yet, to perpetuate "the blessing of Abraham" (Genesis 28:4) through this son and his offspring. When the older twin, already enraged, overheard Isaac express to Jacob his dislike of Esau's two wives, he went to his grandfather's out-of-wedlock son, Ishmael, and took as his third wife, Mahalath, a daughter of his own family's 'outcast,' to spite his parents.

Fleeing from his angry brother (Genesis 35:1), Jacob rested overnight in Luz (Genesis 28:19) and dreamed about a ladder footed on the earth and reaching heaven, with "the angels of God... ascending and descending on it." (v. 12 {cf. John 1:51}) Above it was Yaweh, who introduced Himself as "Yaweh, the God of your father Abraham and the God of Isaac" (v. 13) and promised:

> "...the land on which you lie, I will give it to you and your descendants {who} shall be like the dust of the earth, and you shall spread out to the west and to the east and to the north and to the south; and in you and your descendants shall all the families of the earth be blessed."
> —Genesis 28:13-14

After blessing him and his seed He told Jacob, "I am with you and will keep you wherever you go, and I will bring you back to this land, for I will not leave you until I have done what I have promised you." (v. 15) Waking from this sleep Jacob sensed the spiritual presence and awesomeness of Yaweh and named the site where he had the dream בֵּית אֱלֹהִים [Bethel], which translates 'house of God' and represents "the gate of heaven." (v.17) In contemporary soldiers' term he structured a 'fox hole conversion': after fulfillment of five qualifications he vowed "Yaweh will be my God... and of all that You give me עַשֵּׂר אֲעַשְּׂרֶנּוּ [I will definitely give a tenth] to you." (vs. 20-22)

As Jacob approached a well near Laban's land he unexpectedly encountered his uncle's daughter, Rachel, who had herded her flock of sheep towards it. He was instantly so smitten by her that he uncovered the well's head, watered her flock and then kissed her, tearfully explaining his familial relationship to her. She ran to inform her father of this and he "ran to meet" (Genesis 29:13) Jacob with a welcoming embrace and kiss. After Rebekah's son had visited there for a month, Laban offered his nephew an employment opportunity that was to be based on Jacob's stated terms. Now Rachel "was beautiful of form and face," (v. 17) but had an older sister, Leah, who suffered from poor eyesight. Still smitten by her Jacob asserted to his uncle, "I will serve you seven years for your younger daughter Rachel." (v. 18) Laban agreed with that term and enjoyed Jacob's faithful service for a full seven years.

In claiming the agreed upon term for his service Jacob requested that his uncle give "me my wife, for my days are filled, and אָבוֹאָה אֵלֶיהָ [I will have intercourse with her], evidently the local custom at that time establishing a couple's wedding. But like his sister Rebekah {cf. Genesis 27:6f}, Laban had a trick up his sleeve: because he was sensitive to the social 'norm' that the oldest daughter always married first, that evening he escorted Leah to his nephew who in turn enjoyed complete intimacy with her. I am still baffled as to how Jacob could have been duped into thinking Leah was Rachel, but defer to the phenomenon of 'raging hormones' discouraging voluntary chastity. With his conscience clear having now settled his older daughter's status, Laban a week later promised to give Rachel to his new son-in-law if his nephew worked another seven years for him. Accepting the enticing offer, Jacob received Rachel and became the husband of two sisters. Now it becomes evident to me that polygamy, a state unacceptable to God's will according to Genesis, 2:24, had become an acceptable social convention. Sadly, this three-way 'coupling' arrangement seemed to be acceptable to all three persons involved: Isaac loved Rachel more than he did Leah although the older sister had been favored by Yaweh to bear him four sons

{Reuben, Simeon, Levi and Judah} while Rachel had remained barren. (Genesis 29:18-35)

But in a fit of frustration the younger sister took matters in her own hand, just as her husband's paternal grandmother had done: she gave her maid, Bilhah to Jacob "as a wife" (v. 4) so that she "too may have children." (v.3) Her maid produced Dan and Naphtali but was then replaced by another of Rachel's maids, Zilpah, who bore him Gad and Asher. Later through a trade deal with her husband for mandrakes Leah bore him Issachar, Zebulun and a daughter, Dinah. At last God did open Rachel's womb and she bore to Jacob a son, Joseph. (Genesis 30:1-24)

During the second seven-year contract Jacob faithfully tended and fed all of Laban's livestock while at the same time craftily expanded his own flocks of speckled and spotted goats and sheep as well as of totally black sheep; mastery of animal husbandry and care gained over the next seven-year period enabled Jacob to become "exceedingly prosperous..." (v. 43)

In response to the qualified promise (Genesis 31:13 {cf. 28:18-22}) Jacob had made some twenty years ago (v. 41) Yaweh assured him, "I will be with you," just after advising him to return to Isaac because of Laban's unfriendly face (Genesis 31:2,5) which became evident after he had learned of his son-in-law's successful breeding program. In confiding with his two wives of his plan to depart from their homeland Jacob professed:

> "...the God of my father has been with me...your father has cheated me and changed my wages ten times. However, God did not allow him to

> hurt me...God has taken away your father's livestock and given {them} to me."
> —Genesis 31:5,7,9

Jacob even later professed to Laban that "the God of my father, the God of Abraham, the fear of Isaac" (v. 42) had protected him from all of Laban's abuse over the twenty years but Yaweh had not yet become Jacob's God, as he had qualifiedly promised. (Genesis 28:21) It seems as if Jacob still had not yet been publicly walking in the steps of his grandfather's faith {cf. Romans 4:12; Hebrews 11:8}.

Jacob with his family, livestock and possessions left without Laban's awareness to return to his father in Canaan, but not before Rachel had stolen her father's "household idols." (Genesis 31:19)

When they were three days gone Laban learned of his loss and immediately pursued them, taking seven days to catch up with them. Warned by God not to "speak to Jacob מִטּוֹב עַד־רָע [either cheerfully or hurtfully] (v. 24)," Laban informed his nephew that warning had been given him by "the God of your father" (v. 29) but then asked him why he had stolen his gods. (v. 30) Unbeknown to Jacob what Rachel had done, he assured Laban that the person possessing his stolen gods would "not live" (v. 32). Rachel, though, deceived her father so that he could not discover his missing idols, which her husband also had not known. Strongly suspicious that Laban wanted to take his two daughters back to Paddan-aram, Jacob vented his anger at his uncle for the cruel treatment given him for the labor he had performed in order to marry Laban's two daughters; but in doing so he confessed that "the God of my father, the God of Abraham and the fear of Isaac had...been for me" (v. 42)

Yet even here, there still was no profession of "my God." To mend this rift Laban proposed as a covenant, the agreement medium Yaweh had first made with mankind, "If you mistreat my daughters or if you take wives besides my daughters...God is (our) witness" (v. 50). His son in law affirmed: "The God of Abraham and the God of Nahor, the God of their father, judge between us." That phrase Moses succinctly described as "Jacob swore by the fear of his father Isaac." (v. 53) To seal this covenant Jacob "offered a sacrifice" (v. 54) and all of Laban's kinsmen joined him for the meal.

Content with that covenant, Laban left his family in peace and returned home the next morning; in peace as well Jacob and his family continued their sojourn to Isaac's land. It was now over twenty years since Jacob and his mother had deceived his father and consequently fled his twin brother's anger. Over that time he must have experienced some guilt and regret for what he had done, but Moses avoids any mention. As he travelled on he encountered Yaweh's angels, which not only reminded him of His command to go back to his father but also encouraged him to humbly make peace between himself and Esau: "perhaps he will accept me." (Genesis 32:20) When he sent messengers to Esau to inform him that "your servant Jacob {would like to} find favor in your sight" (vs. 4-5), they returned with Esau's response: "he is coming to meet you and four hundred men are with him." (v. 6) Fear and distress immediately took hold of him "for I fear him, lest he come and attack me, the mothers with the children." (v. 11) He implored "God of my father Abraham and God of my father Isaac, O Lord" (v. 9) to remember His promise that he would prosper and his descendants would be as innumerable as sea sand. He then decided to offer as an appeasement to his estranged brother a plethora of his productive animal stock but chose not to accompany this offering.

That evening when Jacob was alone, "אִישׁ / *LXX*: ἄνθρωπος [a man] יֵאָבֵק [wrestled] with him until daybreak" (v. 24) and purposefully dislocated his thigh. In spite of that discomfort he refused to release his adversary "unless you bless me." (v. 26) This is the blessing the stranger offered him: "Your name shall no longer be Jacob but [Israel.]" (v. 28) To commemorate his 'draw' with Yaweh he named the site פְּנִיאֵל [the face of God] because "I have seen God face to face, yet my life has been preserved." (v. 30)

After leading his family across the ford of the Jabbok stream, Jacob had spent the rest of the night alone until he encountered אִישׁ [a male person {אָדָם is a "human being irrespective of sex"[34]}] This encounter is like the time when Yaweh appeared to Abraham disguised (Genesis 18:1-3,9-10) as three אֲנָשִׁים {plural of אִישׁ } [males.]

Now it might be that the "man" (v. 24) was one of the "angels of God {who} met him" (Genesis 32:1) earlier

---

34. The Analytical Hebrew and Chaldee Lexicon, Benjamin Davidson, editor, page 7

that same day, Moses does not mention what had compelled Jacob to contend in the dust with him. This activity, יֵאָבֵק, is the *nif'al* form of אָבַק, derived from אָבָק [fine dust], and is translated "*dust(ing) each other* by wrestling"[35] The implication to me is that this struggle, a bridging of the spiritual world with the created one, rests in Jacob's divinely given name יִשְׂרָאֵל [Israel], for it acknowledges he "had striven with God and with men and...prevailed"(v. 28), the literal translation for Israel being "he strives with God," not "God contends" as the NAS presents. The contention was so fierce that even though the angel had dislocated his thigh, thereby disabling his leg hold, Jacob remained strongly competitive, refusing his adversary's plea, "Let me go, for the dawn is breaking." (v.26) Jacob agreed to do so only when his adversary would bless him. The angel יְבָרֶךְ [pronounced a blessing] on him (v. 29) in such a way to enable Israel to realize, "I have seen God face to face, yet my life has been preserved." (v.30) Yaweh had indeed prevailed only by inflicting temporal harm on Jacob but graciously acknowledged 'a draw', i.e., a match tie. Jacob sought the man's blessing probably because he had sensed he could not prevail.

> Yaweh...will punish Jacob according to his deeds...
> Yes, he שָׂרָה [contended/strived] with the angel and prevailed; he wept and sought His favor; he found Him in בֵּית־אֵל [Bethel {dwelling of God}.]
> —Hosea 12:2-4

---

35. The Analytical Hebrew and Chaldee Lexicon, Benjamin Davidson, editor, page 5.

I assume that Jacob received His blessing while still holding fast onto His angel. The angel's acknowledgement that "dawn was breaking" (v.26) I consider to be moot because of the perception that Yaweh's emissary did not want to encourage Jacob's stubborn persistence to cause him injury beyond a dislocated thigh. That Jacob had not known at the onset that this physical engagement had been initiated by Yaweh's angel could well indicate his inability to cope with overwhelming guilt of deceiving his father, overwhelming anger with his father-in-law and his anticipated fear of confronting the rage of his twin brother, even though Esau had reneged on his promise to give to Jacob his legal inheritance by right of his eldest-son's status.

The significance of this night event is divine in essence: here is Yaweh directly or substitutionally gripping Jacob's body in order to force his whole being to into submission to Him. Jacob, however, was stubbornly resisting until the angel dislocated his thigh as His compassionate way to prevail upon him to confess his sinful deeds to fulfill the purpose of this wrestling 'match': to be at oneness, i.e., in the state of being unified, with Yaweh. At oneness is the Old Covenant's foreshadowing of atonement, the reconciliation of God and mankind through Jesus Christ, "Who knew no sin {in order to be} sin on our behalf, that we might become the righteousness of God in Him." (2 Corinthians 5:21). Recognizing this divine reconciliation compelled Israel to proclaim, "I have seen God face to face, yet my life has been preserved." (v. 30)

Soon after his families' train had entered the land of Penuel, Jacob saw in the distance Esau and his four hundred men coming towards him. Fear compelled him to rearrange his line of travelers so that Rachel and Joseph would walk behind Leah and her sons who in turn would be shielded by his servants and their kin from the anticipated threats of the approaching group of men. Then Jacob, bravely leading the train, deeply bowed seven times as he approached his twin brother. Suddenly Esau ran towards Jacob and embraced and kissed him - and then they both wept. The 'older' brother marveled at the quality and quantity of Jacob's retinue and told him his proffered present was not necessary because he already had possessed "plenty." (Genesis 33:9) But Jacob implored him to take the gift because "now I have found favor in your sight...for I see your face as one sees the face of God." (v. 10) How should this last phrase be understood: a} 'as I look at your face I see God's face' or b} 'I see your face as one {that} sees the face of God'?

Jacob's "you have received me favorably" (v. 10) points me to option a} because 'Israel' was recounting his recent experience of having been received favorably by God and his life still preserved after he had "seen God face to face..." (Genesis 32:30) I sense Esau had understood his twin brother this same way inasmuch he did relent by accepting Jacob's gift.

After pleasant talk had consumed the brothers, Esau departed from Jacob's presence – unfortunately a parting without either's expressed sorrow or regret of the past. His destination was Seir, a mountainous region stretching between the Dead Sea and the Gulf of

Aqaba in the northwestern region of Edom. This is the last of Moses' narrative which deals with Esau, leaving me with the impression that forgiveness for the deceit performed by Jacob was neither sought nor given and thus they remained unreconciled to one another for the rest of their lives.

> Yaweh:
> "But now listen, O Jacob, My servant, and Israel, whom I have chosen...Do not fear, O Jacob My servant...I will pour out My Breath on your offspring and My blessing on your descendants... Thus says Yaweh, the King of Israel and his Redeemer, the Lord of hosts..."
> —Isaiah 44:1-3,6

As written in His book of life, Yaweh's promise to Abraham and repeated to Isaac, "I will greatly multiply your seed as the stars of the heavens," (Genesis 22:17;26:4) implicitly becomes modified by His choosing only Israel's seed as the future beneficiaries of His gracious love:

> "Will I not," declares Yaweh, "destroy wise men from Edom and understanding from the mountain of Esau?"
> —Obediah 8

> {To the descendants of Jacob:} "I have loved you," says Yaweh. But you say, "How have you loved us?" "(Was) not Esau Jacob's brother?" declares Yaweh. "Yet I have loved Jacob; but שָׂנֵאתִי [I have hated] Esau and I have made his mountains a desolation {cf. Ezekiel 35:15} and

> his inheritance for the jackals of the wilderness {cf. Joel 3:19}...(Edom {cf. Genesis 25:30}) may (re)build, but I will tear down and will call them the wicked territory and the people toward whom Yaweh is indignant forever."
> —Malachi 1:2-4

> ...for though (the twins) were not yet born and had not done anything good or bad, in order for God's purpose according to (His) choice might stand, not because of works but because of Him Who calls, it was said to her, "The older will serve the younger."
> —Romans 9:11-12

Though throughout human history all of God's 'image-bearers' have been, as well as will be, fully accountable to Him for all their thoughts and deeds, the book of life directs Yaweh in dispensing His compassion graciously and selectively:

> Yaweh to Moses:
> "I will be gracious to whom I will be gracious and will show compassion on whom I will show compassion.
> —Exodus 33:19 {cf. Romans 9:15}

> ...just as the Father raises the dead and gives them life, even so the Son also gives life to whom He wishes.
> —John 5:21

> So then (God) has mercy on whom He desires and He hardens whom He desires.
> —Romans 9:18

Having been thrown out of Abraham's extended family, the father-in-law/son-in-law 'team' {cf. Genesis 28:8-9} has treated the Patriarch's family up to the present time with bitterness, bigotry and fear {cf. Exodus 15:15; Deuteronomy 2:4}, all in accordance with His book of life. Such antagonism {cf. Genesis 16:12} has become worldwide and today evidences itself in the Islam faith's professed hatred of Israel and Christianity. Esau's departure from his brother, however, was somewhat abrupt and Moses had not included any mention of a prior reconciliation between them - His book of life it seems had contained other plans for mankind's future {cf. Genesis 28:9, 36:43.}

When he finally returned to Canaan, Jacob acquired from Hamor, the local "prince," (Genesis 34:2) a piece of land on which he built an altar and named it אֵל֙ ׳לֹהֵ֣י יִשְׂרָאֵ֑ל [God, the God of Israel.] (Genesis 33:20) To me this signified Israel's formal, public acclamation that Yaweh was his God (the fulfillment of Genesis 28:20-21) and the altar was constructed for the praise and worship of Yaweh as well as for the burnt offerings of thanks to Him – a refinement of 'calling upon His name.'

As the family of Israel slowly adapted itself to the land of Canaan, Hamor's son, Shechem became so attracted to Dinah, the daughter of Jacob and Leah, that he "lay with her by force" (v. 2), an act her angry brothers alleged was "נְבָלָה [a crime/wickedness] "in Israel" (v. 7) {note: the first time יִשְׂרָאֵל has been applied to identify a place, i.e., Canaan, instead of Jacob.} Shechem pleaded with her brothers to let him wed their sister but they cited that action as a חֶרְפָּה [willful disobedience to or open disrespect for their God's rules] because he was uncircumcised. For the sake of peaceful assimilation in Cannan the brothers proposed consent but with this condition: "you will become like us...every male of you be circumcised...and we will take your daughters and we will live with you and become one people." (vs. 15-16) Hamor, Shechem and most of the males from the prince's town accepted that condition and the circumcisions were performed but without any invocation of Yaweh or mention of the contents of the Covenant associated with it {cf. Genesis 17:1-14.} (vs. 22,24) Two days later, two of Jacob's sons, Simeon and Levi, stormed into the town, slayed all the male population, weakened by the ritual's slowly receding pain and returned Dinah to Leah's tent; the other brothers "looted the city because they had defiled their sister." (v. 27) Jacob was livid at Simeon and Levi, fearful that his entire household could be destroyed, but the two sons countered, "Should he treat our sister as a harlot?" (v. 31)

Later in time the voice of God commanded Jacob to move his entire household to Bethel where he was to erect His altar as a compliment to the rock pillar he had oiled over 20 years ago at the start of his flight from Esau's anger. This return marks fulfillment of his earlier vow to Yaweh: "I {will} return to my father's house in safety, then Yaweh will be my God." (Genesis 28:21) To prepare for this return visit, Jacob ordered his household and staff to surrender to him all the "foreign gods' (Genesis 35:2) stolen from Laban as well as to purify themselves and put on cleaned garments. He then buried all the idols "under the oak which was near Shechem." (v. 4)

When he and his family had returned to Bethel {cf. 28:19} in Canaan (Genesis 35:6), Yaweh told him, "You shall no longer be called Jacob but Israel {cf. Genesis 32:28}" (v. 10) and then reiterated the promises He had covenant with his grandfather, specifically about land and the establishment of many גּוֹיִם [peoples {cf. Isaiah 1:4.}] (v. 35) In gratitude Israel set up another pillar on which he poured both a libation and then שֶׁמֶן [organic oil extract.]

Then on the next trek, this time to Ephrath, known as Bethlehem (v.19), Israel's favored wife died, i.e., "her soul {had departed}" (v. 18, while giving birth to their second son, whom she named during her labor Ben-oni {"son of my sorrow"} which after she died he changed to Benjamin {"son of the right hand"} (v. 18), possibly indicating 'a special place of honor' in Jacob's heart, for as he later declared to ten of his sons:

> "My son shall not go down with you, for your brother is dead and he alone is left. If harm should befall him on the journey you are taking, then you will bring my grey hair down to Sheol in sorrow."
> —Genesis 42:38

After burying Rachel in Ephrath Israel continued his journey to see his father and while briefly pausing near Eder he learned that Reuben, his oldest son by Leah, יִשְׁכַּב אֶת־בִּלְהָה [lay carnally with Bilhah] (v. 22), Rachel's maid as well as Jacob's concubine who bore his sons Dan and Naphtali, but Moses never mentioned any consequence Reuben might have suffered for his indiscretion. Concubinage persisted, paving the way for social acceptance of polygamy, an offense to Yaweh {cf. Genesis 2:18,21-24.}

Finally after a twenty-plus year absence from his father, Jacob met Isaac, then in his one-hundred-eightieth year. Without mentioning any apology by Israel to Isaac for deceiving him, Moses very briefly covers the old father's death and subsequent burial in the presence of his twin sons. (v. 29)

Chapter 36 is devoted to the genealogy of Edom's familial tribal chiefs and kings Esau, also called Edom {cf. 25:30}, begot after he had settled in the hill country of Seir (v. 8) with Canaan's two daughters and Ishmael's daughter. The Edomite kings reigned "before any king reigned over the sons of Israel." (v.31)

JOSEPH

The brevity of Genesis 37:1 infers to me that Israel had settled down on his father's property in Canaan and enjoyed full use of the assets now in his possessions as the recognized birthright holder. That title had not been by birth but through deceiving his own father, two acts of disobedience {two separate acts of disobedience to Yaweh included in the Ten Commandments Moses would read some three hundred years later to the people of Israel in their flight from Egypt to the land He had promised their Patriarch. Such is, however, merely one example of God patiently striving with sinful men He had formed in His image: what Jacob had meant for evil God had meant for good (Genesis 50:20) because He had loved him (Malachi 1:3) when writing His book of life.

    Joseph, the older son Rachel had begotten for Jacob, at the age of 17 gave to his father "a bad report" concerning his four brothers born by Bilhah and Zilpah, this time acknowledged by Moses as Jacob's נְשֵׁי [wives] (v. 2) instead of פִּילַגְשִׁים [concubines] (Genesis 35:22.) Israel loved Joseph "because he was the son of his old age." (v.3) But why not Benjamin too? Was it because

Joseph's relationship with his father had predated for a long time Benjamin's birth? Or had Jacob been constantly associating Benjamin with Rachel's death? Another quandary regards "all his sons" (v. 3): did "all" include Joseph's full brother, Benjamin? Moses provides no guidance for any answers. Thus it is safe to say that under Jacob's sizeable 'tent' there existed jealousy, resentment and scorn of Joseph by "all" his brothers: "they hated him and could not speak to him in peace," about which Moses portrayed Jacob as being very unaware.

Joseph, for reasons Moses had not mentioned, shared this dream with his brothers, inciting even greater hatred among them: "we were binding sheaths in the field and lo, my sheaf rose up and also stood erect; and behold, your sheaves gathered around and bowed down to my sheaf." (v. 7) Later, after relating to his brothers a second dream he had remembered, he then shared it with his father: "the sun and the moon and eleven stars were bowing down to me." (v. 9) In response, Israel exclaimed to him, "Shall I and your mother and your brothers actually come to bow ourselves down before you to the ground?" but then only kept in his heart that moment of his rage. (v. 11)

Soon thereafter Joseph travelled over 45 miles to check up on his brothers at his father's request. Seeing their brother in the distance, the brothers became so enraged with jealousy that they "plotted against him to put him to death." (v. 18) The oldest brother, Reuben, pleaded for Joseph's life because he wanted to "rescue him out of their hands, to restore him to his father." (v. 22) Was

Reuben truly concerned for Joseph's safety or was he still smarting from having been caught sleeping with Jacob's concubine {cf. Genesis 35:22}?

With murder in their intention the brothers "stripped Joseph of... the varied colored tunic" (v. 23) with which Israel had favored him (v. 3) and thrust him into an empty water pit. Realizing that killing him was both risky and profitless (v. 26), they decided instead to sell him.

While the brothers were savoring the notion of profit while eating a meal, a caravan of יִשְׁמְעֵאלִים [Ishmaelites {cf. Gen. 16:12}] came into their distant view. When later a group of that caravan, מִדְיָנִים [Midianite {Midian was the son of Abraham and Keturah, Sarah's successor (Genesis 25:2)}] traders passed nearby, the brothers, without Reuben's knowledge, lifted Joseph out of the pit and "sold him to הַיִּשְׁמְעֵאלִים [the Ishmaelites], who then took Joseph down to Egypt where "the Midianites sold him...to Potiphar (v. 36)," the captain of Pharaoh's bodyguard.

Following their sale of Joseph the brothers dipped Joseph's tunic in goat's blood and then in Jacob's presence asked him in a rather cold-hearted manner to verify if "it is your son's tunic." Israel did so and opined, "A wild beast has devoured him; Joseph has surely been torn to pieces." (v. 33) Refusing the gestures of comfort from all his sons and daughters, Israel wept to himself, "I will go down to Sheol in mourning for my son." (v. 35) But for the moment, though, he still had Rachel's other child to enjoy: Benjamin.

Afterwards, Judah, Leah's son, left his brothers to go down to Adullam, where he saw and became intimate with a daughter of Shua, a Canaanite (Genesis 38:2), who bore him three sons: Er, Onan and Chezib. At the appropriate time Judah selected Tamar to be Er's wife, but his first born son "was רַע [evil {cf. Genesis 6:5, 8:21}] in the sight of Yaweh, so Yaweh took {Er's} life." (v. 7) Obsessed with the assurance of his second-generation heir, Judah implored Onan יַבֵּם ["raise up seed to {Er}"] (The Analytical Hebrew and Chaldee Lexicon, Benjamin Davidson, editor; p. 291] by "go(ing) into" {cf. v. 2} Tamar. Onan, however, knowing "that the seed would not be his...(he) wasted his seed on the ground in order not to give offspring to his brother. That knowledge suggests a form of primogeniture had existed at that time as a Hebrew familial custom which possibly survived with Noah. Displeased by Onan's refusal to honor his father, Yaweh "took his life also." (vs. 9-10)

Judah then promised to give in marriage his last son to the widowed daughter-in-law once he had matured – but he either forgetfully or purposely never did.

Bitter at Judah for breaking his promise to her, Tamar, disguised as a temple prostitute, enticed him sexually to the point where he "went in to her and she conceived by him" (v. 18), still without recognizing her as his widowed daughter-in-law. However, before surrendering herself to him, she was able to bargain for a kid from his flock to be given her as a fee. Craftly she extracted from him as an assurance for his delivering her an infant lamb a עֲרָבוֹן [pledge] comprised of his personal seal, cord and staff, which he readily provided her when departing from her. Days later, when he tried to have the promised kid delivered by a trusted friend, the pledge would not be returned because the disguised harlot had "removed her veil and put {back} on her widow garments." (v. 19) Tamara had disappeared with the pledge as well as with a child newly "conceived by him" (v. 18) within her. At the end of the prior paragraph I wrote that Judah "either forgetfully or purposely never" gave his last son in marriage to Tamar. But now it seems more conceivable that he was suffering from a lapse of memory inasmuch as he had not recognized the harlot's personhood as that of the woman he had personally selected {cf. v. 6} to be his daughter-in-law consecutively with his three sons.

Now some three months later Judah יֻגַּד [was told] that Tamar "כַּלָּתֶךָ [had played the harlot and (was) with child by זְנוּנִים [whoredom]." (v. 24) For me the intriguing question here is: who informed him? Having "arose and departed" (v. 19) quickly after her father-in-law had satisfied himself, she had removed the traditionally recognized appearance of a prostitute, i.e., a veil hiding her face, and donned her widow garments again. If no one had seen this clothing change or her toting away Judah's pledge, how could she have become maligned as a harlot, particularly a pregnant one? Judah's response to that information seems to answer my quandary: "Bring her out and let her be burned!" (v. 24)

Only Tamar could benefit from that confrontation because of his pledge still in her possession. Thus to me it seems Tamar had been the source of this rumor Judah had eventually heard.

As merely an 'aside', I would like to point out how rampant and socially unacceptable prostitution could have been back in Israel's era:

1. the varying vocabulary for this activity:
    (v. 15) [harlot] זוֹנָה
    (v. 21) [קְדֵשָׁה [prostitute, harlot] (v. 21)
    (v. 24) [play the harlot] כַּלָּתֶךָ
    זְנוּנִים [whoredom] (v. 24);

2. the traditional tribal code, like the civil one for witchcraft in colonial Salem, Mass. times, a suspected whore had to be burned for her immoral activity, apparently without any legal guidance or process.

Relevant to today's social reality, Tamar's situation begets this question: for a widow (and not a divorcee) would it be offensive to Yaweh to have had a 'post-marital' affair with a widower? Moses's narrative thus far has revealed female prostitution only as a traditional social morality breach punishable by death, not as evil or a sin.

In response to this report Judah ordered "הוֹצִיאוּהָ [*hiphil* plural imperative of יָצָא {bring her forth}] and may she תִּשָּׂרֵף [be burned!]" (v. 24) His reaction appeared to be that of a family patriarch wanting to discern any potential disgrace a member's immoral character could cast on his family inasmuch as verses 8 and 11 indicate Tamar had joined Judah's family when she became Er's wife and later remained as such after she had become his widow. Just prior to her appearing before her father-in-law, she sent Judah's pledge to him with this message: "I am with child by the man to whom these things belong... הַכֶּר־נָא [gaze at, I pray] and see whose signet ring and cords and staff are these." (v. 25) Immediately her father-in-law recognized them and professed to another person present, "She is more righteous than I כִּי־עַל־כֵּן [because] I did not give her to my {third} son..." (v. 26) Still, though, no answer as to why - forgetfully or purposefully? In the last mention of Judah Moses strangely and unexpectedly informs us that "he did not have relations with her again," but not telling us whether or how Tamar's father-in-law would care for her and her baby.

At 'full term' Tamar learned that she would give birth to twins, so her midwife marked with a scarlet {thread} a hand jutting out of her birth canal to establish the first-born male's claim to birth rights, but it unexpectedly and quickly withdrew itself back into the canal just as the second baby became fully born, thus taking from the one born right after, still wearing the red thread, the right of the first born. He was metaphorically named פֶּרֶץ [Perez, translated a breach {defined: the failure to observe a law or code of conduct.)]

This unexpected 'race to birth' had cost the second born son his right to the rightful claims of a first-birth male:

> According to the Law of Moses, the firstborn may be either the firstborn of his father, who is entitled to receive a double portion of his father's inheritance (compared to the other siblings), (Deuteronomy 21:17) or the firstborn of his mother.

Sensitive to this 'breach,' she named her second son Zerah, which translates "dawning or brightness." So "Tamar (Judah's) daughter in law bore him (i.e., Judah {cf. Ruth 4:12}) Perez and Zerah" (1 Chronicles 2:5), which appears to not have been Onan's understanding {cf. vs. 8-9}. Now I must confess that reflection on the full content of chapter 38 does perplex me because I am wondering why Yaweh's Breath in Moses had inserted it just after the commencement of Joseph's tribulations; maybe, though, when I finish Genesis I might have an answer.

The theme, however, for chapter 39 is וַיְהִי יְהוָה אֶת־יוֹסֵף [Yaweh was with Joseph (vs. 2,3,5,21,23)] and his master, Potiphar, "saw" that and acknowledged by appointing him manager of his entire household. But the "Hebrew slave's" (v. 17), "handsome in form and appearance" (v. 6) a detriment for him due to his master's wife unsuccessful flirts with him and subsequent lies about it. Seeing the spurious evidence to her lie (vs. 12,16,18), Potiphar became enraged and had Joseph put in the jail in which הַמֶּלֶךְ [the king] {identified as פַּרְעֹה [pharaoh] in Genesis 40:2} had confined his enemies. (v. 20) Misfortune seemed to envelop more and more of Joseph's even though Yaweh was with him at all times. The apparent irony here is dismissed, though, by him with this divinely reasoned explanation: my brothers "meant evil against me {but} God meant it for good..." An 'echo' of this appears in Proverbs 16:4: Yaweh has made everything for its own purpose, even the wicked for the day of evil.

Both perspectives He has employed in His *modus operandi* for administering sovereignly the earthly lives of His image bearers: for example, the evil plot of Potiphar's wife He worked out to be goodness for Joseph because the chief jailer appointed him to be supervisor over all his fellow prisoners - "and whatever he did Yaweh made to prosper." (v. 23)

Sometime later two of Pharaoh's officials, the cupbearer and baker, perturbed the king enough for them to be imprisoned where Joseph was now supervising. He was put "in charge of them…and they were in confinement for some time." (Genesis 40:4) One night both of the officials experienced puzzling dreams; when they had awakened, they felt sad because they wanted some idea of what their separate dreams meant. When they expressed their concern to Joseph, he responded, "Do not פִּתְרֹנִים [interpretations] belong to God?" (v. 8) and quickly begged they share with him what they could remember. After the cupbearer related to him what he remembered, Joseph said, "This is the פִּתְרֹנוֹ [interpretation]… within three more days יִשָּׂא פַרְעֹה אֶת-רֹאשֶׁךָ [Pharaoh will lift up your head {i.e., give you liberty}] and restore you to your office." (v.13) Seeing that Joseph had interpreted favorably (v. 16), the chief baker then told him what he had remembered and Joseph in turn responded: "This is פִּתְרֹנוֹ [the interpretation]… within three days יִשָּׂא פַרְעֹה אֶת-רֹאשְׁךָ מֵעָלֶיךָ [Pharaoh will lift up your head by hanging you" on a tree. (v. 19) It's needless to mention that he did not tell the baker what he had said to the cupbearer when concluding interpreting his dream: "please do me a kindness by mentioning me to Pharaoh and get me out of this house." (v. 14) However, though all that Joseph had interpreted turned out to be true, "the chief cupbearer did not remember... but forgot him." (v. 23)

Two full years had transpired when Pharaoh one night had two separate dreams, about which תִּפָּעֶם רוּחוֹ [his disposition was disturbed] (Genesis 41:8) so he commanded an assembling of his magicians and wisemen to assemble to hear and solve the meanings of his two dreams. After none of the attendees could offer an interpretation, the official cupbearer meekly recalled to Pharaoh a true dream interpretation he had received from "a Hebrew youth" (v. 12) in "the dungeon..." (v. 14) Pharaoh then ordered Joseph to be "hurriedly brought {to} him..." (v.14) Properly attired and groomed Joseph arrived and told the king, "{While} it is not in me, God will give Pharaoh a favorable answer." (v. 16) Practically without a pause the king began to divulge both his dreams to the Hebrew youth. After Pharaoh had related his dream experiences, Joseph interpreted both dreams to represent two halves of actually one dream which focused on what God "is about to do" (v. 25) globally (v. 56-57): seven years of abundance due to favorable climates followed then by seven years of a severe famine, for which no one will think to prepare in advance out of the abundance preceding it (vs. 29-31). Joseph then advised:

> "Now as for the repeating of the dream to Pharaoh twice, that the matter is determined by God and God will quickly bring it about...let Pharaoh take action to appoint overseers in charge of the land and let him חִמֵּשׁ [exact {demand/ command} a fifth part] of the land of Egypt in the seven years of abundance."
> —Genesis 41: 32,34

The king and his servants immediately saw the Godly wisdom (v.39) Joseph had volunteered and Pharaoh appointed him "over my house, and according to your command all my people shall do homage; only in the throne I will be greater than you." (v. 40) As a seal of this appointment the King put his signet ring "on Joseph's hand {cf. Esther 3:10} and clothed him in garments of fine linen and put the gold necklace {cf. Daniel 5:7,16,29} around his neck." (v. 42)

Pharaoh also dubbed him with the Egyptian name of Zaphenath-paneah and then "gave him Asenath, the daughter of {a priest for the Egyptian deities} as his wife." (v. 45)

Now as commander of his own advice, the thirty-year-old Hebrew set out to harvest and store "in every city" storehouse (v.56) one-fifth of all "the food from its own surrounding fields" (v. 48) for the duration of the seven-year abundance period. Just prior to the end of abundant harvests Asenath bore him two sons; the first he named Manasseh [making forget] because "God has made me forget all my trouble and all my father's household" (v. 51) and the second Ephraim [fruitfulness] in acknowledgement that "God has made me fruitful in the land of my affliction." (v. 52.) Joseph had wisely stored one-fifth of all the crops harvested in Egypt in its city warehouses so that when the famine became severe "over all the face of הָאָרֶץ [the earth]" (v. 56) while "וּבְכָל־אֶרֶץ [in all land] of Egypt there was bread." (v. 54)

Very soon "כָּל־הָאָרֶץ [all of the earth] began entering Egypt to buy grain from Joseph" (v. 57), whom all foreign traders deemed "הַשַּׁלִּיט [the ruler over the land {of Egypt.}" (Genesis 42:6) After learning of Egypt's harvest surplus, Jacob sent his ten sons down there to replenish his family's depleted crop supplies. Success for this mission required the brothers to deal directly with Zaphenath-paneah, so when they entered his presence they "יִשְׁתַּחֲווּ־לוֹ אַפַּיִם אָרְצָה [bowed down to him, faces (to) ground]" (v. 6 {cf. 37:6-7}) in order to conduct business with him. He instantly recognized them as his mean brothers and anger swelled up within him, in spite of the "forget...all my father's household" nuance in the name he had given his son Manasseh. (41:51) "...disguis(ing) himself to them (v. 7), i.e., through an interpreter (v. 23), he started accusing them harshly for being spies. In denying his charge they claimed to be "twelve brothers, the sons of one man in the land of Canaan; and behold the youngest is with our father today, and one is no more." (v.13) This revealed to Joseph that since his family had considered him dead, he could remain 'hidden' to them, and so he continued harping on the charge of spying so much that he invoked "the life of Pharaoh" (v. 15) with the order, "you shall not go from this place unless your youngest brother comes here!" (v. 15) Thus he confined nine of them for three days in prison for being spies while instructing the tenth to return to Canaan in order to bring Benjamin down into Egypt.

Pharaoh's "lord of the land" (v. 30) softened after the third day and offered to release eight more to take Jacob's needed grain to Canaan and then bring Benjamin down to Egypt "so your words may be verified and you will not die." (v. 20) Then he averred: "Do this and live, for

I fear הָאֱלֹהִים [God.]" (v. 18) And so they did. Because הָאֱלֹהִים seems to be a non-Hebrew, stilted, impersonal rendering of אֱלֹהִים coupled with the traditional Hebraic employment of 'fear,' had Joseph purposefully spoken that way to his interpreter or had his interpreter tried to be diplomatic by adding the definite article הָ? Either way, though, did work since it kept Joseph's identity from being revealed while delivering a persuasive impact on them as they prepared for their sojourn back to Canaan: the mention of "the fear of God" 'unseared' their consciences, forcing them to admit to one another, "Truly we are guilty concerning our brother, because we saw the distress of his soul when he pleaded with us, yet we would not listen; therefore this distress has come upon us." (v.21) And then Reuben replied, "Now comes the judgment for his blood." (v. 22) Joseph indirectly 'overheard' that conversation because his brothers had not been aware "כִּי [that] an interpreter was between them." (v. 23) And when his interpreter told him, he "wept" (v. 24) because Zaphenath-paneah had now become aware that Reuben, his oldest brother had at least sought to protect him from the other nine brothers.

Just before their departure, Zaphenath-paneah "took Simeon from them and bound him before their eyes," (v. 24) and had his stewards fill the brothers' sacks with the grain they had bought together with the money they paid for it as well as provisions for their sustenance on the trip. On the first evening of their trip the brothers' hearts sank after one had discovered that his purchase money lay in one of his grain sacks. Now in fright the nine shouted to one another, "What is this that God has done to us?" (v. 28) Having arrived back in Canaan they anxiously related to Israel their trading experience with the lord of Egyptian land, but excluding discovery of one's purchase money in his sack. But still in their father's presence, they discovered that all their purchasing money was interspersed in their sacks while emptying the grain they had bought, As a result "they .v) bocaJ ylralucitrap ,(53 .v) "[diarfa erew] וַיִּרְאוּ yltnamada eh ylkciuq rof ,(63 refused to let Benjamin be taken with his nine brothers to Egypt: "his brother is dead and he alone is left. If harm should befall him {the remaining "son of his old age" (Genesis 37:3)}...then you will bring my gray hair down to Sheol in sorrow." (v. 38) At this point I am surprised Joseph had not made any attempt to learn about his father's wellbeing before {cf. 43:27} demanding Benjamin be brought down to Egypt. Also, by stuffing all the purchase money for the grain in his brothers sacks before they left for Canaan, was he not aware of a possible adverse effect it could have on Jacob? And when he had quickly recognized his ten brothers, Joseph most certainly would have recalled Benjamin as being father's "son of the right hand." (35:18) Could Joseph, after a thirteen-plus-year absence from his younger brother, have become jealous of Benjamin in spite of Genesis 37:3? Whatever reasons he may had been mentally entertaining, though, is not yet evident to me and so we must plow ahead into chapter 43 in hopes of discovering them.

As the famine became more severe in Canaan and was rapidly consuming Israel's food supply, he ordered his nine sons to return to Egypt but they reminded him that the ruler over the Egyptian land had warned they would not see his "face unless your brother is with you." (v.5) Reluctantly Jacob agreed and sent all ten brothers back to Egypt with home-grown products as a present for the land ruler plus double the money which had mysteriously appeared in the brothers' sacks when they had returned to Canaan. Israel then offered them his blessing: "may אֵל שַׁדַּי [God Almighty] grant you compassion in the sight of the man, that he may release to you your other brother and Benjamin." (v. 14)

Upon arriving back in Egypt the brothers explained to Joseph's steward the returned-money situation but the steward responded: "אֱלֹהֵיכֶם וֵאלֹהֵי [Your God and the God of your father] has given you treasure in your sack; כַּסְפְּכֶם, בָּא אֵלָי [your silver went in for you i.e., was intended for you.]" (v. 23) Right after saying that, the steward reunited Simeon with his brothers. Joining the brothers at noon for a meal in his house, Joseph, upon inquiring for the first time, learned that his father was alive and well, at which point all his brothers "bowed down in homage" (v. 28) to him {cf. 17:7-8.} Seeing Benjamin close up for the first time in over thirteen years, Joseph, "deeply stirred" (v.30), graciously greeted him with, "May אֱלֹהִים [God] be gracious to you, my son,"(v. 29) then excused himself temporarily to weep in his chamber. Whether his tears indicated a joy for reuniting with his mother's only other son or a sadness for missing some thirteen years of Benjamin's growing up, Moses gives us no hint.

Now at the meal a social intolerance soon became evident to the sons of Israel: "the Egyptians could not eat bread with the Hebrews, for that was abhorrent to the Egyptians." (v. 32) Consequently, Joseph was first served at his own table, then his Egyptian guests at their own table and lastly the brothers at their own, "seated before {Joseph}, the first-born according to his birthright and the youngest according to his youth, and הָאֲנָשִׁים [the men] looked at one another in astonishment." (v. 33) Here הָאֲנָשִׁים has to be the eleven brothers, who were astonished at who could have known the birth order of Israel's sons, rather than the Egyptian guests whose own table had been setup and served to represent a physical separation from the Hebrews. It seems to me that Zaphenath-paneah, formerly Joseph the Hebrew slave, had his own table to indicate his second-in-command status, which in turn permitted him the freedom to take "portions... from his own table" to his brothers so they could feast and drink "freely with him" (v. 34) without provoking his Egyptian guests.

After the meal Joseph instructed his steward to fill each brother's sack with food and "his money" (Genesis 44:1) but also to place in Benjamin's sack the silver cup he customarily used "for divination." More regarding divining will soon be discussed below.

At daybreak the eleven brothers left on donkeys Joseph's house but not too far from the city his steward, under his specific orders, intercepted them and demand to know, "Why have you repaid evil for good." (v. 5) Thinking the steward was referring to the money in their sacks in their last return trip to Canaan, the stunned brothers became very apologetic, repeating what they had already explained when returning the money upon their arrival the day before. Not accepting any of what they professed, he demanded to search each brother's sack, which he did, "beginning with the oldest and ending with the youngest..." (v. 12) Pointing to the silver cup he discovered in Benjamin's sack, the steward accused the youngest brother, "You have done wrong in doing this!" (v. 5) Dejected, Israel's eleven sons returned with the offended steward to the house of Zaphenath-paneah, who caustically scolded them, "Were you not aware that such a man as I נַחֵשׁ יְנַחֵשׁ [definitely perceives enchantment]?" (v. 15) The same verb combination [נַחֵשׁ יְנַחֵשׁ] had been used by his steward when he had overtaken them outside the city. (v. 5) The *LXX* translates twice this verbal couplet: οἰωνισμῷ οἰωνίζεται. In Genesis 30:27 Moses dictated that Laban had used נִחַשְׁתִּי to translate not in the sense of 'to divine' but in that of "to perceive," i.e., to identify by means of one's senses. Thus, inasmuch as nothing Moses had narrated this far informs me that the brothers could associate the silver cup with the practice of divination, I'm puzzled by Joseph's obtuse question. Did he mean to convey, "What makes you think I would not have missed this cup?"

Or could this be his 'back door' way of reminding them about their hatred and jealousy they had of their seventeen-year-old brother after he had related and interpreted to them two dreams he had experienced {cf. 17:5f}? Regardless, though, there is no doubt that Joseph's rhetorical question to Pharaoh, "Do not interpretations belong to אלהים [the Hebrew God, not an Egyptian deity]?" (40:8) indicates that he knew God had endowed him with the gift of dream interpretations. In other words, Yaweh's interpreting specific dreams by means of His Breath through Joseph was not divination, about which some three centuries later Yaweh spoke to Moses, "You shall not practice divination..." (Leviticus 19:26) and "...anyone who uses divination...is detestable to Yaweh..." (Deuteronomy 18:10-12) Thus because of this Godliness in Joseph, I am compelled to accept that verses 5 and 15 state Zaphenath-paneah enjoyed very much perceiving enchantment from what his silver cup would offer: the fruits of the vines.

Now Judah immediately went on the defense by offering all eleven of them as his slaves but Joseph refused:

> "The man in whose possession the cup has been found, he shall be my slave; but as for you, go up in peace to your father." (v. 17)

Acknowledging Joseph as an "equal to Pharaoh" (v.18 {cf. 37:9-10}), Judah sought to remind him about their father's strong reluctance for letting the youngest son come to Egypt: "when he sees that the lad is not {with us} he dies...Thus your servants will bring...our father down to Sheol in sorrow." (v. 31) After adding, "we became surety for the lad to my father" (v. 32), he begged Joseph to indenture himself instead of Benjamin. Becoming bereft with emotion in the presence of his staff, Joseph ordered them all out of the room and commenced wailing, so loud that "the household of Pharaoh heard." (v. 2) When he confessed his true identity to his eleven brothers and enquired about his father's wellbeing, his brothers נִבְהֲלוּ מִפָּנָיו [were terrified before him.] Sensing that, he asked them to come closer to him and sought to provide loving comfort to the guilt-ridden men:

> "...do not be grieved or angry with yourselves... God sent me before you to preserve life...to preserve for you {the family of Israel} a remnant in the earth and to keep you alive by a great deliverance...it was not you who sent me here but God, and He has made me...ruler over all the land of Egypt." (vs. 5,7,8)

Joseph then urged them to hurry back to Jacob both to inform him of rose from being an Egyptian a slave to Pharaoh's 'right-hand man' as well as to urge him to come to Egypt without "delay." (v. 9) Then Pharaoh encouraged them to return to Canaan and bring the entire family of Israel back to Egypt to settle securely in the best land in all of Egypt, Goshen, as the king's gift of appreciation to Zaphenath- paneah . After showering Israel's sons with a multitude of foods, garments, donkeys and wagons, Joseph sent them off with these wise parting words: "Do not quarrel on the journey." (v. 24) These were wise words in that they would have to become united truth-wise inasmuch as they will have to speak it when they tell him, "Joseph is still alive." (v. 26)

After learning that his favored son (37:3) was still alive and wanted him to come to Egypt, Jacob's "רוּחַ [feeling (mood)]... revived" (v. 27) in anticipation of seeing him before he dies. So Israel's seventy-member (Genesis 46:27) family left Canaan as soon as feasible with all their belongings. While passing through Beersheba he stopped and "offered sacrifices to the God of his father Isaac" (v. 1) "Yaweh spoke to him "in visions of the night... 'do not be afraid to go down to Egypt for I will make you a great nation there. I will go down with you to Egypt and I will also surely bring you up again; and Joseph will close your eyes.'" (vs. 3-4) So Jacob's family continued on their trip to Goshen, the directions for which Judah had gone ahead to obtain from Joseph. In due time Zaphenath-paneah anxiously rod his chariot to Goshen and upon arriving "fell upon {Israel's) neck and wept on his neck a long time." (v. 29) Finally, in reaction his father declared to him and his family, "Now let me die, since I have seen your face, that you are still alive." (v. 30) This statement foreshadows what more than a millennium later Simeon, while holding the newly born Jesus in his arms in the temple with Joseph and Mary present, had "blessed God...

> 'Now Lord, let Your bondservant depart in peace according to Your word {cf. v. 26}, for my eyes have seen Your salvation, which You have prepared in the presence of all peoples: a light of revelation to the Gentiles and the glory of Your people.'"
>
> —Luke 2:29-32

**At the end of his reuniting with Jacob, Joseph said he would inform Pharaoh that his father's family wishes to do their shepherding in Goshen and then urged them to confirm their shepherding livelihood to the king should he ask, because "every shepherd is loathsome to the

Egyptians." (v. 34) But interestingly, though, it makes me wonder who had been tending the king's livestock (Genesis 47:6) as well as the "horses,,,flocks...herds {cattle}...and the donkeys" (47:16-17) Zaphenath-paneah later into the middle of the severe famine had started buying from the impoverished Egyptian farmers for the sake of the country's economy. Yet as he had anticipated, Joseph and five of his brothers did have an audience before Pharaoh as did Jacob, who " יְבָרֶךְ [kneeled towards] the king. (vs. 7,10) the king. In response the monarch instructed Joseph to "settle your father and your brothers in the best land, let them live in the land of Goshen." (v. 6) Joyfully Joseph settled the family of Israel in Goshen, "gave them a possession in...the best of the land...of Rameses, as Pharaoh had ordered" (v. 11) and provided his family with ample food in spite of famine's severity (vs. 12- 13.)

Verses 13-26 provide this overview of Joseph's management skills:

- he amassed all monies raised from the sale of food in Egypt during the start of the famine into Pharaoh's treasury;
- when all the citizens' money had been depleted, he swapped stored up food for their livestock;
- the next year he represented the monarch in purchasing all the land of Egypt (except the priests' allotment) and relocated the Egyptian citizens, now his slaves (vs. 19,25), to Egypt's cities;
- as part of the land sale, he provided all the people seeds by which to sew their king's lands, the

> harvest of which would belong to them except for a 1/5th portion going to Pharaoh;
> - any food need would be procurable by the funds generated from the land sales.

> Now Israel {Jacob – cf. v. 29} lived in the land of Egypt in Goshen and they {Jacob and his sons} acquired property in it and were fruitful and became very numerous. (v. 27)

The significance of this verse is two-fold. First, it indicates the fulfillment of the promise Yaweh made to Israel in a vision (46:2-3) and second, it displays Moses's 'poetic license' of using 'Israel' in either an individual sense or a communal one. "When the time for Israel to die drew near…{as a sign of} kindness and truth" (v. 29) Joseph placed his hand under his father's thigh and "swore" (v. 31) that he would bury Jacob in Abraham's and Isaac's {cf. v. 30} burial site in Canaan. Shortly thereafter Jacob, bedridden now with failing vision, recounted to Joseph all of Yaweh's promises to him (vs. 29:13-15, 35:6-12) and then claimed Zaphenath-paneah's sons, Ephraim and Manasseh, as his own sons in order to incorporate them as the beneficiaries of God's promise; this formal act in effect transferred to them his own first-born son's birthright, because Reuben "had defiled his father's bed. (1 Chronicles 5:1 {cf. Genesis 35:22}) When Joseph's young {cf. v. 12} sons appeared before Israel, he kissed and embraced them but when preparing to give them his blessing, Jacob had placed his right hand on the head of Ephraim, the younger son, much to the father's consternation. Joseph tried to correct his father's hand placements but Jacob was adamant for he already had intended to put Ephraim before Manasseh" (v. 20), precisely in the same order he had mentioned earlier to Joseph (v. 5.) Israel's reasoning, the "younger brother shall be greater than" the older brother (v. 19) interestingly perpetuates the prophecy Yaweh had spoken to Rebekah, his mother, at his birth: "the older shall (i.e. Esau) serve the younger (i.e., Jacob.)" (25:23) Another item of interest to me is the phrase with which Jacob had paralleled, "The God who has been my shepherd," in his blessing of Joseph: "הַמַּלְאָךְ הַגֹּאֵל [the angel redeeming me] from all evil." (v. 16) Though subtly implied by Abraham's intended sacrifice of his only son to God, the gracious gift of redemption for a sinner now became clearer in Jacob's blessing. God had commanded the patriarch, "Take now…your only son, whom you love…and offer him…as a burnt offering…" (Genesis 22:2) In all of Genesis only two types of burnt offerings were apparently made: a "dedicatory" (Genesis 4:4) or a "praise and thanksgiving" offering. (Genesis 8:20-22) {Evangelical Dictionary of Theology, p. 789}

> מַלְאַךְ יְהוָה [angel of Yaweh]…said to Abraham…"I know that you fear God since you have not withheld your son, your only son, from Me. Then Abraham raised his eyes and looked and behold behind {him was} a ram caught in the thicket…and Abraham…took the ram and offered him up for a burnt offering in the place of his son." …The לְאַךְ יְהוָה called to Abraham a second time

> from heaven... "because you...have not withheld your son, your only son, indeed I will greatly bless you and I will greatly multiply your seed as the stars of the heavens...And in your seed all the nations of the earth shall be blessed because you have obeyed My voice."
> —Genesis 22:11-13,15-18

Abraham had positively responded for he had a strong faith in God, as manifested in what he had told his servants when they separated {"we will worship and return to you,"} (v. 5) as well as when Isaac asked him where the lamb to be sacrificed was {"God will provide for Himself the lamb for the burnt offering..." (v. 8) As reward for Abraham's faith and trust in, as well as obedience to, Him, Yaweh had redeemed the patriarch and Isaac from sin's grip {cf. John 8:34}, thereby reconciling and atoning them to Himself. The consequential scope of the blessing (v. 18) was that all of Abraham's seed would become what He said to Moses some three hundred years later: עַמִּי [My people.] (Exodus 9:1)

God's 'last-minute' substitution of a ram is the foreshadowing of Yaweh's sending Jesus, His only begotten Son, to earth in order to serve as the substitute sacrifice for all the sinners whose names appear in His book of life. The Son obediently did so by assuming all the saints' sins when nailed to a cross in order to suffer two-fold: slow, fatal torture while simultaneously His Father's countenance being turned away from Him in anger. Like Abraham's ram, Jesus substitutionally bore all His believers' sins and voluntarily experienced

extreme physical pain as well as the grief of rejection by and anger of His Father. God's gift by Christ to the saints (John 3:16) is each's personal salvation, their freedom from sin and its consequences. Though Isaac was aware of the promises Yaweh had made to his father, they instead were conveyed to Jacob in a dream (Genesis 28:12-15), not by the one he had deceived, his father. His response to that revelation was similar to today's 'foxhole conversion: "If God will be with me... and I return to my father's house in safety, then the Lord will be my God." (vs. 20-21) Jacob did indeed return to his father's home safely.

Genesis 49:28 informs us that the first twenty-seven verses of that chapter focus on the blessings Jacob יְבָרֶךְ [had pronounced] to each of his twelve sons, to "everyone with the blessing appropriate to him {i.e., attributable to his own doing.}" While each of his "blessings" displays a father's appreciation of his child, they all tend to be prophetic in character because they entail specific impacts on each son's descendants:

<u>To Reuben</u> - "Preeminent in dignity and...power...you shall not have preeminence because you went up to your father's bed, then you defiled it {cf. 35:22}..." (vs. 3-4)

Jacob's rebuke of Reuben raises this question: was the father possessive of his concubine or did the position of concubine acquire a socially moral aspect? Definition of concubine includes: "In certain societies...a woman contracted to a man as a secondary wife, often having few legal rights and low social status." (The American Heritage Dictionary) In other words, she was a slave as well as a party to marital infidelity. Regardless of the answer, two consequences resulted: Reuben had lost his oldest-brother's leadership {cf. 42:22} and Jacob had denied him of the firstborn's privileges.

<u>To Simeon and Levi</u> - Your "swords are implements of violence" and I don't want any responsibility or disgrace for whatever they harm. Your anger is a threat to human life {cf. 34:25-30} as well as to the debilitation of an ox. Cursed is your anger for it is fierce and cruel and consequently your inheritances as well as descendants (in) Israel will be divided among those of my other ten sons' {cf. Joshua 19:21:1-42.}

<u>To Judah</u> - "Your brothers shall praise you…and bow down to you." (v. 8) His lion instincts will establish his military prowess and his role as חָקַק [lawgiver {cf. Numbers 24:17; Psalm 60:7,108:8}] will prevail up to the coming of שִׁילֹה [Shiloh] to (whom) is the obedience of the peoples. He ties…his donkey's colt to the choice vine…He washes his garments…in the blood {cf. Isaiah 63:2} of grapes. His eyes are darker than wine and his teeth whiter than milk." (vs. 10-12)

"Shiloh" translates as pacificator/bringer of peace and represented in Jacob's era the precursor of the awaited Messiah to come {cf. Isaiah 9:6; Ezekiel 21:25-27.} In 1977 at Westminster Theological Seminary Dr. Meredith G. Kline, the Old Testament lecturer, said 1] because covenants in Abraham's time were often made by cutting a donkey as the sacrifice, "Shiloh" was going to suffer; 2] the man Jesus rode a donkey {cf. Zechariah 9:9; Mark 11:2} to signify the coming shedding of blood for the covenant God's Son had 'cut' with His Father to sanctify the completed book of life (1:3-4); and 3] the descriptions of "Shiloh's" eyes and teeth represented "a paradise motif."

Various questions arise concerning Jacob's blessing for Judah:

1. When had Jacob learned of "Shiloh" - when God had appeared to him in Bethel (35:8-13) or "in visions of the night" from Him (46:2-4) or had he been filled "by His Breath" to mention it without any prior knowledge? I am unable to discover whether Moses had addressed that.
2. Had Judah and his brothers any prior knowledge of "Shiloh" inasmuch as this word appears only once in all the Scriptures? Moses is silent about that possibility as well.
3. Did Jacob and his sons have any understanding as to why a pacificator/bringer of peace was necessary and desirable for them since life in Canaan and Egypt had seemed at that time peaceful for the entire family? Had they been informed by oral history of what God had covenanted with Noah:

> (Even though) "the intent of man's heart is evil from his youth...I will never again destroy every living thing...while the earth remains, seedtime and harvest, and cold and heat, and summer and winter, and day and night will not cease."
> —Genesis 8:21-22

"...while the earth remains" to me definitely conveys that life on earth is not to be eternal, just as He earlier had succinctly "said : 'My Breath will not strive with man forever.'" (Genesis 6:3) Two verses later He "saw... that every intent of the thoughts of (man's) heart was only evil continually" (v. 5) and was justly compelled to destroy all of mankind except Noah and his immediate family. Now up to the 49th chapter of Genesis I am able to recall only one divine law divinely expressed to man: verse 17 in chapter 2. There are, however, four events in oral Hebrew history describing חָטָא לַיהוָה [sin against Yaweh]:

I: Genesis 4:7 — Yaweh to Cain: "חָטָא [sin] is crouching at the door וְאֵלֶיךָ, תְּשׁוּקָתוֹ [and to you {is} its desire – cf. 3:16], but you must master it." Yaweh's response to his murdering his brother, Abel, is so severe that he exclaims to Him: "from Your face I will be hidden and I will be a vagrant and a wanderer on the earth." (v. 14) This punishment foreshadows Jesus's separation from His Father He will merit for bearing on the cross all the sins committed by those whose names have been written in the book of life {cf. Matthew 27:46 and Mark 15:34.} Moses does not inform us much about the first family for we do not know the ages of Cain and Abel when the murder had occurred, though it had happened before Seth was born. But Moses portrayed Abel intelligent enough to realize the scope of Yaweh's punishment on him. And Adam and Eve at least at that moment knew what their Creator considered man-made destruction of a human being. So at least one offense to Yaweh now had become known by the first family as it expanded exponentially up to the time of Noah.

II: Genesis 13:13 — Abram, when settling in Canaan learned the "the men of Sodom were wicked exceedingly and חַטָּאתָם [sinners] against Yaweh." In the *Septuagint* ἁμαρτάνω {cf. John 5:14} is the translation for חָטָא.

III: Genesis 18:20 — "Yaweh said, 'The outcry of Sodom and Gomorrah is indeed great and חַטָּאִים [their sin] is exceedingly grave.'" His anger was such that it brought about instant destruction of both communities.

IV: Genesis 20 — Warned by God in a night dream that Abimelech would become "a dead man" {v. 2} if he "touched" (v. 6) Abraham's 'sister,' the king was kept by Him "from חָטָא [sinning] against Me." (v. 6) Then in righteous indignation Abimelech yelled at Abraham, "how have חָטָאתִי [I sinned] against you, that you have brought on me and on my kingdom a great חָטָא [sin?]"

Genesis 39:9 — In defense Joseph to Potiphar, his enraged master, pleaded his innocence: "How then could I do this great evil and חָטָאתִי [sin] against God?" Here Joseph had appealed to his fear of God in order to counter what he had been accused of doing to Potiphar's wife.

Now it stands to reason that because sin with consequences is the common thread shared by the above four incidences, oral Hebrew history would most certainly have included these events to provide a divine influence and guide for every human's walk. And as a reasonable consequence, many peoples' consciences during that era would have become sensitive in one degree or another that the sin(s) they had committed had jeopardized their relationships with Yaweh. Up to the first 48 chapters of Genesis Moses has merely hinted that a burnt offering was man's means to establish or restore his 'good standing' with the Creator, but then Jacob had become inspired to casually mention Shiloh, the future pacificator/bringer of peace whom "the peoples" (v. 10) would obey when he wields Judah's scepter and staff. I hesitate to call Israel's inspired blessing to Judah a prophecy because Moses had not mentioned that Jacob had attributed its origin to Yaweh. Yet Shiloh appears to be the conceptual precursor of מָשִׁיחַ [the appointed, Messiah {the anticipated deliverer and king of the Jews}], originally the accepted Hebrew title for priests {cf. Leviticus 4:3,5,16} but then evolved (Psalm 60:7, 108:8) to include "Yaweh's anointed" {cf. 1 Samuel 16:6; 2 Samuel 1:14; Psalm 2:2; Isaiah 45:1; Habakkuk 3:13.}

It seems possible that Shiloh refers back to Melchizedek, king of שָׁלֵם [Salem {"righteousness... peace" (Hebrews 7:2)}], whom Moses identified as "כֹהֵן [priest] of God Most High" (Genesis 14:18), the first mentioned functionary of an "order" (Psalm 110:4) comprised of eternal priests "designated by God." (Hebrews 5:10) Abram appreciated the king's offering of bread and wine and respectfully gave him a tenth of "all the goods of Sodom and Gomorrah and all their food supply." (v. 11) It's interesting to note these two symbolic gestures foreshadowed and then became principal practices of the Christian faith.

As for his tribe's future, Jacob in effect vested leadership of his twelve sons' families (v. 16) on his fourth son by forecasting that שִׁבְטֵי [staff's emblem of authority] and מְחֹקֵק [poel participle of מָחַק – to smash, crush, strike through, implying a ruler's stout-stick weapon symbolizing authority] would become his. (v. 10)

To Zebulun — Jacob said he would live on the southeastern coast of the Mediterranean Sea, south of Sidon {cf. Joshua 19:11-12}, and would provide a safe harbor and thriving commerce for many ships {cf. Deuteronomy 33:19.}

To Issachar — Jacob likened this son to a scrawny donkey willing and fit to bear burdens of hard labor in areas suitable for growing crops as well as providing him pleasant rest.

To Dan — Jacob predicted Dan יָדִין [would govern] his {family} as one of Israel's tribes and would wisely and swiftly protect it from marauding enemies. (v. 17) But then Jacob, apparently weakened by his talking, said parenthetically to Yaweh, "לִישׁוּעָתְךָ [For Your help] I wait."

To Gad — Jacob predicted shysters יְגוּדֶנּוּ [would have an effect on him] but he was going to עָקֵב [take by the heel, i.e., defraud {cf. Jeremiah 9:4(3)}] them. This is the same verb Esau used when complaining to Isaac {cf. Genesis 27:36} about Jacob's trickery against him at birth {cf. Genesis 25:26} as well as defrauding him of his birthright.

To Asher — לַחְמוֹ [what he swallows greedily] will be nourishing but rich and he will merchandise delights fit for a king to surrounding communities.

To Naphtali — Jacob likened him to a hind being set free {an act of which} speaks aloud words of beauty. In describing Naphtali's endowed 'gift of the tongue' Jacob had employed a simile: the hind, a female deer, was capable of placing the hooves of her back feet onto the spot where those of her front feet had just left and thus would display nature's beauty when she was engaged in free flight.

To Joseph — Israel lauded him as a fruitful בֵּן [son], a fruitful בֵּן [descendant] near a watery spring, whose בָּנוֹת [daughters] will spread throughout the land. Though "archers," i.e., his brothers, "bitterly" sought to harm him, physical and mental strength came to him from אֲבִיר [the mighty One {cf. Psalm 132:2, Isaiah 1:24,49:26}], רֹעֶה [the Shepherd {cf. Psalm 23:1,80:1}, אֶבֶן יִשְׂרָאֵל [the Stone of Israel {cf. Psalm 118:22; Isaiah 28:16; Ephesians 2:20 .}] He had been sustained מֵאֵל [by the God] of his father, שַׁדַּי [the Almighty {cf. 28:3,48:3}], by the Persons emanating from Yaweh would shower. Possibly spoken by Israel another way: The willful care of Joseph had been manifested מֵאֵל [by God], by אֲבִיר, שַׁדַּי {cf. 39:2-3,21,23} through His divine voice {cf. Genesis 1:3}, personified as רוּחַ אֱלֹהִים [Breath of God], and His Son [רֹעֶה {cf. v. 24; John 10:11)] and stone [אֶבֶן], first of Israel (v. 24 { cf. Psalm 31:3,62:2,6}) and then of his bride, the Church {cf. Matthew 16:18.}

Jacob then professed that the blessings he had received from Him had been more abundant than those his ancestors had enjoyed and prayed it would be the same for Joseph, "the one distinguished among his brothers." (v. 26) Earlier, before this gathering had taken place, Israel had promised him "one portion {cf. Joshua 24:32, John 4:5.} more than your brothers, which I took from the hand of the Amorite with my sword and my bow." (Genesis 48:22 {cf. Ezekiel 47:13})

To Benjamin — Israel likened his youngest heir's reputation and character to that of a wolf: a hardworking hunter/gatherer who dutifully provided for those within his scope of responsibility. (v. 27)

The blessings Jacob had pronounced resembled father-to-son greetings and/or salutations and most displayed keen personal knowledge based on close relationships and were tempered with rebuke, praise as well as visions of the future for most of the twelve.

For the first time Jacob had referred his twelve sons collectively as שִׁבְטֵי יִשְׂרָאֵל [tribes of Israel] (vs. 16), then later as שִׁבְטֵי יִשְׂרָא שְׁנֵים [twelve tribes of Israel.] (v. 28 {cf. Exodus 24:4, 28:21, 39:14}) Over 147 years his 'family' (defined as all the descendants of a common ancestor) had evolved into individual 'tribes,' which anthropologists define as human social organizations based on a set of smaller groups of common descent, language, culture, ideology and self-government. What is interesting to note here is that the Ancient Hebrew noun for 'tribe' [שֵׁבֶט] is the Chaldee derivative of שֵׁבֶט [scepter], the instrument of authority Jacob had bestowed on Judah. (v. 10)

To conclude this plenary session Israel commanded them collectively to fulfill specific instructions for his burial (vs. 29-32). And not that much later, after living 17 years in Goshen "he drew his feet into the bed and breathed the last and אָסַף [was taken away {cf. 25:8}] to his people" (v.33), to Abraham, Sarah, Isaac, Rebekah and Leah in the cave which Abraham had purchased in Canaan for Sarah's burial.}

While for 70 days "the Egyptians wept for him" (Genesis 15:3), the process of embalming Jacob required 40 days. Having personally instructed Joseph and his brothers to return to Canaan, Pharaoh sent along with them the elders {political appointees} not only of his household but of the rest of Egypt as well. All that had been left behind in Goshen were "the little ones...flocks and...herds" (v.8), though only temporarily.

Having fulfilled Israel's burial instructions and begun their journey back to Goshen, Joseph's brothers became fearful that he would vent his wrath on them for what they had done to him in the past. So they contrived this fib to be sent ahead to him: "Your father charged before he died, saying, 'Thus you shall say to Joseph, "Please forgive, I beg you, the transgression of your brothers and their sin, for they did you wrong."'" Upon learning of this request Joseph wept because personal, familial reconciliation was foremost on this mind, as it was made apparent as well on his brothers' minds when they lay before him and humbly professed their servitude to him. (vs. 17-18) Yet immediately the second most powerful living Egyptian explained to his humbled brothers that they must not fear him but instead only God. (v. 19) Moses, inspired as well, described Joseph's inspired revelation as to how Yaweh's sovereignty in the spiritual realm interacts physically with all human lives, past, present and future: whatever evil every man does He employs for good. (v. 20 {cf. Genesis 20:6,16-18; Proverbs 16:4; Romans 9:13-18}) To celebrate his reconciliation with Israel's household Joseph promised them care and comfort in the land of Goshen.

Sometime later, when he had reached the age of one hundred and ten, Joseph had sensed his life was soon coming to its end (thirty-seven years earlier than had Jacob's) he gathered the remnant of his brothers to express his burial wishes and bless them with this prophesy:

> "God will פָּקֹד יִפְקֹד [visit to take care of] you and bring you up from this land to the land which He swore on an oath to Abraham {cf. 13:15,17;15:13}, to Isaac {cf. 26:3} and to Jacob {cf. 28:13;35:12}." (v.24 {cf. Hebrews 11:22})

In compliance with his wishes, the favored (37:3) and distinguished (49:26) son of Jacob, known also as a grandson of Isaac as well as a great grandson of Abraham, "was embalmed and placed in a coffin in Egypt" (v. 26) which "the sons of Israel brought up {and buried} at Shechem, in the piece of ground which Jacob had bought {cf. 33:19.}..." (Joshua 24:32)

This concludes the initial phases of Yaweh's account, the absolutely unerring 'His-story', of the establishment of creation's foundation and of His role as sovereign administrator in time and space up to circa the early second millennium before Christ. The focus of בְּרֵאשִׁית [Genesis] is God's interaction with His creation at the commencement of "the seventh day" (Genesis 2:2-3.) To his brothers Joseph had explained God's *modus operandi*, the way He involved Himself personally with man in earthly reality: "{while} you meant evil against me, God meant it for good in order to bring about {goodness}..." (Genesis 50:20) The American patriot Benjamin Franklin, though a doubter of Jesus's divinity, just prior to his death wrote a Congregationalist minister: "I believe in one God, creator of the universe.

That he governs it by his Providence."[36] I, a believer in the deity of Jesus Christ, like to think that my title for this chapter, Yaweh's Sovereign Reign Over Life, parallels Franklin's 'providential governance of the universe,' even though I had crafted that title at least a year prior to seeing Franklin's letter.

A good example of Yaweh's reigning over life is Abraham's visit to Gerar, where he feared for his safety because he had sensed that "no fear of God" (Genesis 20:11) was there and thus his wife's beauty had jeopardized his safety after he had presented Sarah as his sister to King Abimelech. The monarch unexpectedly יִּקַּח [took away] her from her husband but "had not come near her" (v. 4) when God spoke to him in a dream, "you are a dead man because of the woman whom you have taken, for she is married...I know that in the integrity of your heart you have done this and I also kept you from sinning against Me; thus I did not let you touch her" (vs. 3,6) since He "had closed fast all the wombs of the household of Abimelech." (v. 18) God had 'entered' reality and kept Abimelech from taking Sarah as a wife because that would have been sin for various reasons: Abraham had withheld full truth regarding Sarah and thereby entrapped the king into potentially sinning for 'lying' with a married woman as well as callously thrust his wife into a potentially compromising sin of 'lying' with the king, all of which offended Yaweh. What Abraham unwittingly but selfishly orchestrated as evil God meant for good. A very similar crisis Abraham

---

36. Dark Agenda, David Horowitz, Humanix Books, 2018

had caused with Sarah appears in Genesis 12:10f, which you are free to consult on your own.

Then there are two incidents when God 'entered' His creation to be with Jacob. The first occurred when Jacob, all alone by "the ford of the Jabbok" (Genesis 32:22), had wrestled to a stalemate a stranger unknown to him. When the stranger asked to be released, Jacob requested a blessing from him first. The stranger then 'blessed' him with the name Israel, which literally translates 'he who strives with God.' In response Jacob named the place Peniel [the face of God] for "I have seen God face to face, yet my life has been preserved." (Genesis 32:30) Another time God appeared to Jacob when he had come from Paddan-aram, and blessed him, saying, "Your name is Jacob; you shall no longer be called Jacob, but Israel shall be your name." (Genesis 35:9-10)

Now during this same post-flood era God had involved Himself personally with the life of Job, a man "in the land of Uz..." (Job 1:1) [Note: The person named Uz was the son of Aram, who was Noah's grandson through Shem (Genesis 10:22-23) and another Uz was the firstborn of Nahor {Abram's brother} and his wife Milcah {the daughter of Abram's other brother, Haran. (Genesis 11:29)} (Genesis 22:21) Thus Uz in Job 1:1 is a person's name, not a place's name {cf. Jeremiah 25:20, Lamentations 4:21.}]

Now because Job "was blameless, upright, fearing God and turning away from evil" (Job 1:1), Satan boldly posed a serious challenge to Yaweh: "Does Job fear God for nothing? Have you not hedged in [שׂוּךְ] him and his house and all {described by Job in vs. 29:2-6} that he has...? Put forth Your hand now and touch all that he has; he will surely curse You to Your face." (1:9-11) Yaweh responded: "all that he has is in your power, only do not put forth {your} hand on him." For some time afterwards severe losses, familial as well as economic, befell him, but through all these drastic reverses "Job did not sin nor did he blame God." (1:22) Satan then modified his challenge to Yaweh: "Skin for skin...all that a man has he will give for his life... put forth Your hand now and touch his bone and his flesh – {Job} will curse You to Your face." (2:4-5) God answered: "he is in your power, only spare his life." Satan departed and inflicted Job with boils all over his body. When his wife advised him to curse God and die, he asked her. "Shall we indeed accept good from God and not accept adversity?" In all this Job did not sin with his lips. (2:9-10) At the end of this wager with Satan, God declared that his servant Job had "spoken of (Him) what is right" (42:8) and restored to him all that His hand had removed while suffering under Satan's power. "Yaweh blessed the latter {days} of Job more than his beginning." (42:12)

In early life men learned to trust one another by making {literally "cutting"} בְּרִית [a covenant], an ancient agreement between two parties that bound each maker to fulfillment of specific objective(s) and was made binding by both makers walking through and back a path outlined by a few halved animal carcasses:

> Abraham took sheep and oxen and gave them to Abimelech and the two of them made a covenant...
> And he said, "You shall take these seven ewe lambs from my hand in order that it may be a witness to me that I dug this well" {in Beersheba.}"
> —Genesis 21:27,30-31

[Note: Going unnecessarily further, Abraham "called upon the name of Yaweh, the everlasting God" (v. 33) for Him to witness the covenant he had made with Abimelech in Beersheba and then planted there a tamarisk tree to mark the site of their agreement. Calling upon the name of Yaweh, attributed first to Seth (Genesis 4:26), was man's means of establishing and enjoying a personal relationship with Him in order to praise Him as well as to implore His help. Such a call was invalid for anyone not maintaining the graciously established enmity with Satan (cf. 3:15.)]

> Abimelech and his two officers to Isaac, "We see plainly that Yaweh has been with you, so we said, 'Let there now be an oath between...you and us and let us make a covenant with you.'"
> —Genesis 26:28

> Laban to Jacob, his son-in-law, concerning unity within their family: "...let us make a covenant, you and I, and let it be a witness between you and me."
> —Genesis 31:44

Yaweh also made covenants, though universally for man's benefit, either graciously or qualified by man's fulfillment of its stipulations:

> The first covenant, that of grace was Yaweh's promise to "put", i.e., establish, deep-seated hostility forever between the serpent (Satan's

disguise) and Eve as well as all of mankind within her womb. {cf. Genesis 3:15}

Noah was righteous and blameless; he too "walked with God." God covenanted with Noah to save him, his wife and three sons if (works) he would build an ark based on His specifications and fill it with a male and a female of all creature species. {cf. Genesis 6:9}

God to Noah: "I Myself will establish My covenant {of grace} with you and with your descendants after you: ...neither shall there be a flood to destroy the earth."
—Genesis 9:9,11

He also made a few covenants with Abra(ha)m:

A covenant {of grace} that promised land "from the river of Egypt {to} the river Euphrates" {"all the land of Canaan" (v. 17:8)} for his descendants, but only after a four-hundred-year enslavement in a strange land.
—Genesis 15:6-21

A covenant {of works} for his descendants' everlasting possession of the land of Canaan as well as for being their God if each male in his household was circumcised.
—Genesis 17:10

As well with Isaac:

"I will establish my covenant {of grace} with (Isaac) for an everlasting covenant for his seed after him {cf. 26:2-5,24-24} (Genesis 17:19,21) - "בַּעֲבוּר [because of] My servant Abraham."
—Genesis 26:25

The first godly character described by Moses was that of Enoch, who for 365 years had "walked with God" (Genesis 5:22), i.e., had lived a godly life, and apparently had been recognized as a prophet (Jude 14.) He had not died; instead "he was not, for God took him" (v. 24), possibly in a similar manner as He had done with Elijah (cf. 2 Kings 2:11.) But the fullest description of man's personal relationship with Yaweh at the commencing phase of "the seventh day" is that of Abr{ah}am, which Yaweh had explained when He יֵרָא **[had appeared] to Isaac:**

> **He "harkened to my voice {cf. Exodus 15:26} and kept** מִשְׁמַרְתִּי **[My charge (what is to be observed)],** מִצְוֹתַי **[My commandments],** חֻקּוֹתַי **[My expectation] and** תּוֹרֹתָי **[My instruction.]"**
> **—Genesis 26:2,5**

In order to understand how God had discerned and assessed the patriarch's character, we need descriptive examples of what Abra{ha}m had "kept":

A] מִשְׁמֶרֶת **— a charge, what is to be observed {cf. Leviticus 8:35}**

> Abram obeyed Yaweh's charge to leave his home and relatives and move to the land of Canaan. Because of His promise that all this new land would be for his descendants, Abram built an altar, upon which he later called on His name {cf. Genesis 12:1-7, 13:4}.
>
> Yaweh's covenant {of works} with Abraham for his descendants' everlasting possession of the land of Canaan as well as being their God to be manifested by each male's circumcision;

after His appearing He יַעַל [rose up] and shortly afterwards Abraham complied fully {cf. Genesis 17:1-14, 24-27}.

"Take now your son, your only son, whom you love, Isaac, and go to the land of Moriah and offer him there as a burnt offering on one of the mountains..." (Genesis 22:2) God נִסָּה [tested by tempting] Abraham; his obedience to Him was being 'proved' like a metal is when its ore is exposed to extremely high heat. Here Yaweh was seeking to perfect the patriarch's obedience, loyalty and faithfulness to Him. Abraham's strength emerged in his words to his aids: "I and the lad will go yonder and we will worship and return to you." (v. 5.) Isaac dutifully followed his father but knew something was not right: "where is the lamb for the burnt offering?" (v. 7) Yet his father replied, "God will provide for Himself the lamb..." (v. 8) but after he had built an altar, bound and laid Isaac on it top of the wood, he stretched out his hand and took the knife to slay his only son. Amid Isaac's trust and silence the voice of Yaweh's angel complimented his father: "now I know that you fear God, since you have not withheld your son, your only son from Me." (v. 12) Abraham worshipped God by naming the place of his test "the Lord will provide" {cf. 1 Corinthians 10:13.}

And through His angel Yaweh expanded on the covenant he had made earlier with Abraham (15:6-21.) He trusted, and had confidence in, Yaweh that He would deliver on his promise (Gen. 12:7; 13:14-17) and thus provide continuance of Isaac's life because his son was the only means to enjoying descendants.

In his old age Abraham had charged the oldest servant of his household to find a bride for Isaac among the patriarch's relatives in Haran, encouraging him in this task with:

> "Yaweh, before Whom I have walked, will send His angel with you to make your journey successful…"
> —Genesis 24:40

B] מִצְוָה — a commandment {cf. Exodus 15:26; 20:2-7}

> Yaweh to Abram:
> "Walk before Me and be blameless' {cf. Romans 4:12}…and Abram fell on his face…"
> —Genesis 17:1,3

> Yaweh:
> "יְדַעְתִּיו [I have regarded/cared for him {Abraham}] to the end that he has commanded his children to keep the way of Yaweh by doing righteousness and justice."
> —Genesis 18:19

> Abraham circumcised his son Isaac when he was eight days old, as God had commanded him.
> —Genesis 21:4

C] חֻקּוֹת — statutes   **D]** תּוֹרָה — laws {cf. Exodus 13:9}

> I am unable to discern any statute or law He had prescribed and thus have to assume that his 'walking before Yaweh' {cf. Genesis 24:40} had exposed him to them.

On a stopover in Gerar Abraham had feared for his safety because he had been able to discern that "no fear of God" (Genesis 20:11) was existing there. Abraham had 'modeled' for Isaac how to build an altar as well as when to call upon the name of Yaweh (26:25); yet his grandson, Jacob, apparently had not acquired that fear of Yaweh when he had left Isaac to visit his uncle, Laban, in Haran {cf. 28:20-22.} The "fear of God" was mentioned by Moses six times in Genesis {directly in 20:11, 22:12 and 42:18 but indirectly in 28:17, 31:42 and 31:53} and 13 times in his other four 'books.' This 'call to faith' also appears well over a hundred times in the later Old Testament books. One's "fear of God", according to Proverbs 29:25, is that person's trust in and of Him and as a verb, its imperative conveys a gentle urgency for one to submit his life fully to Yaweh.

Any time I reflect on the "book of the generations of Adam" in Genesis 5 I'm intrigued to learn:

- How did Moses know all that information?
- If not by Yaweh's Breath what was his source?
- If by ancient word-of-mouth, how directly, considering his growing up in Pharaoh's household?
- If by preserved 'records', how were they authored, compiled, updated, protected and made available to him?

Because my faith positively compels me to accept God's Word as absolute truth, I firmly believe the source to be His Breath.

Now everything God created had purpose for life; each thing made possessed a specific function to interact with the functions of other things. For instance:

- **In addition to providing heat for all vegetation, the sun offers vitamin D as support for man's immune system;**
- **The moon effects the oceans' tides;**
- **Weather all over is influenced by the Atlantic Ocean's north and south Gulf Streams.**
- **Satan's persuasive influence He uses to strengthen an individual's obedience to Him.**
- **Yaweh has made everything for its own purpose, even the wicked for the day of evil {cf. Ephesians 6:13}. (Proverbs 16:4)**

Prior to the beginning, creation of life's foundation had already become a reality; Yaweh's traits of omnipresence {cf. Matthew 18:20}, His being and working everywhere simultaneously, and of πρόγνωσις (foreknowledge), among others, enable the Author to present His book of life within the confines of created time and space. Jesus said, "rejoice that your names are recorded in heaven." (Luke 10:20) Luke's inference that the saints are already in the book is affirmed by Paul: "...while we were enemies, we were reconciled to God through the death of His Son..." (Romans 5:10) All those reconciled to God by Jesus' death had their names written in God's book before the foundation of the world: "For those whom He foreknew, He also predestined to become conformed to the image of

His Son..." (Romans 8:29) Thus even the names of those not yet conceived have already been recorded by God. And just as comforting, the total outcome of creation at all times is precisely as Yaweh wills {cf. Colossians 1:9} and plans, "after the counsel of His will." (Ephesians 1:11)

> ...God was in Christ reconciling the world to Himself, not counting their trespasses against them...
> —2 Corinthians 5:19

WHAT WENT WRONG

In order for me to properly address what did go wrong, I first need to highlight what had 'gone right.' The determining factor of that phase consists solely on the Creator's assessment of His creation of life.

> God, after He spoke long ago to the fathers in the prophets in many portions and in many ways, in these last days has spoken to us in (His) Son...
> —Hebrews 1:1-2

God had spoken through Moses almost four millennia ago in order to inform His image bearers what pleased as well as displeased Him. In the beginning of John's gospel we learn that His Son was the "Word...In Him was life; and the life was the light of men." (John 1:1,4) The "light" was Jesus' conception as the 'second man' as well as the humility of His earthly existence and death in order to guide to eternal life all who believed both Him as well as in Him; He was not the "light" of Genesis 1:3-4, which Chapter 2 asserts is the divine book of life which radiated absolute truth. The book of life specified that reality commence on the divinely created earth as its foundation. (vs. 1:1-10) The rest of Genesis is Moses's history of creation according to personal inspiration by Yaweh's Breath and thus is absolute truth as well.

Now Moses dictated that at the end of the "sixth day" the Creator pronounced all that He had made was טוֹב מְאֹד [exceedingly agreeable]/ *LXX:* καλὰ λίαν [exceedingly good] (Genesis 1:31):

וַיַּרְא אֱלֹהִים אֶת-כָּל-אֲשֶׁר עָשָׂה, וְהִנֵּה-טוֹב מְאֹד

[And God looked at all that He had made and undoubtedly/certainly {it was} exceedingly agreeable]

καὶ εἶδεν ὁ θεὸς τ ἀπάντα, ὅσα ἐποίησεν,
καί ἰδο ὐκαλ ἀλίαν.

[And the God observed all which He created and lo(!) it was good exceedingly]

While the focus of Genesis is on life's beginning within the solar system, its termination, the final phase God had authored in His book of life, is subtly implied in the covenant He had "cut" with Noah: "never again shall the water become a flood to destroy all flesh." (Genesis 9:15) The nuance to me rests in what Yaweh purposefully omitted: His use of fire or earthquake to destroy all flesh as well as matter. Jesus' millennia later indirectly confirmed this:

"The heavens [ὁ οὐρανὸς {cf. Genesis 1:1; Matthew 6:26,16:2-3}] and the earth will pass away..."
—Matthew 5:18,24:35; Luke 21:33

At the end of each of the first five days as well as up to the creation of man in the sixth, Moses dictated וַיַּרְא אֱלֹהִים, כִּי-טוֹב . (Genesis 1:4,10,12,18, 21,25) According to Davidson's The Analytical Hebrew and Chaldee Lexicon, כִּי is "supposed...to be primarily a relative pronoun" like אֲשֶׁר / ὅσα [that] but in this quote it serves as a relative conjunction to indicate what Yaweh had observed as being good at the end of each "day" was a serial accumulation of what He had created/formed up to the end of that respective *yohm*. But at the end of day six He examined all that He had accomplished and was pleased "to see" that the fulfillment of His 'master plan for life was טוֹב מְאֹד / καλὰ λίαν [very good.]

טוֹב מְאֹד / καλὰ λίαν is a divine assessment: anything "very good" to Him, 'a perfection of perfections,' is agreeable and acceptable and therefore perfect. However, man's word to describe perfection is תָּמִים with its various nuances:

Upright, righteous	(Genesis 6:9; Deuteronomy 18:13)
Blameless	(Genesis 17:1; Proverbs 2:21; Ezekiel 28:15)
Without blemish	(Exodus 12:5, 29:1; Leviticus 19 times, Numbers 17 times, Ezekiel 11 times)
Complete	(Leviticus 23:15, 25:30)
Sincere	(Judges 9:16,19)

Though Moses used the adjective תָּמִים in Deuteronomy 32:4 to express completeness and perfection, Yaweh chose טוֹב, which is neither moral {in opposition to evil - cf. Genesis 2:9,17,3:5,22,50:20; Psalm 25:8} nor positive / desirable in nature {cf. Genesis 2:18; Numbers 10:29,32.} It instead indicates that God's creating and forming efforts conformed completely and perfectly to what His book of life, the "light" of Genesis 1:3-4, had specified. תָּמִים פָּעֳלוֹ [{His} work {is} perfect, without blemish] / *LXX:* ἀληθινὰ τὰ ἔργα αὐτοῦ [His work {is} true.] (Deuteronomy 32:4 {cf. 2 Samuel 22:31; Psalm 18:30(31),19:7(8)}) Since the *LXX* counterpart for תָּמִים, ἀληθινὰ [real, true, trustworthy], is rather bland, τέλεια would seem to have been more appropriate: perfect, complete, without spot or blemish. American Heritage Dictionary's[37] definition for 'perfect' includes:

- being wholly without a flaw;
- lacking nothing essential to the whole;
- complete of its nature;
- without blemish or defect;
- completely suitable for a particular purpose;
- excellent and delightful in all respects.

From here on, then, in discussing what comprises His טוֹב מְאֹד , (1:31) כָּל consistently presupposes the translation of "divinely perfect":

1. The foundation for life: waters (v. 2) and "the light" (v. 5), Yaweh's fully exhaustive 'blue print' specifying and directing His creating and forming;

---

37. https://ahdictionary.com/word/search.html?q=perfect, Viewed 3/27/23

2. Earth's atmosphere, dry land and seas (v. 10);
3. All kinds of flora for all uses, above and below the seas (v. 12)
4. The heavens [ὁ/ הַשָּׁמַיִם οὐρανὸς], which exists above the earth's troposphere all the way out to the edge of the solar system and produces the gravitationally bound system comprised of the moon and the eight planets that either directly or indirectly orbit the sun (v. 18);
5. All creatures in the sea and air (v. 21) as well as on and in the ground (v. 25);
6. God created man {females with two X chromosomes in their cells and males with X and Y chromosomes in their cells} in His own image and as His 'vice regent' to רָדָה [rule over/subdue] all the flora and fauna in the air and oceans as well as on the ground (vs.1:26; 2:5). "God created human beings to reflect and image {H}im by loving the things {H}e loves."[38]

On the seventh day יְהוָה אֱלֹהִים [Yaweh God] engages in caring simultaneously for the past, present and even future of all life in His creation; from the creation of time to its termination He reigns freely outside, over and within it and administers a perfect control of everything, including all of Satan's activities. Yaweh never experiences the "past" or the "future" as do all life's creatures; God supremely reigns forever only in the

---

38. Politics & Evangelical Theology, Brian G. Mattson, self-printed; 2020, page 213

'present,' hence יְהוָה, His personal name to all mankind. From the perspective of human incomprehensibility, God is capable of functioning simultaneously within and during all three periods, the past, present and future; throughout the Old and the New Testaments as well as after the end of time Yaweh "is" and executes simultaneously all that He plans. As He asserts:

> "...there is no one like Me, declaring the end from the beginning and from ancient times things which are not done, saying 'My purpose is established and I accomplish all My good pleasure.'"
> —Isaiah 46:10

His book of life focuses constantly on all phases of life; it is not restricted by any chronological progression because His omnipresent character simultaneously attends to planning, creating, administering, governing and caring for all of life's needs in freedom from the constraint of created time.

I confess that my very simplistic explanation of God's ability and character defies all human understanding, especially His traits of foreknowing and foreordaining. All of Yaweh's traits transcend all things men's minds have been created to comprehend; in other words, only He can understand Himself. According to Peter all believers "are foreordained {chosen beforehand} according to the foreknowledge of God the Father, by the sanctifying work of {His} Breath, that {they} may obey Jesus Christ and be sprinkled with His blood." (1 Peter 1:1-2) Even before Yaweh created and formed man, all those He foreordained to enjoy eternal life with Him had already had their names written in His book of life. As Paul explains, all believers "obtain...an inheritance having been predestined according to His purpose Who works all things after the counsel of His will." (Ephesians 1:11) In other words, each believer is foreordained by Him to receive the gift of His Breath, the fulfillment of Christ-like sanctification and eternal life with Yaweh:

> {literal translation}...with fear and trembling work out your salvation, for it is God putting into operation in you both the to intend and the to be in operation for the realization of {His} intention.
> —Philippians 2:12-13

Just try to imagine the uncountable number of souls over whom He is dispensing lovingkindness and encouragement, endowing them with distinct abilities and "not allow{ing them} to be tempted beyond what {they} are able, but...will provide the way of escape also, that {they} may be able to endure it." (1 Corinthians 10:13) I believe Jesus bore on the cross once for always {cf. Hebrews 9:28,10:10; I Peter 3:18} all the sins committed by every soul "whose {name is} written in the Lamb's book of life." (Revelation 21:27)

A great example of divine foreknowledge is the fulfillment of a warning Jesus during His earthly ministry had predicted: "Simon, Simon, behold, the opponent/ enemy demands for himself to sift you {i.e., Peter and his fellow apostles} like wheat {i.e., by trials and temptations.}...I tell you, Peter, the cock will not crow today until you have denied three times that you know me." By means of His ability to foreknow He knew was certain the silent cock would indeed crow after this disciple had lied three time {cf. vs. 57,58,60.} His foreknowledge has been completely incorporated in the book of life. Even though He foreknows the outcome of every conceived human's life, His justice requires every individual's accountability of disobedience to Him.

I readily admit my confusing and weighty statements above are illogical as well as difficult to comprehend when trying to bridge their phrases together to 'venture' a description of Yaweh, but for me the only way I know how to explain His foreknowing and foreordaining is by focusing on the first couple's obedience and accountability to Him. I'm forced to 'tread very lightly' because of these two germane questions continually nagging me: 1] did God foreknow the first couple would disobey and 2] had He prepared them to see through the serpent's deceptive challenge to His authority?

Now let's address first WHY the What went wrong. Contrary to the implicit 'realism' present in Genesis 1:31, one of the "creeping things" God had created (1:24), a particular הַנָּחָשׁ [the serpent {large snake}], used a human voice to employ its trait of being עָרוּם [crafty, cunning, sly.] With Yaweh's sovereign knowledge {cf. Job 1:7-8} this particular snake was a treacherous creature capable of exploiting a position of trust in order to betray it. Though Adam and his helpmeet had become familiar with the created existence (3:1) of such a large snake {cf. 2:19}, Eve apparently had not been startled by a talking one, possibly because she assumed that "with God all things are possible." (Matthew 19:26) At this point the narrative has yet to mention Adam. The snake's initial question is to Eve, which she forthrightly affirms. Coldly and smugly it responds אֶל־הָאִשָּׁה [to the woman, not to the couple] with a terse, haughty denial of what the Creator had warned Adam {cf. 2:17.} From a trickery perspective it then appeals to Eve's naivety by highlighting the benefit to her if she were to eat the forbidden fruit: she would be like her Creator since she would instantly come to know what good and evil were. (v. 5)

> ...the phrase "the tree was desirable to make wise" is what magnetized Eve...Why would Eve be hungry for wisdom, when she was in a perfect relationship with the one who was and is the ultimate source of everything that is wise? Why wasn't God's wisdom enough for her? What attracted Eve was not just wisdom but *autonomous wisdom*, that is, wisdom that did no require reliance on and submission to God...2 Corinthians 5:15 reads: "and He died for all, that they who live should no longer live for themselves, rather for Him who died and rose again on their behalf." In that moment in the garden, Eve is living for herself, and because she is, she will disobey God and eat what he has forbidden.[39]

Looking reflectively at the tree of good and evil, Eve became lured by the tree's delightful appearance and its delicious produce as well as by the curiosity of

---

39. Do You Believe?, Paul David Tripp, Crossway, Wheaton, IL. 2021, page 269-270

gaining a new, unknown wisdom; she succumbed by eating what she could take from its fruit. (v. 6) As the result she either had become callous about what she had just done or was cluelessly unaware that she had just disobeyed her Creator. Moses then continued his narrative:

וַתִּתֵּן גַּם־לְאִישָׁהּ עִמָּהּ, וַיֹּאכַל

[and she gave also to her husband along with her, and he ate]

Thus it does seem that Adam had indeed been in Eve's presence when the serpent had begun his conversation with her. That means he heard fully what the large snake had been saying to her, yet according to Moses first man had not contested the veracity of its asserted denial of the exact punishment Yaweh had decreed עַל־ הָאָדָם [to man.] (v. 2:16)

So based on the assumption that chapters 2 and 3 of Genesis Moses had dictated in a linear progression of earthly time, the first man was alone when God put him in the garden of Eden to cultivate. It was only after He had pronounced the prohibition of, and resulting consequence for, eating "from the tree of the knowledge of good and evil" (v. 2:17) that the Creator had terminated the man's solitude by forming his helpmeet. Thus, for Eve to have been able to inform the serpent of what "God has said" (v. 3:3), the inference to me is that either Adam had repeated that warning to her or Yaweh had similarly warned her after she had come into being. While Eve's 'helpmeet' function tended to encompass servitude, discipleship, apprenticeship, and nurturing, the two assumption we need to accept are that both humans knew the wording of His warning and they understood what their death would entail; and therefore, the serpent's "You surely shall not die" (v. 3:4) apparently had not been immediately corrected or challenged by either listener. The couple's intelligence had been focusing on learning, acquiring and memorizing agricultural skills. The Lord's warning had confirmed that the essence of their intelligence was void of all morality, that they had lacked all knowledge of good & evil; the serpent's words had also acknowledged this by means of its baiting untruth: "{if you do so,} you will be like god, knowing good and evil." (v. 5)

When warning first man alone, I believe Yaweh surely knew that while Adam's heart and mind lacked all knowledge of evil, he did possess an inkling of doing 'good' by being obedient, because first man was fully aware of his total dependence on Him. Also, Moses's silence compels me to wonder whether Adam as the cultivator of Eden had acquired familiarity of all the trees within it, except for their God-given names. Vs. 2:16-17 leads me to accept the divinely named tree in His warning had been visually indicated to Adam by the Law Maker, Whose righteousness would require 'full disclosure' by Him. Then in v. 3:3 Eve confirmed that this same tree grew "in the middle of the garden," knowledge she most likely had garnered from first man. The Hebrew letter starting v. 3:6 is not כ [when] but the *vov consecutive,* indicating continuing relevance to the prior sentence, i.e., "and so" or "and then," specifying that she had suddenly become attracted to its produce both for consumption as well as for acquiring wisdom and knowledge.

Genesis 2:9 tells us that both the tree of life and the tree of the knowledge of good and evil were growing together "in the midst of the garden" but in v. 3:3 Eve confirmed only the latter tree was "in the middle of the garden," implying both humans had not known the name God had bestowed on the former tree. I'm just wondering if they had known God's name for the tree of life, would they have appreciated the need for eternal life prior to their gaining the knowledge of good and evil? And after that fateful 'bite just for the picking,' and the instant attainment of the knowledge of good, would they then have realized their need for eternal life? Thus it would make sense their newly gained wisdom and knowledge had not contained what Yaweh secretly knew, particularly the tree of life's name nor its location.

Adam had been formed by the hand of Yaweh as a sinless (cf. Genesis 1:31) image [Genesis 1:27] of Himself; Eve, too, was sinless inasmuch as He had formed her out of a rib belonging to Adam. Though only creatures, not divine, they were initially created with the Christ-like character: "in (them) there (was) no sin" [I John 3:5]; they "knew no sin" [II Corinthians 5:21]; they "committed no sin." [I Peter 2:22] While God's decree of Genesis 2:17 might not have been the only prohibition He had given them, through the serpent's deceit the prohibited fruit became for them too great an allurement to resist, due either to its anticipated flavor or to possibly they becoming "like God" (Genesis 3:5.) Eve, followed by Adam, bit into that fruit, thereby instantly becoming sinners endowed with the knowledge of good and evil. The penalty for their sin, as Yaweh had warned, was a death sentence for each.[Genesis 3:19] By this 'foundational' sin Adam and Eve abruptly altered their relationship with Yaweh (cf. Romans 2:5,5:16,8:20) as well as precluded for all humanity the opportunity for eternal life (Genesis 3:22-24):

> Then the Lord saw that the wickedness of man was great on the earth, and that every intent of the thoughts of his heart was only evil continually.
> —Genesis 6:5

> Then the Lord saw...that every intention/inclination of his heart was only evil continually.
> —Genesis 8:21

> ...through one man sin entered into the world, and death through sin, and so death spread to all men, ἐφ' ᾧ all sinned.
> —Romans 5:12

The interrogative ἐφ' ᾧ is comprised of ἐπί and the dative of ὅς, which The Analytical Greek Lexicon translates "wherefore, why." Then the inference here is: in Adam "all sinned" [cf. 1 Corinthians 15:22], which is a statement of consequence, not of causation. In other words for Romans 5:12, through the first couple's defiant deed, every human was, is and will be conceived with sin in his/her body and viewed by Yaweh as a sinner:

הֵן־בְּעָווֹן חוֹלָלְתִּי; וּבְחֵטְא, יֶחֱמַתְנִי אִמִּי.

> **David:**
> "Behold, with sin/iniquity I was born, and my mother conceived me with sin."
> —Psalm 51:5{7}

The phrase "born in sin" tends to address a circumstance causing or leading up to the birth, like incest, infidelity or rape, but due to David's desire for "a clean heart" (verse 10), the preposition ב more likely meant to be translated "with" in order to indicate the immoral integrity of David when merely a conceived fetus: a sinner. David has confessed that he was born a sinner – well before he could even sin. "...through the one man's disobedience (all) were made sinners" (Romans 5:19) and as the consequence, "in Adam all died."(I Corinthians 15:22)

> David doesn't have a problem with sin only when he does something wrong, because sin is a part of his very nature. Sin was as much a part of David's nature when he came into this world as the fact that being a biological male is part of his nature...David is confessing that sin is a condition he inherited at birth. It is as much a part of his spiritual constitution as the physical characteristics that he inherited from his parents are part of his physical constitution.[40]

---

40. Do You Believe?, Paul David Tripp, Crossway, Wheaton, Il. 2021, page 272

The first couple's sin has stained all mankind because each individual conception was, is or will be formed by Adam's future sperms fertilizing Eve's 'pyramiding egg chain':

> Mark Stoeckle at Rockefeller University and David Thaler at the University of Basel: mitochondrial DNA, snippets of DNA that reside outside the nuclei of living cells, are passed down by mothers from generation to generation.

All embodied souls in every succeeding generation after the first couple are destined to die-to-die (Genesis 2:17) because all of mankind had been compacted within Adam and Eve when the couple had eaten the forbidden fruit:

> David:
> ... I was brought forth in iniquity, and in sin my mother conceived me.
> —Psalm 51:5

> ...just as through one man sin entered into the world, and death through sin, and so death spread to all men, because all sinned...death reigned from Adam until Moses, even over those who had not sinned in the likeness of the offense of Adam...through one transgression there resulted condemnation to all men...
> —Romans 5:12,14,18

Each human being has been, is or will be conceived a sinner, and those fortunate to survive birth continue to be a sinner, even though he or she could not yet

sin. Man sins because he is born a sinner; the natural effect of his or her immoral nature is that from birth on, both are predisposed to sinning. Adam's guilt has been attributed to all mankind. Every human is viewed by Yaweh as having sinned in Adam and thus deserves the same punishment He had meted out to first man: death in order to die.

Secondly, we need to comprehend How the What went wrong. The warning Yaweh gave to Moses "from the midst of the fire" (Deuteronomy 5:4) on Mount Horeb: "You shall not do at all what {the Israelites} are doing here today: every man doing whatever is right in his own eyes." (Deuteronomy 12:8) But even after Joshua had died, having brought the tribe of Israel into their promised land, "every man did what was right in his own eyes." (Judges 17:6,21:25) The absence of a king to rule over Israel implicitly perpetuated this immorality because there was no prophet to fulfill Moses's role as intermediary between Yaweh and the tribes of Israel. There was no longer a moral being ruling them and, consequently, they strayed from what Moses had instructed their forefathers by instead determining individual sets of moral principles. "In his own eyes" means 'in his mind' and became the only source for determining what is right and what is wrong. The creature in Yaweh's image had now asserted independence when deciding what moral principles should influence his actions.

> Trust in Yaweh with all your heart and do not lean on your own understanding.

> ... Do not be wise in your own eyes. Fear Yaweh and turn away from evil.
>
> —Proverbs 3:5,7

The source for knowing goodness and evil had now resided in man's mind, not in the divine statutes spoken by Him to Moses. The prevailing attitude among the Israelites began to evolve into 'I'll listen to God but I will make up my own mind.' Here is man esteeming himself above his Creator by asserting an ability to know what is best for him. Calling on the name of Yaweh and offering burnt offerings had become subalternate to the emerging practice of "every man doing whatever is right in his own eyes." (Deuteronomy 12:8; Judges 17:6,21:25); man had become a self-idolator, the determiner and controller of his own being:

> The idol of self is the ultimate idolatry. It is the idol from which every other form of idolatry flows. If you worship yourself, you will then exchange worship and service of God for worship and service of created things.[41]

As one result Godly wisdom became less sought after; knowing, understanding and fearing, i.e., believing and obeying, Yaweh was no longer the primary focus of mankind's mind. This emerging

---

41. Do You Believe?, Paul David Tripp, Crossway, Wheaton, IL. 2021, page 270

mindset deprecated the value attributed in the past to fearing Him:

> ...the beginning of wisdom; a good understanding have all those who do *His commandments*.
> —Psalm 111:10

> ...the beginning of knowledge...
> —Proverbs 1:7

> ...is a fountain of life that one may avoid the snares of death.
> —Proverbs 14:27

Another result became mankind's developing inability to deal in a godly manner with whomever he encounters, including Satan and his angels (Revelation 12:9):

> A person's deeds and words portray and convey his true character, i.e., they "distinguish... himself."
> —Proverbs 20:11

> Jesus told the multitudes, "you will know {false prophets} by their fruits."
> —Matthew 7:20

> And this is my prayer: that your love may abound more and more in real knowledge and discernment, so that you may be able to discern what is best and may be pure and blameless for the day of Christ...
> —Philippians 1:9-10

> ...do not believe every animating force but examine/scrutinize the animating forces {to see} to see if they are by God, because many false prophets have gone out into the world.
> —1 John 4:1

The **WHAT**, then, was that Noah's issues had practiced self-determination and self-idolatry in rebellion against their Creator's authority. Next is the **HOW**, the originating factor for the What going wrong: Satan's νοήματα [schemes, purposes {cf. 2 Corinthians 2:11}] all attack man's relationship with Yaweh by means of deceptive, divisive, destructive tactics.

> And Yaweh said to Satan, "Have you considered My servant Job?...all that he has is in your power, only do not put forth your hand on him."
> —Job 1:8,12

> Jesus to Peter:
> "...Satan ἐξῃτήσατο [has asked to sift you like wheat."
> —Luke 22:31

These verses immediately make me wonder why God had given הַשָּׂטָן / ὁ Σατανᾶς [the accuser / opposer] a dominant role in the book of life. God allowed the devil Satan's actions not for His own amusement but for fulfillment of His will by testing and correcting individuals tempted by this ungodly spirit and his angels (Revelation 12:7), his legions of τὰ πνεύματα τὰ ἀκάθαρτα [the unclean animated forces] (Mark 5:13 {cf. Matthew 10:1; Mark 1:23,5:2}), πνεῦμα δαιμονίου ἀκαθάρτου [an animated force of an unclean devil.] (Luke 4:33) "...the days are evil" (Ephesians 5:16); "Your adversary, the devil, prowls about like a roaring lion, seeking someone to devour." (1 Peter 5:8)

The Father's Son even engaged patiently with the devil but was never persuaded by his rational-though-deceptive rhetoric:

> Jesus:
> "the ruler of the world...has nothing in Me"
> —John 14:30

> Jesus "has been tempted in all things as we are, yet without sin."
> —Hebrews 4:15

For His glory as well Yaweh had included Satan and his angels (Matthew 25:41; Luke 4:33-35; Jude 6-8; Revelation 12:9) in the book of life and accordingly let the adversary be disguised as a talking creature to deceive the naïve, passive, undiscerning first couple with its persuasive allurement, "you shall be like God..." (Genesis 3:5) In the Apostle John's Revelation evil spiritual characters interacted within reality because "God has put it in their hearts to execute His purpose...until the words of God should be fulfilled."(v. 17:16) The voice emanating from "a beast coming up out of the sea" (13:2) belongs to Yaweh's spiritual adversary, Satan [הַשָּׂטָן], who priorly enjoyed a spiritual relationship with Him as the first two chapters of Job and Zechariah 3 relate. But scholars reckon Job had been written between 300–400 BC whereas Genesis had

been completed between 1440-1400 BC, which infers additional Godly revelations during that millennial gap provided more clarity as to who and/or what the talking serpent was. Yaweh, for His glory granted Satan the freedom to deceptively tempt the first couple into disobeying His 'law,' just as with David and Paul:

> Then Satan stood up against Israel and moved David to number Israel.
> —1 Chronicles 21:1

> ...there was given me a thorn in the flesh, an angel of Satan, to afflict me – to keep me from exalting myself...I entreated the Lord three times that it might depart from me. And He said to me, "My grace is sufficient for you, for power {cf. Philippians 4:13} is perfected in weakness."
> —2 Corinthians 12:7-9

•••

Note: I do not think his 'thorn in the flesh' was intense sexual desire because of this: "But if they (i.e., the unmarried) do not have self-control, let them marry; for it is better to marry than to burn with passion. (1 Corinthians 7:9)

•••

The WHY "what went wrong" is important as well to appreciate. The first couple's lack of responsive resistance to the serpent's "You surely shall not die" displayed their lack of discernment and judgment to recognize and resist its defiant attitude toward their Creator. Their ignorance,

Moses's narrative compels one to deduce, was based on their inability to know "good and evil" (3:5); and yet from the philosophical perspective, did accountability to the Creator hold these two souls created in His image to be responsible even for what they did not know? Or during their entire past had they faithfully obeyed all that He had instructed because they had not yet been confronted by the purveyor of evil? I'm inclined to believe that this was His initial introduction to them of the potential for their loss of being 'beings' and thus in His eyes it was His extreme test their of their continuing their faithfulness to Him. As I've read and heard in the past, Adam and his wife, when they initially encountered "the adversary", each possessed a free will to do whatever he or she had decided, not the propensity for either sinning against or obeying their Creator. But I also have to acknowledge that Yaweh foreknew the outcome of their exposure to the talking serpent, the consequence of which pervades all of His book of life. Humanly speaking, that seems as if Adam and Eve had followed His 'script' of life and thereby had no 'free will.' Such is just one of the eternal mysteries surrounding our great Creator:

> Yaweh:
> "Behold the man has become like one of Us, knowing good and evil; and now, lest he stretch out his hand and takes also from the tree of life and eat and live forever...."
> —Genesis 3:22

Lack of the knowledge of evil prevented the first couple from questioning the serpent's words; i.e., they knew no reason why not to trust it!) just as lack of knowledge prevented them from seeking to obey God. Satan was fully aware of their 'moral deficit' and used evil deceit and convincing bait to 'hook' them.

Finally we come to the WHAT of "what went wrong." Now immediately after they had eaten the forbidden fruit Yaweh expelled the first man out of the garden, which I assume had to include Eve inasmuch as she had been formed to be his helpmeet. The first couple had defied and thereby חָטָא [sinned] against their Creator. Divine justice and righteousness demanded a very severe penalty, which by advanced warning culminated in a future loss of life for not only both of them but also for all future generations residing in Adam's sperm and Eve's ova:

> "...I Yaweh your God am a jealous God, visiting the iniquity of the fathers upon the sons to the third and fourth generation of those that hate me...
> —Exodus 20:5

> Yaweh is long-suffering, and of great mercy, forgiving iniquity and transgression, and by no means clearing the guilty, visiting the iniquity of the fathers upon the sons to the third and fourth generation.
> —Numbers 14:18

> "...I Yaweh your God am a jealous God, visiting the iniquity of the fathers upon the sons to the third and fourth generation of those who hate Me...
> —Deuteronomy 5:9

> **Ah, Lord Yaweh! You...repay the iniquity of the fathers into the bosom of their sons after them.**
> **—Jeremiah 32;17-18**

In Paul's words (Romans 5:12), πᾶσα ἡ κτίσις [all the creation {of mankind – cf. Romans 8:21-22}] had sinned. In other words, throughout the rest of time every human soul conceived in the fallopian tube is to be deemed a sinner by Yaweh, but for the exception {cf. Matthew 1:18} of the "gift" He gives ὁ κόσμος [the world.] (John 3:16-17)

> David:
> "There is no one who does good, not even one."
> —Psalm 14:3

> ...as it is written, "There is none righteous, not even one."
> —Romans 3:12

> ...all have sinned and fall short of the glory of God.
> —Romans 3:23

> ...just as through one man sin entered into the world and death through sin, and so death spread to all men because all sinned...
> —Romans 5:12

To paraphrase Isaiah 59:2: original sin separates every image-bearer of God from Him and hides His face from every human. As the result πᾶσα ἡ κτίσις [all the creation] lost Yaweh's טוֹב מְאֹד [very perfect] assessment, which His book of life, "the light" of Genesis

1:4, resolutely addressed by planning the covenant between God the Father and His only begotten Son for salvation unto eternal life of many named sinners from the consequences of their second deaths. Such is the out-working of the spiritual 'symbiotic' relationship between foreknowledge and foreordainment:

> God "predestined us to adoption as sons through Jesus Christ to Himself, according to the kind intention of His will, to the praise of the glory of His grace, which He freely bestowed on us in the Beloved."
>
> —Ephesians 1:5-6

His adoption of the many is assured and manifested in each believer's personal ἐν Χριστῷ Ἰησοῦ {in Christ Jesus} relationship {cf. Philippians 4:13.} Through Satan's devious deception Adam and Eve had gained knowledge of good and evil but such wisdom all their future descendants could ever aspire to acquire could only be by Yaweh's Breath ἐν Χριστῷ Ἰησοῦ.

'Nature' originally involved intrinsic characteristics; earth's flora and fauna developed on their own accord. But with the advent of modern scientific method, nature has become a passive reality, organized and moved by divine laws, and often refers to geology, wildlife as well as to the processes associated with inanimate objects, i.e., to the way that particular types of things exist and change of their own accord, such as the weather and geology of the Earth. The divinely perfected components of the earth, its atmosphere, dry lands and seas, comprise collectively all of nature's inorganic composition, including the forces and processes producing and controlling every phenomenon of the material world continually in the evolving state as a geologic by-product of tectonic plate displacement and subsidence, i.e., of the sudden sinking or gradual downward settling of the ground's surface with little or no horizontal motion. Ever since the foundation of/for life became reality (Genesis 1:1-10), nature has been influencing all underground, under-ocean as well as ground-surface disturbances, including the entire weather system.

The universe is comprised of a countless number of galaxies, one of which is our solar system, the environment Yaweh had created for life "in the beginning." Mankind's understanding of his environment and its dynamics barely touches the interactive intricacies He instituted around and within it. Here, for example, are two observations alluding to 'superhumanly' developed 'mechanics' uniquely for the operation and maintenance of life in the solar system:

> "...the magnetic north pole consists of a large molten (2700 degrees F) mass of iron ore under the earth's surface. For decades this mass was located in the Hudson Bay of northern Canada. Until recently, its movement was limited to inches a year. It currently resides under the Artic Circle and is moving toward Russian Siberia...a mass of iron at 2700F would have a definite effect on the polar ice above.
>
> "...the earth makes a yearly orbit around the sun, and...the earth spins on its axis once every 24 hours...the earth is tilted some 20 degrees-

plus on its axis, thus creating the seasons...as the earth makes its yearly trip around the sun...the earth wobbles on its axis...(and) begins to spin down. This wobble affects the earth's tilt toward (and away from) the sun. This wobble is called 'the procession of the equinox'...This scientific fact has been known for centuries...If the angle of the earth changes its exposure to the sun, there would be a corresponding temperature that would affect both positive(ly) and negative(ly), A single (360-degree) rotation of this 'procession' takes approximately 26,000 years to complete. Just one degree of this 'procession' takes around 72 years...the last ice age in the Northern Hemisphere ended around 12,000 years ago...if 12,000 year ago the Northern Hemisphere was under ice, the earth has been warming ever since...The earth is going to continue its cycle of warming for another 1,000 years..."[42]

"A group of astronomers has discovered one of the biggest planets ever found orbiting a massive and extremely hot two-star system, despite previously believing that such an environment was too inhospitable for a planet to form in. The planet was discovered by Markus Janson, a professor of astronomy at Stockholm University, and colleagues... 'Named b Centauri (AB)b or b Centauri b, the planet is an alien world experiencing conditions completely different from what we face here on Earth and in our Solar System...It is 10 times more massive than Jupiter, making it one of the most massive planets ever found. Moreover, it revolves around the binary star at a staggering 100 times greater

---

42. "Magnetic north pole: Not 'true north'" in Letter to Editor of The Epoch Times, March 24, 2021

distance than Jupiter does from the Sun, one of the widest orbits discovered yet,' astronomers explained. Janson said the discovery of the planet around the two-star system completely changes what astronomers previously believed about massive stars hosting planets, and shows that they can, in fact, form in such severe star systems. Prior to its discovery, scientists had been unable to detect any such object around a star more than three times as massive as the Sun. ("Astronomers Discover Massive Planet 10 Times Bigger Than Jupiter", by Katabella Roberts; The Epoch News, December 9, 2021)

Whether left on its own or through divine intervention {cf. Genesis 7:10f}, millennium after millennium nature has exercised and maintained its function as Yaweh intends – perfectly; the laws of nature are immutable. However, the sins committed throughout life by Yaweh's 'resident managers,' i.e., all of mankind, have become embedded in all aspects of creation – and continue to be so:

> A life well lived is lived with the understanding that you don't belong to you... It's not natural to approach your responsibilities and relationships in light of God's purpose. It's natural to be moved by your own desires and to define a good day as a day when you got what makes you happy.[43]

Here, then, follows mankind's sins which have affected varying aspects of Yaweh's creation of life: οἱ οὐρανοὶ

---

43. Do You Believe?, Paul David Tripp, Crossway, Wheaton, IL. 2021, page 202

A] Earth's atmosphere, dry land and seas (Genesis 1: 10):

1) On the second day Yaweh created "the expanse" (Genesis 1:6-7) and called it שָׁמַיִם / οἱ οὐρανοί [heavens, i.e., the cosmos] (v. 8; cf. Psalm 148:4) but then on the fourth day He created the solar system (vs. 14-16) with lights "to govern" day and night; He purposed the earth's existence to fully depend on the sun's and moon's physical influences. Man's solar system performs perfectly as long as its Creator wills so – as does His created earth. In other words, nothing goes wrong within and on earth unless He wills it so. Scientists claim the earth's surface has experienced many life forms as well as temperature changes, polar reversals, tectonic activities of varying intensities, and asteroids, comets and rocks straying from within the universe. All such activities fall within His will and abilities, indicating that nothing unexpected or unnoticed 'goes wrong.' This raises a poignant question: is our atmosphere in danger of faltering? In current-event jargon, is our climate being threatened by mankind's misuse of the world's natural elements like oil, coal and natural gas? Throughout life the heavens and the earth have experienced cataclysmic surface damage via geological plate shifts, earthquakes and volcanic eruptions, not one of which has permanently affected the atmosphere's original functioning. Neither have satellite traffic and clusters, jet plane exhaust contrails, the treatment of oil, chemical and sewage wastes.

Comedian George Carlin in his 1992 HBO special declared how "audacious" it was for mankind to think it can alter what God had made. Skepticism, "the life blood of science" (Dr. Joseph Mercola) of the climate crisis exists among a profoundly large group of respected scientists. Throughout life the heavens and the earth have experienced cataclysmic surface damage via geological plate shifts, earthquakes and volcanic eruptions, not one of which has permanently affected the atmosphere's original functioning. Neither have satellite traffic and clusters, jet plane exhaust contrails, the treatment of oil, chemical and sewage wastes.

"The earth has gone through cycles of warming and cooling throughout history...Some scientists believe that galactic cosmic ray flux or solar activity play bigger roles in climate change than man-made carbon dioxide emissions. ("Global Warming Versus Carbon Dioxide Versus humans", p. A20 of Epoch Times; February 24, 2021) Yet, "Earth today has a protective magnetic field generated by electric currents from the motion of molten iron in the planet's core, shielding the surface from cosmic rays and charged solar particles."[44]

Centuries ago hurricanes and tornadoes were considered acts of an angry god but today they are the result of 'climate change.' Its advocates practice "active idolatry {because} mankind wants to be like God and do not want Him to tell it what to do." (Catholic Bishop Charles J. Chaput on Fox News network's "Tucker Carlson Tonight"; May 28,2021) In his June, 2020 PDF book Apocalypse Never – Why Environmental Alarmism Hurts Us All Michael Shellenberger asserts that climate

---

44. "Mars Quakes! Tremors Detected on Red Planet", The Wall Street Journal, 2/25/2020

emergency is based on various lies and is not supported by science. As editor Gerard defines this movement as "a secular religion...a kind of climate theology {which} has replaced traditional Christianity as the ultimate authority over human behavior...The climate imperative is science-based, the opposite of religion. Its bishops are Nobel-winners; its biblical texts are peer-reviewed papers."[45]

According to global-warming 'evangelizers' CO2 in the atmosphere acts like glass by trapping heat and thereby effecting the temperature increase. The mid-19th century Industrial Revolution's dependence on fossil fuels exponentially increased CO2 emissions, causing an imagined 'greenhouse effect.' But over the longer term of the geologic record there is no proof that rising CO2 has caused rising temperatures. There have been million-year periods both when CO2 levels and atmospheric temperatures were higher as well as when they were lower. Proponents of this evolving quasi-religious movement, i.e., global warming → climate change → climate crisis, tend to promote this theory (not truth!) with a fervor of Chicken Little: "The sky is falling!" Another interesting perspective is "Medical Journals Committing Malpractice With Climate Change Public Health Crisis Misdiagnosis", an article by H. Sterling Burnett in the 9/14/21 edition of The Epoch Times.

Unfortunately, what science proposes today is both imprecise as well as a threat to the common good of mankind and frustrates any establishment of global unity to deal with elusive alternatives. Such

---

45. The Wall Street Journal, page C4, 9/21-22/2019

had not been the case in the 1970's and 80's when the majority of governments and industries worked together to eliminate harmful industrial pollutants. The 2021 climate policy's drive to lower emissions has focused on substantially reduced dependency on coal, oil and natural gas for energy production, which nature over millennia has made available to mankind for its survival. A friend with chemical engineering credentials informed me that the use of fossil fuels to keep warm and generate thermal energy has nothing to do with Global Warming and Climate Change. Our interpretation and our sense of Global Warming and Climate Change (and our sense of "time", as well) has everything to do about the rotation of the earth about its axis, about the rotation of the earth around the sun, and the fact that the earth's axis is not perpendicular to the Sun's radiation (therefore, the seasonal variations). These are the constants that basically keep the Earth's Environment in "Thermal Equilibrium" on a short time basis because of its size and distance from the sun.

Centuries ago hurricanes and tornadoes were considered acts of an angry god but today they are the result of 'climate change.' Its advocates practice "active idolatry {because} mankind wants to be like God and do not want Him to tell it what to do." (Catholic Bishop Charles J. Chaput on Fox News network's "Tucker Carlson Tonight"; May 28,2021) In his June,[46] Michael Shellenberger asserts that climate emergency is based

---

46. 2020 PDF book Apocalypse Never – Why Environmental Alarmism Hurts Us All

on various lies and is not supported by science. As editor Gerard defines this movement as "a secular religion...a kind of climate theology {which} has replaced traditional Christianity as the ultimate authority over human behavior...The climate imperative is science-based, the opposite of religion. Its bishops are Nobel-winners; its biblical texts are peer-reviewed papers."[47]

Alluding to Le Chatelier's principle, meteorologist Joe Bastardi on "Tucker Carlson Tonight" on September 8, 2021[48] addressed the politicization of 'global warming': "Any system that has something foreign introduced to it, or excessed, naturally tries to fight back... The sun, the oceans, the stochastic {having a random probability distribution or pattern that may be analyzed statistically but may not be predicted precisely} events, the very design of the system always try to fight back... Weather and climate are nature's eternal search for balance she cannot alter because of the very design of the system."

"The earth has gone through cycles of warming and cooling throughout history...Some scientists believe that galactic cosmic ray flux or solar activity play bigger roles in climate change than man-made carbon dioxide emissions.[49] Yet, "Earth today has a protective magnetic field generated by electric currents from the motion of molten iron in the planet's core, shielding the

---

47. The Wall Street Journal, 9/21-22/2019; page C4
48. Tucker Carlson Tonight, 9/8/2021 (Joe Bastardi)
49. "Global Warming Versus Carbon Dioxide Versus humans", page A20 of Epoch Times, 2/24/2021

surface from cosmic rays and charged solar particles."[50] Based on noncontroversial data, "a report from the World Wildlife Fund – chillingly subtitled 'A crisis raging out of control?' – concedes midway through that 'the area of land burned globally has actually been steadily declining since it started to be recorded in 1900.'...Perhaps the best example of unwarranted media histrionics came in response to Australia's 2019-20 fire season. Papers plastered their covers with images of the destruction, capped with headlines such as 'Apocalypse Now', 'Terror Coast' and 'This is what a climate crisis looks like.' Yet satellite measurements show that total burned area that fire season was one of the lowest Australia had seen in the last 120 years."[51]

A refutation to zealous 'global warming' advocacy is "Willow Shrubs Grew in Greenland 500 Years Ago, on Land Long Covered by Glaciers"[52], which explains credibly how prehistoric Chinese mariners were able to cartograph a complete map of Greenland while sailing around the globe[53]

Today, green radicalism has become the ideological driving force frightening the West's social, economic and health cultures into bending their knees at 'the greeniac altar.' Power-and-money-hungry political and business members of the world are religiously and

---

50. "Mars Quakes! Tremors Detected on Red Planet", 2/25/2020, The Wall Street Journal
51. "Climate Activists Blow Smoke on Wildfire Fears", 10/28/21, The Wall Street Journal Op-ed by Bjorn Lomborg
52. The Epoch Times, 8/25/21
53. cf. 1421, The Year China Discovered America, Gavin Menzies William Morrow Paperbacks, 2008

energetically glauming methods to prevent what they perceive as an unnatural, lethal warming of this planet. They blame their peers for abusively using the basic elements Yaweh had created to produce energy: wood, coal, oil and natural gas. Their preventative technics are aggressively, recklessly and uneconomically pursued, with little or no concern for planning an affordable transitioning and manufacturing of their replacement products. A good example is the electric powered automobile, the making of which involves the manufacturing of large batteries, the development of thousands of charging stations, expansion of power plants to supply those stations with electricity produced from the processing of elements other than wood, coal, oil and natural gas. The economic alternative source, nuclear power, poses its own concerns: cooling towers, leakage, atomic waste disposal and duration of the facility's structure. But all this is futile because it's based on man's belief that there exists an inherent flaw in what Yaweh created and man has to correct it. I can't understand why the scientists are ignoring the real cause of global warming: the 'hardscaping' of the earth's surface by building roads, driveways and parking lots out of oil-based materials. Pursuit for eliminating the unnatural (and unproven) 'greenhouse effect' by $CO2$ in the atmosphere is far from globally united due to China's and India's economic challenges. Thus the goal of those countries and states committed to stopping $CO2$'s threat to life on earth both are hindered by these two large nations and pose economic hardship and instability on the committed entities. The war against 'climate change' is a subtle political ploy which ultimately establishes domination of the elitist 'global warming' believers over the remaining citizenship, the end game of Marxism leading to the destruction of family, faith and individual freedom. If all the thinking, planning, resources and time for dealing with what I consider is a 'political con game' instead be devoted to dealing with and overcoming all the problems only on earth. After all, the heavens belong to Yaweh whereas He has appointed mankind as earth's 'resident manager,' fully accountable to Him:

> The heavens are the heavens belonging to Yaweh,
> but the earth He has given to the sons of men.
> —Psalm 115:16

It's commonly accepted that space commences 62 miles above sea level and below it is the stratosphere, which begins some 30 miles above the earth's surface. The troposphere, the 12-mile-high area directly covering the earth, is the area in which ozone acts as a greenhouse gas, trapping heat. Though seeming unscientific, I prefer to treat the politics of climate as only an earth problem; after all, whatever belongs to Yaweh is divinely maintained. "As world leaders consider how to limit greenhouse gases, they depend on what computer climate models predict...While vital to calculating ways to survive a warming world, climate models are hitting a wall. They are running up against the complexity of the physics involved; the limits of scientific computing uncertainties around the nuances of climate behavior; and the challenge of keeping pace with rising levels of carbon dioxide, methane and other greenhouse gasses. Despite significant improvements, the new models are still too imprecise to be taken at face value, which means climate-change projections still require judgment calls...models remain prone to technical glitches and are hampered by an incomplete understanding of the variables that control how our planet responds to heat-trapping gases."[54]

The politically driven climate crisis in today's world is demanding too much attention, resources and sacrifices in return for future and unconvincing changes to the way western man has lived for decades. In my opinion, world leaders are using the climate issue to avoid having to deal with the continuing social problems within their bailiwick: mental health, homelessness, drug addiction as well as abject hunger and poverty. This neglect does not manifest love to Yaweh and must therefore be purposefully converted and transformed so that all mankind focuses on loving their neighbors as themselves {cf. Matthew 22:37-39}, serving as their keepers {cf. Genesis 4:9.} I believe Psalm 115:16 is telling man to leave alone all that is above the troposphere, because Yaweh had already perfected the way for its perpetual care, and to concentrate instead on his accountability to the Creator for the maintenance and care of the earth's surface. I have a major concern for the rapidly diminishing tree population. In God's creation plan trees all over the world depend on CO_2 for sustenance and

---

54. The Wall Street Journal, 2/7/22, pages A1 and A9

hence this balance: the more trees there are, the less CO2 exists. Yet modern civilization's drive to populate and enhance living conditions all over has resulted in massive deforestation and increasing numbers of blacktop/cement roads and parking areas. Psalm 115:16 to me is calling for man to replenish all the missing timber deforestation has carelessly brought about.

It was the year 1958, to be precise, when NASA first observed that changes in the solar orbit of the earth, along with alterations to the earth's axial tilt, are both responsible for what climate scientists today have dubbed as "warming" (or "cooling," depending on their agenda). In no way, shape, or form are humans warming or cooling the planet by driving SUVs or eating beef…Earth's climate has *always* been changing, and is in a constant state of flux due to no fault of our own as human beings…In 1982…the National Research Council of the U.S. National Academy of Sciences adopted Milankovitch's theory as truth, declaring that orbital variations remain the most thoroughly examined mechanism of climatic change on time scales of tens of thousands of years and are by far the clearest case of a direct effect of changing insolation on the lower atmosphere of Earth…to sum the whole thing up in one simple phrase, it would be this: The biggest factor influencing weather and climate patterns on earth is the Sun.[55]

---

55. https://www.agricultureportal.co.za/index.php/farming-news/africa-world/3260-nasa-admits-that-climate-change-occurs-because-of-changes-in-earth-s-solar-orbit-and-not-because-of-suvs-and-fossil-fuels, Viewed: 3/27/23

To close the discussion regarding climate control I would like to offer the following view provided by Joe Wang, Ph.D., a head scientist for Sanofi Pasteur's SARS vaccine project in 2003:

> At the Munich Security Conference on Feb. 18, Bill Gates was asked to assess where we are at in beating the pandemic. He replied: "Sadly, the virus itself, particularly the variant called Omicron, is a type of vaccine. That is, it creates both B-cell and T-cell immunity."... Maybe Mr. Gates, whose foundation funded the development and distribution of COVID-19 vaccines around the world, was sad because of any deaths that occurred? It doesn't appear so, as he continued:"[Omicron] has done a better job getting out to the world population than we have with vaccines...That means the chance of severe disease – which is mainly associated with being elderly and having obesity or diabetes – those risks are now dramatically reduced because of that infection exposure."...Was Gates sad because Omicron beat the vaccines in generating protective immunity, thereby preventing the ability of COVID to spread – meaning there would be no need for any future COVID vaccines? {i.e.,} naturally occurring Omicron brings an end to the pandemic... Vaccines {had been} rapidly developed and the emergency use of them was pushed out. There were vaccine drives and clinics, and before long boosters became part of the scenario. Then came vaccine mandates, even for people who had acquired natural immunity, followed by vaccination of children. Meanwhile, the silencing of any negative information about

vaccines, including vaccine safety, continued. Now Gates is looking ahead to the next pandemic and even faster vaccine development and rollout: "Next time, we should try and make it—instead of two year we should make it more like six months. ... It took us a lot a longer this time than it should have." When it turned out that vaccination failed to defeat COVID and it was instead conquered by Omicron, Mr. Gates found it sad. Humans missed a great opportunity to show that we are the true masters of the world... Human history is a history of survival in harsh, natural conditions. Some in their efforts to survive discovered how to live in peace and harmony with nature, while others who fought and won regarded themselves as triumphant against nature. Mao Zedong famously said, "It is so rewarding (with endless joy) to fight against heaven, against earth, and against people. According to Mao and his comrades, when dealing with natural disasters, humans must win, and win decisively, through cleverness and persistence. It would not be a complete win if humans got help from nature, which would instead bring shame to all involved. When I grew up in communist China I believed that, guided by Mao's teachings, science and technological advancement could provide solutions for all the problems humanity could possibly face... As a young man brainwashed by the doctrine of communism, I dreamt of engineering genes to solve all the world's problems, such as diseases, food shortages, environmental disasters, etc. I thought that since nature caused so much trouble for humans, it was up to geneticists like myself to change nature by engineering the genes of all creatures to be exactly what we humans would like them to be... In November 2018, when Chinese scientist He Jiankui announced he had created the world's first genetically edited babies Lulu and Nana, I realized that this crazy scientist could have been me if I'd stayed in China...Communism coupled with advanced technology has created types of human beings that have never existed on Earth before. Besides us regular humans who have existed for thousands of years, there are now people like He Jiankui, with his God-like powers to engineer human beings, and there are the engineered people like Lulu and Nana. Chaos will be the new norm if things like genetic engineering or nuclear technology are not tightly regulated... There was debate in the United States in 2014 about lab research that increases the virulence, ease of spread, or host range of dangerous pathogens—what is known as gain-of-function (GOF) research. The debate was triggered by the creation of a chimeric coronavirus, providing a bat coronavirus with an additional function of infecting humans (sounds familiar, but this is different from SARS-CoV-2 as we know it). Many scientists argued that GOF research was too risky. As a result, it was banned in the United States in October 2014. However, such research continued in other countries, especially in China. If you can engineer babies, you can engineer viruses...Scientific research must be guided by the highest moral principles and with enough scrutiny to avoid human-wrought catastrophes, such as from nuclear technology or genetic engineering. The idea that man and nature are one harmonious body, as ancient Chinese believed, makes more sense than the fighting mentality the communist system taught me. I have learned to appreciate nature and accept whatever it has in store for me... It seems that Mr. Gates and many others of his ilk have not yet found peace with nature. Using their money and power, they want to achieve a complete win in a war against nature. My advice to Mr. Gates, for a better approach, is that humans work in tandem with nature and find harmony with nature. Do not pick fights with nature. We may win a fight here and there, but we will never win in a war against nature. Omicron has played a decisive part in assisting human efforts to end the pandemic, so be grateful, thank Mother Nature for the gift, and happily move on.[56]

Dr. Wang's closing remark echoes this truth: while nature does not need any improving, audacious humanity surely does:

"Oil and gas prices are soaring amid fears of reduced global supply...In the U.S., consumers are increasingly dismayed by rising gasoline prices...Why not do everything possible to expand American energy production instead?... But if Mr. Biden says no, we'll know he's siding with his climate emissary John Kerry and the progressive left against the urgent economic and Strategic interests of the United States."[57]

---

56. "Pandemic Lessons Learned: Omicron Vs Bill Gates", theepochtimes.com, 2/26/2022
57. "A Question for President Biden", The Wall Street Journal, 3/15/2022

Nature is administered by Yaweh and involves all aspects of His creation, including the constant functioning and interaction within and between the earth, the sun, nine planets and millions of asteroids, comets and meteoroids. A growing concern of man's audacious daring is his rapid exploration and settlement of our upper atmosphere with a variety of satellites. The purposes for such launches are both positive and negative, from assessing weather, bridging communications and studying the solar system to posing physical as well as digital threats as well as destruction both to the peaceful satellites or to surface areas on earth. While mankind seeks the spawning and facilitation of technological advancements, his methodology rarely employs risk aversion. To date I don't believe there is a 'world space regulator' in existence to regulate "36,500 pieces of junk larger then 4 inches in Earth's orbit…'Deep space is about to go through the transition low-Earth orbit went through 30 years ago,' {astronomer Jonathan McDowell} said… 'People have put junk into higher orbits…and just kind of forgotten about,' said {astronomer Bill Gray}… {today} a four-ton hunk of space junk will careen into the lunar surface at nearly 5,800 miles an hour, pulled there by the moon's gravity…the impact should mark an inflection point in the discourse over humanity's stewardship of space…" ("Lunar Impact Stirs Concerns over Space Junk" by Aylin Woodward, *The Wall Street Journal***, March 4, 2022, p. A17) Ignored possibilities of unintended consequences or responsibility to anticipate and plan for them. The scientists of tomorrow have their eyes on the possibilities of outer space – not on**

the poverty, ill health and war victimhood constantly thrusted on and experienced by much of the world's population.

2) Unfortunately, earth's resident managers' rebellion has harmed the seas, the oceans and the waterways for centuries by recklessly discharging fertilizers, pesticides, sediment and unnatural trash, all of which block sunlight, choke fish, seagrass and coral and cause surges of algae and coral-eating starfish. Foundries, factories and mining operations have been threatening the earth's air with mercury and other toxic particular matter; Nuclear and power plants' waste water as well as communities' and the homeless people's sewage have been jeopardizing earth's supply of fresh water. A few of the earth's major countries still pollute the earth's air as well as its fresh water aquifers and natural reservoirs. Mankind is accountable to earth's owner for the maintenance and sustenance of all living forms. Although many elements of the earth still face serious survival threats, mankind can serve itself well by first getting to know and thereby obey the Creator, unite together in love and commitment and execute the cures necessary to please the earth's Owner:

> For even though they knew God, they did not glorify Him as God or give thanks; but they became futile in their speculations and their foolish heart was darkened.
> —Romans 1:20-21

> The twenty-four elders to Yaweh: "Your wrath came, and the time... διαφθεῖραι [to cause

to decay {cf. Luke 12:33; 2 Corinthians 4:16; 1 Timothy 6:5}] those who διαφθεῖραι [cause very bad damage to {cf. Rev. 8:9}] the earth."
—Revelation 11:18

{God's glory expressed in Psalm 19:1} has been retained to stimulate in you the most significant, intimate, profound, and formative of all human functions: worship. This account is meant to drive you to what you were created for. It is written to take you to the core of your humanity and to there discover your true identity...This glory display is retained for you so that you would own your identity... you and I are meant not only to find God, but also to finally find ourselves. We are required to deal with him... to release us from our bondage to us...to forsake your reliance on your own wisdom and power.[58]

"Climate-change moralists love humanity so much in the abstract that they must shut down its life-giving gas, coal, and oil in the concrete. And they value humans so little that they don't worry in the here and now that ensuing fuel shortages and exorbitant costs cause wars, spike inflation, and threaten people's ability to travel or keep warm...The moral of Biden's oil madness? Elite ideology divorced from reality impoverishes people and can get them killed."[59]

It appears to me that our efforts to change the Earth's climate just don't work. They're based on the idea that reducing carbon dioxide (CO_2)

---

58. Do You Believe?, Paul David Tripp, Crossway, Wheaton, IL. 2021, pages 204-6
59. "The Green Immortals" by Victor Davis Hanson, The Epoch Times, 3/16/2022, pages A15

emissions will reduce global warming. That idea has never been tested. Not once. But we're all-in on this approach anyway, even thought early results are, as they say, disappointing. We can begin to see now that the idea was way too simplistic to bet our energy future on. Here's one reason why this approach is wrong. The oceans store vast amounts of CO2. Like in a can of soda, the gas is released when {it is} warmed. So warmer temperatures mean warmer oceans, which mean more CO2 released, which means still warmer temperatures and still more CO2. This death spiral can't happen. If it did, it would have occurred millions of years ago, and we wouldn't be here. Yet we continue down the road of "CO2 is the problem." There's clearly more to global warming – much more. We haven't begun to understand the dynamics. Our focus on CO2 comes under the heading of :do something, even if it's the wrong thing."[60]

B] The earth's flora (v. 12), birds, fish (v. 21) and fauna (v. 25):
  1. Man's harm of the earth's flora occurs when pesticides are applied for the protection of crops and flowers from invading insects and weeds. Unintended harm occurs with the use of GMO's (genetically modified foods) to improve the timing and quality of crop yields: insects (like bees) are not attracted to the crop, thus diminishing bees' presence to pollinate as well as not attracting

---

60. "CO2 Isn't the Problem", a letter in Opinion section of The Epoch Times, 9/7/22

insects upon which birds need to survive, resulting in the creation of a man-made ecology. Interestingly, agricultural science appears to alleviate the effects of Yaweh's punishment on Adam and Eve (Genesis 3:17-19) as well on their seed {cf. Exodus 34:7.}

2. Climate changers' major means to generate 'clean' energy are wind turbines and clusters of solar panels, both of which pose constant threats to birds in flight. This unintended consequence remains acceptable because of the politically claimed existential threat to mankind's future.

3. Man, earth's 'resident manager' (Genesis 1:26,28), hurts all kinds of non-human life:
   a. Farming of cattle, pigs, chickens and fish for meat markets involve unsanitary, hostile environments and inappropriate, foreign feed;
   b. Cruelties of animal racing and fighting;
   c. Treatment of animals in varying research facilities, like the Gain of Function project in a Wuhan, China lab funded by the NIH to form deadly unnatural viruses by recklessly altering nature.
   d. "Detected deforestation in the Brazilian Amazon reached a high for the month of February following a similar record the prior month... Deter {the Brazilian space agency} data last month showed January registered 166 square miles of deforestation, more than quadruple the level in the same month last year...the uptick could be a worrisome sign for months

to come, with loggers and legislators eager to make headway before...the October election." ("Record Deforestation Seen in Amazon", *The Wall Street Journal*, March 12-13, 2022; p. A12)

e. A food source for much of avian and reptile wildlife is being threatened by the release of genetically altered mosquitoes:

> "Million of genetically modified mosquitoes are set to be released...in an effort to reduce the number of real, disease-carrying invasive mosquitoes...The mosquitoes were made by UK-based biotechnology firm Oxitec, which is funded by the Bill and Melinda Gates Foundation, in an effort to combat insect-borne diseases... Oxitec's new technology consists of genetically-modified male mosquitoes, which do not bite, that will be released into the wild where they are expected to mate with females, that do bite. In mating with them, they will pass on a lethal gene that will effectively ensure their offspring die before reaching maturity.[61]

One of the world's richest individuals, Bill Gates, actively opposes meat protein for human consumption, attacks CO_2 as a toxic gas because it effects climate change and promotes global population control. As of June, 2022 he is heavily invested in United States land, owning 269,000 acres, of which 242,000 are farmable[62]

---

61. "Genetically Modified Mosquitoes Set to Be Released in California and Florida", by Katabella Roberts, theepochtimes.com, 3/9/2022
62. "Tucker Carlson Tonight", 6/22/2022, on Fox News.

C] Creation of the human race (Genesis 1:26-27): Some so-called "human ancestors" fossils are actually made up of bone fragments, which are not scientifically sound and do not provide complete proof that humans evolved from apes.

Dr. Charles Oxnard, professor of anatomy and human biology at the University of Western Australia (UWA) and professor at the University of Chicago and the University of Birmingham in the United Kingdom, wrote in his 1987 book published by the University of Washington Press "Fossils, Teeth, and Sex: New Perspectives on Human Evolution" that Lucy (whose skeleton was discovered in East Africa in 1974) had nothing to do with the ancestors of humans, but was a type of extinct ape of the "southern archaeopteryx Alfalfa species," which had the long, curved fingers and toes typical of arboreal primates.

Based on the theory of evolution, a certain gene mutation in the original species is required for the species to evolve. While most gene mutations are harmful, the probability of a beneficial mutation is only about 1 in 1000.

Then, the mutation must not only be compatible with other genes in the original species itself, but also survive natural competition and be able to reproduce. The chance for a mutated but beneficial gene to be stable and expanding in the population is almost zero. There's not enough time in the universe!

The journal Nature published a study of drug resistance of bacteria by scientists at Boston University and Harvard University. They found that some strains of bacteria with strong drug resistance would sacrifice themselves to increase the overall drug resistance of the bacteria, thus improving its chances to survive. In other words, nature does not exactly follow the cruel competition law of "survival of the fittest;" even microscopic bacteria display self-sacrificing altruistic behavior.[63]

1. The Theory of Evolution is a hypothesis {proposed explanation made on the basis of limited evidence}, not an axiom {proposition regarded as being self-evident} and its 'achilles heel' is the absence of any mention regarding its genesis in life. It persists as Science's refutation of man being formed in Yaweh's image.

2. Evil attacks on the divinely established relationship for man (v. 27), a male (v. 27), and for woman (v. 2:22), a female (v. 1:27): "עַל־כֵּן (therefore, because) / ἕνεκεν τούτου [*LXX* - on account of, by reason of this thing] man shall leave his father and his mother and shall cleave to his wife; and they shall become one flesh." (v. 2:24) This is an implicit mandate inspired by Yaweh's Breath into Moses' awareness and memory and its outworking later became generalized by Paul: the husband loves his wife regardless (Ephesians 5:25) and his wife respects her husband regardless. (Ephesians 5:33) On page 86 of his 2020 self-published Politics & Evangelical Theology, Brian G. Mattson wrote:

---

63. "As Science Develops, More Holes Show Up In Evolutionary Theory", by Dr. Yuhong Dong; https://www. theepochtimes.com, 4/25/2022

"The institution of marriage provided women dignity and protection. It provided men a safe, healthy, responsible, and fruitful avenue for their sex drives." But over time the sanctity of marriage had become debased by many who had opted for unrestrained sexual rebellion and self-idolatry.

3. The first recorded deviation of this divinely established paradigm was the introduction of פִּלֶגֶשׁ **[a concubine] (Genesis 35:22; 25:6; 42:22; 36:12), a woman who cohabited with a married man but bore a lower status than did his wife or wives. Soon other rebellious deviations surfaced:**

Now the men of Sodom were wicked exceedingly and sinners against God.
—Genesis 13:13

Yaweh; "The outcry of Sodom and Gomorrah is indeed great and their sin is exceedingly grave."
—Genesis 18:20

Yaweh to Moses:
"You shall not lie with a male as one lies with a female; it is an abomination...a man who lies with a male as those who lie with a woman, both of them have committed a detestable act; they shall surely be put to death...a man who marries a woman and her mother, it is immorality; both he and they shall be burned with fire...a man who lies with an animal...shall surely be put to death...a woman who approaches any animal to mate with it... they shall surely be put to death."
—Leviticus 18:22; 20:13-16

> **Moses representing Yaweh: "A woman shall not wear man's clothing nor shall a man put on a woman's clothing, for whoever does these things is an abomination to Yaweh your God."**
> **—Deuteronomy 22:5**

During his mission to the Gentiles centuries later, Paul warned against the practice of "degrading passions" {in defiance of God}: the women exchanged the natural function for that which is unnatural, and in the same way also the men abandoned the natural function of the woman and burned in their desire towards one another, men with men committing indecent acts..." (Romans 1:26-27) Then in his second letter to the church in Corinth the 9th verse of chapter 6 reads:

> ...the unrighteous shall not inherit the kingdom of God...neither πόρνοι [fornicators, impure persons], nor εἰδωλολάτραι [idolaters (worshippers of idols)], nor μοιχοὶ [adulterers, unfaithful persons], or μαλακοὶ [effeminate persons, instruments of unlawful lust], nor ἀρσενοκοῖται [homosexuals.]"
> "For this is the will of God...that you abstain ἀπὸ τῆς πορνείας [from sexual immorality."
> **—1 Thessalonians 4:3**

> **God made Sodom and Gomorrah "an example to those who would live ungodly thereafter..."**
> **—2 Peter 2:6**

> **...Sodom and Gamorrah...indulged in gross immorality and went after strange flesh...**
> **—Jude 7**

4. Divorce
Marriage is only a 'life' concept:

Jesus:
"For in the resurrection they neither marry (the groom – cf. 24:38) nor are given in marriage (the bride), but are like angels in heaven."
—Matthew 22:30; Mark 12:25; Luke 17:27

Jesus said to them, "The sons of this age marry and are given in marriage {γαμοῦσιν καὶ γαμίσκονται}, but those who are considered worthy to attain to that age and the resurrection from the dead, neither marry nor are given in marriage {γαμοῦσιν καὶ γαμίσκονται};"
—Luke 20:34-35

But:

"...I hate divorce," says Yaweh, the God of Israel...
—Malachi 2:16

Jesus:
"...He who created {man and woman} from the beginning made them male and female and said, 'For this cause a man shall leaves his father and mother and shall cleave to his wife, and the two shall become one flesh' {cf. Genesis 2:24}...What therefore God has joined together, let no man χωρίζω [divide, separate]...Because of your hardness of heart Moses permitted you to divorce your wives; but from the beginning it has not been this way. And I say to you, whoever divorces his wife, except for immorality, and marries another woman commits adultery."
—Matthew 19:6,8-9

> ...to the married I {Paul} give instructions, not I but the Lord, that the wife should not χωρίζω [separate] her husband, but if she does leave, let her remain ἄγαμος [unmarried] or else be reconciled to her husband...
> —1 Corinthians 7:10-11

> "...biblical design for marriage is under assault {also by} the easy divorce culture common...in evangelical circles."[64]

In the first half of the twentieth century divorce began to creep quietly into American culture but well within the last half it has become acceptable and common even ecclesiastically but without any consequential prohibition of remarriage. Sadly, it is estimated that almost 50 percent of all marriages in the United States today will end in divorce or separation, with close to 40 percent involving first marriages.

5. Homosexuality – "the "gross immorality {of pursuing} strange flesh..." (Jude 7):

Homosexuality in the broad sense has existed for millennia and today polarizes human societies worldwide: the 'straights' vs the 'gays.' The prevailing sentiment at least within Western culture is, 'it's a right so live and let live,' while attributable health issues are a concern. And, not surprisingly, it has even infiltrated the 'visible' church for centuries.

---

64. Politics & Evangelical Theology, Brian G. Mattson, self-printed, 2020; p. 74

"In 2015...gay-rights groups reached agreement with the Church of Jesus Christ of Latter-day Saints and other religious groups on a framework that prohibited many forms of discrimination while safeguarding core religious liberties. The Utah Legislature quickly enacted the agreement in law. Our divided polity needs more civil dialogues like this, and more legislators willing to respect their outcomes." ("Freedom of Belief Bridges America's Divides", by William A. Galston; *The Wall Street Journal*, December 12, 2018)

One of the nation's most prestigious liberal arts colleges is advancing a "queer theology" agenda with hopes of destabilizing (through revising The Word, not by challenging historic interpretation!) traditional beliefs about what the Bible says about gender and sexuality. Swarthmore College, founded by Quakers, is offering courses in "queering the Bible" and "queering God." (Queer Theology.com)

"Christianity is a transformative religion in which people really can become new creatures in Christ. And that means even homosexuals can be transformed if they want to be. But that threatens the very core of the homosexual narrative, depending as it does on the myth that homosexuals are born that way and can never change...The homosexual militants know this full well, which is why everywhere they are seeking to make 'conversion therapy' illegal and turn it into a major crime."[65]

---

65. The War Against "Conversion Therapy" by Bill Muehlenberg; December 11, 2018, https://www.agricultureportal.co.za/index.php/farming-news/africa-world/3260-nasa-admits-that-climate-change-occurs-because-of-changes-in-earth-s-solar-orbit-and-not-because-of-suvs-and-fossil-fuels, Viewed: 3/27/23

One notable non-profit group that counters those militants is **Harvest USA**, which counsels and disciples ἐν κυρίῳ those who struggle with ungodly sexual issues.

> The issues currently dividing Christians – sex, sexual identity, the definition of a person – can't easily be isolated from society at large... Rejecting the values of the sexual revolution may not break anyone's leg, but today the breaking of hearts is regarded as equally violent and unacceptable. Examples include the Obama-era contraceptive-coverage mandate. Battles over the legitimacy of same-sex adoption, and vandalism of churches leading up to and following the Supreme Court's decision in *Dobbs v. Jackson Women's Health Organization*... the problems of the early 21st century...can be characterized as a crisis in what it means to be human. Are embryos persons? Are sex differences morally significant? Is "gender identity" different from sex? It's ironic that disagreements about the creature may prove more devastating to the church than those about the Creator.[66]

6. Abortion: Yaweh's Ordinance

On Mount Sinai God had instructed Moses to convey to the wandering Israelites terms of His covenant with them, including this law: "You shall not murder."(Exodus 21:13) Soon thereafter Moses conveyed to the sons of Israel ordinances Yaweh had dictated to him. One of these decrees involved a child within its mother's womb:

---

66. "The Church of the Sexual Revolution" by Carl R. Trueman; Wall Street Journal, 11/11/22, page A17

וְכִי-יִנָּצוּ אֲנָשִׁים, וְנָגְפוּ אִשָּׁה הָרָה וְיָצְאוּ יְלָדֶיהָ, וְלֹא יִהְיֶה, אָסוֹן

—Exodus 21:22

My translation: "If men struggle with each other and strike a הָרָה **[pregnant] woman and** וְיָצְאוּ **[they {i.e., the strugglers} cause to come out]** יְלָדֶיהָ **[<u>his children</u> {plural noun with single masc. suff.}] and there is not** אָסוֹן **[injury.]" Verse 22 then continues: "If an undesired, externally caused miscarriage is not** אָסוֹן **a wrongdoing or a feeling of resentment over something believed to be wrong or unfair, an outrage, the injurer only could be fined by the lost child's father." Then verse 23 continues:**

וְאִם-אָסוֹן, יִהְיֶה--וְנָתַתָּה נֶפֶשׁ, תַּחַת נָפֶשׁ, **which I translate: "But if there is** אָסוֹן **[injury] then you {sing.} render a soul/life for a soul/life" {cf. Leviticus 24:19; Deuteronomy 19:21.}" The** *LXX***'s reading is: ἐὰν δὲ... τὸ παιδίον αὐτῆς μὴ ἐξεικονισμένον, which literally translates: if...the child not unchangeable ἐξ [from] εικονοσ [likeness] μένον [continuing.] Removal of the double negative here renders: if the child is changed.., and implies the injury experienced by the expecting mother and the singular "you" is directed towards the individual sons of Israel. Though murdering a soul guilty for the purposeful murder of another human being is impossible to actualize because only Yaweh can destroy a soul (Matthew 10:28), destroying the life of one who purposefully murders another human being became decreed as administrative law upholding the sixth commandment. Unfortunately, abortion is not** illegal now but should it become a civil crime, it's up to the U. S. governing authorities {cf. Romans 13:1-3} to determine what the penalty should be. The woman's cry, "my body, my choice" prevails – yet there is a slight legal code that seeks to protect a fetus's right: guardian *ad litem*, an attorney appointed by a court to represent the interests of a child, particularly as a designated future trust beneficiary.

Now the third person masculine suffix for יְלָדֶיהָ (v. 22) was breathed out of Moses's mouth by Yaweh and thus infers the translation of "His", i.e., Yaweh's. Moses did not change the suffix to "her" because he considered himself the spokesman for the authoritative Speaker and had remembered a key fact about the founding of life notated by later prophets :

> Solomon:
> "Behold, children are a gift of the Lord, the fruit of the womb is a reward."
> —Psalm 127:3

> David:
> "...You did form my inward parts; You did weave me in my mother's womb...My frame was not hidden from You when I was made in secret... Your eyes have seen my unformed substance."
> —Psalm 139:13-16

> Hezekiah to Isaiah:
> "Thus says Yaweh, your Redeemer and the One Who formed you in the womb...
> —Isaiah 44:24

The structure, personality and life experiences of every embodied soul has been predestined in Yaweh's book of life. David's words encapsulate just how precious every human conception is to Him as well as just how hateful to Him is every murder of His handiwork either in the womb or at the moment of birth.

A soul is each individual's unique core identity in the spiritual realm and by becoming uniquely embodied at conception it thereby physically manifests the soul's personality in life. As the consequence of Adam's and Eve's initial disobedience to Yaweh, every soul in the first couple's future generations has to bear the stain of sin in His judgment; they all are destined to be born sinners in spite of the fact that all the descendants had been uniquely formed by Him in Eve's womb in compliance with the book of life. Yaweh loves all of life because He had created each human life, embodied souls, in immeasurable times and forms in the wombs of women. At the moment of each conception, life uniquely came into being - it becomes manifested as (Leviticus 17:14) as well in (Leviticus 17:11) the fertilized ovum attaches to the wombs wall. The traditional marriage vow, "what God has brought together let no man tear asunder," represents the grounds for His hatred of a divorce (Malachi 2:16), it is reasonable, therefore, to assert that this phrase also serves as grounds for Yaweh's hatred of all abortions, but not of accidental, unintended and involuntary miscarriages.

"Originally passed in 1976, three years after the Supreme Court legalized abortion in *Roe v. Wade*, the Hyde Amendment is named after one of its biggest advocates, the late congressman Henry Hyde. The amendment prohibits federal funding of abortions, and as a rider to the HHS appropriations bill, must be passed each year. There have been various iterations of the amendment's language over the past 40 years, but the current version includes exceptions that allow Medicaid funds to be used for abortions in cases of rape, incest, or the health of the mother – but all other federal taxpayer funding of abortion is banned." (Hyde Amendment.com) Is the Hyde Amendment already the beast's 'foot in the door', thus signifying the worship of him {cf. Revelations 13:16}? In other words, does one's tax-payment check with his and/or her social security number on it make him and/or her a worshipper bearing the number 666 stamped on the payer's right hand or forehead?

The reported number of abortions for 2020 is nearly one million, with the murder of black fetuses approximating 4 times that of white ones. "The Epoch Times" on page A15 of its April 6, 2022 issue carried this headline:

> W(orld) H(ealth) O(rganization) Demands Abortion at Any Time for Any Reason Throughout the World

7. Gender Identity Revolt:

This is an eternal truth: "...in the image of God He created... male and female." (Genesis 1:17) The traits and markers for either gender is permanently engrained in each human body, not only at birth but throughout all of life as well as after life, by biologists, anthropologists and archaeologists. But since the latter half of the twentieth century many individuals as well as medical specialists accept and endorse transgenderism, an individual's freedom and right to claim a gender identity which does not correspond with his/her birth {biological} sex. The opposite, referred to as cisgender, is a person whose sense of personal identity and gender corresponds with its birth {biological} sex. In 2009 the International Transgender Day of Visibility designated March 31 as its annual event to celebrate transgender people and their contributions to society as well as to raise awareness of discrimination faced by transgender people worldwide:

> The Fairfax County School Board in Northern Virginia is considering teaching children there is no such thing as "biological sex" and also that "clergy" are not to be trusted if students have questions...the board's plan is to teach seventh and eighth grade students to embrace transgender identity, but don't tell them about the risks. Advisers voted against telling children about any of the health risks and side effects from 'gender transitioning.'[67]

Puberty blockers are hormone blockers used to help delay unwanted physical changes that do not match a very young person's desired gender identity. Delaying such changes can be an important step in a

---

67. http://www.wnd.com/2018/05/school-board-stunner-there-is-no-biological-sex/ Viewed: 3/2023

youth's elected transition. But because this treatment is unapproved by the FDA, it is only dispensed in hospitals as a 'medical experimentation. Because of the youth's extremely early age as well as of the many grieved regrets of its irreversible nature, hormonal treatment as well as irreversible 'gender reassignment' surgery have to be considered as forms of child abuse due to this absurd contradiction: a person has to reach 18 years of age to be eligible to vote whereas a three year-old unhappy with its birth gender is encouraged as well as free to choose various harmful alterations to what had originated naturally, i.e., had been formed by Yaweh.

> Texas State Rep. James Talarico:
> "...modern science obviously recognizes that there are many more that two biological sexes... six really common biological sexes based on X and Y chromosones – XX (female) and XY (male), but also single X, XXY, XYY and XXXY."[68]

Gender dysphoria usually means a difficulty in identifying with the biological sex in an individual.... The causes of gender dysphoria are not fully clear. (What is Gender Dysphoria? by Dr. Ananya Mandal, MD) Mutations, which result at conception, occur in many forms: Siamese twins, cleft palates, etc {cf. 1 Chronicles 20:6.}

Intersex people are born with any of several variations in sex characteristics including chromosomes, gonads, sex hormones, or genitals that, according to the UN

---

68. "New York Post", 4/27/21

Office of the High Commissioner for Human Rights, "do not fit the typical definitions for male or female bodies". For more information regarding intersex individuals go to https://www.huffingtonpost.com/entry/intersex-hanne-odiele_us_58875dabe4b096b4a2347790.

> Georgiann Davis:
> "...it would behoove all of us to escape these constraints of binary thinking that underline sex, gender, and sexuality. Genitalia are naturally variable and are not predictive of our gender or sexual identities, which are complex and fluid parts of who we are. There are many ways to accomplish your gender and sexual identities both with and without your genitals."[69]

No abnormality {cf. Matthew 19:12}, biological, chemical or behavioral, alters an infant's gender foundation for his or her entire life. As of this writing, Washington State is legally seeking to become the third state (after Oregon and California) to allow parents to select the gender-neutral designation of X on their newly born child's birth certificate. The reasoning behind this unbiblical selection is that it gives the child the right at a later date to decide which gender it wants to be. Thus gender determination is no longer finalized by Yaweh but by human will, thought, desire or 'feeling.' The one 'glitch' I foresee for any child with the X gender designation on its birth certificate is what gender-neutral name its parents can give it at birth.

---

69. https://www.npr.org/sections/13.7/2015/11/19/456458790/what-does-it-mean-to-be-intersex Viewed: 3/2023

The medical professionals who perform transitional surgeries have abandoned their pledges to the Hippocratic Oath, inasmuch as its original began with *"Primum non nocere"*, which translates "First do no harm," though in AD 245 it was altered to "I will abstain from all intentional wrong-doing and harm." The entire medical industry has become evilly stained by the abandonment and neglect of this time-honored oath! This letter in the 10/11/21 "Wall Street Journal" written by a faculty member of the Medical College of Georgia so gently deals with the realty of today's degenderizing aficionados:

> The ACLU is not alone in replacing the term "woman" with "people"...The degenderizing has also been adopted by the American College of Obstetricians and Gynecologists. It is reflected in redactions of position statements that now identify patients previously called "pregnant women" as "pregnant people," "persons" or "individuals." Today, people can select the nominal gender with which they wish to be identified. But having practiced obstetrics for 50 years, delivering more than 10,000 babies, I have yet to see one born to a biological male – rendering the gender de-identification of pregnancy utter nonsense.

8. Work Compulsion:

After blessing the first couple God told them {individually} to "fill the earth and כִּבְשֻׁהָ [bring under control] it and וּרְדוּ [rule over] the fish of the sea and over the birds of the sky, and over every living thing that moves עַל [on and above] the earth." (Genesis 1:28)

As a start, "God placed the man in the Garden of Eden…to…care for it." (Genesis 2:15) The presupposition underlying Adam's role of exercising control over all that Yaweh had created was that the power and authority needed to fulfill this responsibility was subaltern to that of His Creator because of the accountability he owed Him. Adam had been appointed as Yaweh's vice regent over all that He had created. But then this relationship took on a new dimension: first man and his helpmeet inexcusably disobeyed God. The Creator's response to this breach was in justified anger:

> "Cursed is the ground. In toil you shall eat of it all the days of your life. Both thorns and thistles it shall grow for you and you shall eat the plants of the field.
> —Genesis 3:17-18

The participle "cursed" connotes one of two perspectives: having an effect on caused by something bad or overwhelms, devastates. God's choice of wording implicitly indicates both meanings: the earth's surface is now overwhelmed, devastated by aggressively invasive thorns and thistles due to the first couple's shameless disobedience to Him. The consequence is they will have to contend with prickly thorns as well as poisonous-to-livestock thistles in order to sustain their livelihood instead of cultivating and maintaining the garden of Eden. While the latter job might have required attentive labor, its reward was always assured; now laboring becomes brutally arduous, frequently with no assurance of any bounty. Such assurance now is being subtly altered by the socialistic ideology, such as the disastrous consequence of the 2020 pandemic: the post-pandemic extension of $300 per week unemployment assistance in addition to what the unemployed was eligible to receive through state unemployment insurance. The resulting sum of weekly aid was such that it approximated or exceeded what the unemployed had been earning prior to the job-loss, thus encouraging the recipient not to become gainfully employed once again. While the labor market and production were actively heating up, many out of work were no longer qualified or desired by employers, preventing the economy from returning to 'normal' and thereby reducing tax incomes rising to the pre-pandemic level. Man was being paid to not work and not to pay income taxes. Socialism was taking root on US soil, eliminating for the worker the sense of pride derived from earning his or her livelihood and subtly commencing a negative self-image for each.

> Re Genesis 3:23, God "created the ground to be tilled and that in response it would produce economic fruitfulness...industriousness and frugality will result in economic prosperity. Promoting private property rights, ensuring free markets, and not stifling return on investment will result in prosperity because that is {God's} design."[70]
>
> In the "Pepper...And Salt" cartoon of *The Wall Street Journal's* April 14, 2022 edition a forlorn applicant for a job is informed by the interviewer, "We have plenty of job opportunities if pride is not a factor."

---

70. Politics & Evangelical Theology, Brian G. Mattson, self-printed, 2020' pgs. 123-24

The right to work gives man pride, integrity, the true sense of being. It is one of the "rights that we have by nature as human beings...and to store up the product of our labor so that we and our families can eat and live... We have (this right) because we...were born with them sewn by God into our nature, and we cannot find our earthly fulfillment without (it)."[71] The innovations today like AI and robotics are designed to improve production, but with the unintended consequence of replacing, and thereby reducing, the need for human labor.

> **God "created the ground to be tilled and that in response it would produce economic fruitfulness...industriousness and frugality will result in economic prosperity. Promoting private property rights, ensuring free markets, and not stifling return on investment will result in prosperity because that is {God's} design... Welfare states go "against the created design (for they do) not bring fruitfulness, prosperity, and human flourishing."[72]**

9. Natural and synthetic drugs:

Satan's subtly expanding influence manifests itself in the driving force of politics, primarily to rewrite as well as to flip the history and morality of our cultural heritage. One glaring example is the pharmaceutical industry and its dynamic: recognition of a newly discovered disease makes the 'market' fearful and demands a

---

71. "The Way Out" by Larry P. Arnn, President, Hillsdale College; Imprimis, November, 2021; page 7
72. Politics & Evangelical Theology, Brian G. Mattson, self-printed, 2020, pages 123-4, 155

drug to fight it; after extensive research, production and government approval, the expectant 'market' is wooed and bombarded by written, broadcast and digital advertisements; physicians are inadequately informed about the product but their clientele are hounding them for the prescription in order to acquire it at a pharmacy. Such drugs, though legally purchased, often get into the wrong hands and cause all manners of harm. The major threat in the opioid crisis the world faces today are natural poppy plants refined/processed to yield morphine and heroin as well as extremely dangerous synthetic substances, particularly fentanyl. And now the systematic legalization of marijuana (cannabis) is jeopardizing man's health purely for economic reasons. Addicts are treated not as accountable for their abusing drugs but as victims of those substances.

Then there's the plethora of vaccines that have gained control over citizens' health 'for the greater good,' even though the drugs' effectiveness and safety remain questionable enough for the U. S. government to maintain a trust fund in order to underwrite court-awarded damages caused by specified vaccines. Most recently, the Covid-19 pandemic gave birth to a synthetic (i.e., no pathogen but a 'spike protein') which had yet to be tested by the FDA but through selective mandates became publicly administered. But then variants necessitated 'booster' vaccines be required because 'the science' in power denied all possibility of one's natural immunity.

I harp on this subject because I believe φαρμακεία, pronounced *farm-a-kee-a*, is one of the means Satan is employing today to establish his control over all the world. In later Biblical times φαρμακεία represented the use of drugs, medicines, potions or spells for any purpose as well as poisoning, witchcraft, sorcery, magic or enchantment. The English word pharmacy comes from this Ancient Greek word.

Exodus 22:18(17) is one of Yaweh's explicit ordinances: "You shall not allow כָּשַׁף [practice of sorcery, witchcraft] / *LXX*: φαρμακεία [sorceress] to live" and the remaining uses in the Scriptures of כָּשַׁף / φαρμακεία connote a negative, foreboding, evil character:

> כָּשַׁף / *LXX*: φαρμακεία (sorcerers) "by their לַהַט"
> (flames- i.e., dazzlings, delusions)
> —Exodus 7:11
>
> כָּשַׁף / *LXX*: φαρμακεία (sorcerer)
> —Deuteronomy 18:10
>
> כָּשַׁף / *LXX*: φαρμακεία (sorcery)
> —2 Chronicles 33:6
>
> כָּשַׁף / *LXX*: φαρμακεία (sorcerers)
> —Daniel 2:2
>
> כָּשַׁף / *LXX*: φαρμακεία (sorcerers)
> —Malachi 3:5

And then there is חָבַר [to charm, bind with a spell]:

> חָבַר / *LXX*: ἐπαοιδή [enchantments]
> —Deuteronomy 18:11
>
> חָבַר / *LXX*: φαρμακεία [charmers]
> —Psalm 58:5{6}
>
> חָבַר / *LXX*: ἀδικία [deceitfulness, evil]
> —Proverbs 21:9
>
> חָבַר / *LXX*: λοίδορος [slanderer, reviler]
> —Proverbs 25:24
>
> חָבַר / *LXX*: ἐπαοιδή [enchantments]
> —Isaiah 47:9

חֶבֶר / *LXX*: ἐπαοιδή [enchantments]...כָּשַׁף [practices of magic) / *LXX*: φαρμακεία [employment of drugs, medicines, potions or spells for any purpose; poisoning; witchcraft; sorcery; magic; enchantment]
—Isaiah 47:12

φαρμακεία [employment of drugs, medicines, potions or spells for any purpose; poisoning; witchcraft; sorcery; magic; enchantment]
—Galatians 5:20

φαρμακεία [employment of drugs, medicines, potions or spells for any purpose; poisoning; witchcraft; sorcery; magic; enchantment] or φάρμακον [drug, poison, philter {love potion}]
—Revelation 9:21

φαρμακεία [employment of drugs, medicines, potions or spells for any purpose; poisoning; witchcraft; sorcery; magic; enchantment]
—Revelation 18:23

The Alpha and the Omega to John: "But for the cowardly and unbelieving and abominable and murderers and immoral persons and φαρμάκοις [φαρμακεύς - preparer of drugs, poisoner, sorcerer] and idolaters and all liars, their μέρος [destiny {cf. Matthew 24:51;Luke 12:46}] will be in the lake that burns with fire and brimstone, which is the second death."
—**Revelation 21:8**

This last verse clearly indicates that the selling and use of illicit drugs as well as the abusive use and mandated consumption of legal drugs is one of Yaweh's targets destined for destruction. There is no question that what He particularly hates is now a global crisis fueled

by Satan's full strength. For instance, the 'evolution' of illegal cannabis {marijuana) began quietly, and somewhat harmlessly, in the mid-twentieth century and its primary harm on many of the users was its addictiveness as a 'gateway' to serious and illegal drugs. At the turn of the century, though, various states began to legalize marijuana, first only for medical benefit but then for recreational enjoyment, even though its sale and use continue to be considered illegal by the Federal government while it is simultaneously regulating and taxing the state-approved sales.

> But youth nowadays are consuming marijuana more frequently and in higher doses than their elders did when they were young. This is leading to increased addiction and antisocial behavior. THC, the chemical that causes a euphoric high, interacts with the brain's neuron receptors involved with pleasure... But dabs – portions of concentrated cannabis – can include 20 times as much THC as joints did in the 1960's...One in 6 people who start using pot while under 18 will develop an addiction...As they use the drug more frequently to satisfy cravings, they develop psychological and social problems... Prenatal exposure to marijuana has been linked to behavioral problems, mental illness and lower academic achievement in children and adolescents.[73]

Yaweh's image-bearers are life's participants purposed to worship and obey Him; they were called by Him to live in accordance to His commandments - not

---

73. "Cannabis and the Violent Crime Surge" by Allysia Finley, The Wall Street Journal, 6/7/22

to alter what He had created. As Daniel Henniger wrote in his article, "The Devil Resurfaces in Ukraine"[74]:

> Through the ages humanity continues to rebel against God by seeking to 'improve' what He had intended. Evil and Satan, the Devil, "came to be seen as impediments to some forms of private personal behavior. So we demoted evil and expanded the definitions of goodness. But banishing the devil came with a price...Opinions on the nature of evil have differed since at least the Garden of Eden. But...If you give the devil a chance, he will try to destroy you."
>
> A nation that forgets its past has no future. (Winston Churchill)
>
> Queen Elizabeth 2 practiced "an unsophisticated faith and a devotion to duty"[75]

Paul's assessment goes directly to the heart:

> ...the anxious longing of the creation awaits eagerly for the revealing of the sons of God {cf. Isaiah 63:16, Hosea 1:10.} For the creation was subjected to futility {cf. Genesis 3:17-19}, not of its own will but because of Him who subjected it, in hope that the creation itself also will be set free from its slavery to corruption into the freedom of the glory of the children of God {cf. vs. 16-17; 1 John 3:2.} For we know that the whole creation {cf. Jeremiah 12:4,11} groans and suffers the pains of childbirth together until now.
>
> —Romans 8:19-22

---

74. The Wall Street Journal, 4/14/2022, Opinion section
75. Officiating clergyman at the Queen's September 19, 2022 funeral service conducted in St. George's Chapel at Windsor Castle

LIFE TODAY

Satan's 'apostles' methods: trickery and "craftiness in deceitful scheming...the days are evil."
—Ephesians 4:14, 5:16

"Your adversary, the devil, prowls about like a roaring lion, seeking someone to devour."
—1 Peter 5:8

A culture is both a way of living, which preserves a population's arts, beliefs and institutions passed down from generation to generation, as well as distinct codes of manners, dress, language affected by the commingling of rules and cultural meanings associated with activities such as family, education, religion, work, and health care. A culture is comprised of societies of individuals who share those beliefs and practices. Philosophers claim a culture's spirit, i.e., the driving force which sustains and characterizes it, is its unique economy. While I consider its core spirit to be religion, I will offer no defense of that in this discussion. The culture of the US commenced in the early 16th century with the arrival of Bible-believing settlers fleeing Europe for protection from religious persecution. The cultural aspects they contributed to the 'melting pot' resulting among the emerging colonies included individuality, scientific rationalism, capitalism, and the rule of new laws influenced by England's *Magna Carte* and ancient Greek philosophers. Christianity back then dominated the establishment of the colonies' moral and ethical codes of conduct but over time secular humanism, atheism, agnosticism as well as the influx of all the other religions and philosophies in the world have achieved civil and political freedoms to promote their beliefs publicly. Once a Christian nation, the US today is comprised of only a Christian minority; church attendance continues to decline as the age of attenders increases.

Since its emergence on North American soil in approximately the early 17th century, 'American' culture has slowly drifted away from Biblical influence and toward classical and political philosophies, prompted by emigrants drawn to 'the land of the free.' Liberty derived from, and later protected by, armed conflicts has always been the United States' primary draw. The unity and strength of the US culture depend on its synergy (the interaction or cooperation of two or more subsocieties, organizations and/or other agents that produces a combined effect greater than the sum of their separate effects) as well as unique democratic politics (governance activities proposed or rejected by varying parties having, or hoping to achieve, power) needed to uphold a semblance (the outward appearance or apparent form) of unity.

The slowly expanding merger of varying ethnicities with differing social conventions has subtly drawn Americans away from Christianity into agnosticism, secular humanism, Hinduism, Sikhism, Buddhism, Scientology, each one qualifying today as a religion according to definition #4[76]: "a cause, a principle, or an activity pursued with zeal or conscientious devotion." That definition even includes atheism, whose purpose in the US is:

> Since 1963, American Atheists {with more than 230 local affiliates nationwide} *seeks to* protect the absolute separation of religion from government, raised the profile of atheists and atheism in our nation's public and political discourse, and educated Americans about atheism.[77]

The irony here is that the American Atheists organization ignores this fact: all mankind is born with a religious nature because each individual is confronted with this two-fold quandary: who made me and why am I living? Any answer bears a 'religious' element for it either acknowledges or denies God and thereby renders the impossibility of purging "religion from government."

When she had been nominated to the Seventh Circuit in 2017, Senator Dianne Feinstein of California had grilled {Judge Amy Coney} Barrett on her strongly held religious views, suggesting that they would overwhelm

---

76. The American Heritage Dictionary, Third Edition
77. https://www.atheists.org/?gclid=EAIaIQobChMI9OOcofSJ-QIVStqGCh26ig0AEAAYASAAEgLKvvD_BwE

her principles when it came time to interpreting statutes and the law. "The dogma lives loudly within you," she told Barrett.[78]

> The wicked in the haughtiness of his countenance does not seek {Yaweh.} All his thoughts are, "There is no God."
> —Psalm 10:4

> The fool has said in his heart, " There is no God." They are corrupt, they have committed abominable deeds; there is no one who does good.
> —Psalm 14:1

Christianity, which undergirded the original foundation of the American 'way of life,' has become boldly and shamelessly treated as a result of the 2019 Covid-19 epidemic emanating from the NIH-funded project Gain of Function conducted in a Wuhan, China lab. Federal, state and municipal governments imposed severe restrictions on every-day life styles, including the closing of churches:

> But Peter and John answered and said to {the Temple priests and Sadducees}, "Whether it is right in the sight of God to give heed to you rather than to God, you be the judge, for we cannot stop speaking what we have seen and heard."
> —Acts 4:19-20

---

78. Rigged, Mollie Hemingway, Regnery Publishing, Washington, DC, page 174

> But Peter and the apostles answered {the Temple priests and Sadducees}, "We must obey God rather than men."
>
> —Acts 5:29

Paul:
> "For we must all appear before the judgment seat of Christ, that each one may be recompensed for his deeds in the body, according to what he has done, whether good or bad.
>
> —2 Corinthians 5:10

A Michigan high school junior has gone to federal court to fight for his right after he was suspended "for expressing his Christian beliefs and opinions in private text messages outside school...He shared the Judeo-Christian doctrine that homosexual conduct was a sin and that God created only two biological genders – man and woman."[79]:

The Supreme Court justice who drafted the decision that overturned Roe v. Wade decried a "growing hostility" toward religion in the West in his first public appearance after the ruling. "The problem that looms is not just indifference to religion, it's not just ignorance about religion," Alito said, starting his keynote address at the 2022 Notre Dame Religious Liberty Summit in Rome on July 21..."There's also growing hostility to religion or at least the traditional religious beliefs that are contrary to the new moral code that is ascendant in

---

79. Article by Steven Kovac in January 31, 2022 online edition of The Epoch Times

some sectors," the justice said..."One thing I hope they will say is that our country, after a lot of fits and starts, and ups and downs, eventually showed the world that it is possible to have a stable and successful society in which people of diverse faiths live and work together harmoniously and productively while still retaining their own beliefs," Alito added, noting that the fact that Americans can exercise religious liberty has been "truly a historic accomplishment" for the country. In this United States, the Justice said...a "growing hostility" towards religion is threatening the protection of this sacred right across the country. "And the problem that looms is not just indifference to religion, it's not just ignorance about religion. There's also growing hostility to religion, or at least the traditional religious beliefs that are contrary to the new moral code that is ascendant in some sectors," the justice added. Yet, according to Alito, this hostility to religion and religious freedom threatens a range of other fundamental rights. "The exercise of religion very often involves speech, a spoken or written prayer, the recitation of Scripture, a homily, a religious book or article these are all forms of speech they are also forms of religious exercise. If this sort of speech can be suppressed or punished, what is to stop the state from crushing other forms of expression?...On the other hand, if religious liberty is allowed, it will be harder for the state to restrict other speech and other assemblies," Alito said. While most legal academics nowadays believes that "religion doesn't merit special protection," Alito added, "the Constitution of the United States provides a clear answer" to the question of whether religious liberty warrants protection. "Constitution protects the free exercise of religion ... And for judges like me, who think to the belief that it matters what the Constitution says and what it does not say, that is enough," the justice said. "It's the law, and don't ask me why." The justice went further to reflect on religious persecution across the world—such as in Nigeria, Egypt, and India—and, most prominently China, but all were not successful. "During my lifetime, the People's Republic of China did its best to eradicate religion completely. And yet it failed. Just as the Roman emperors who spent centuries trying to destroy Christianity failed," the justice said.

As an example of this, Alito added, was that "the Cultural Revolution did its best to destroy religion, but it was not successful. It could not extinguish the religious impulse."[80]

The 'satanic' irony' of governmental lockdowns in 2020 due to covid-19: Humans are social creatures, but government policies are demanding that people "show their love" by staying away from others, which is contrary to human nature and human need, especially during times of crisis...

What's apparent, however, is that lockdowns, social distancing and other pandemic requirements are interfering with every one of (the five stages of grief),

---

80. "Justice Alito Criticizes World Leaders for Opposing Abortion Ruling, Cites 'Hostility to Religion'" By Gary Bai, The Epoch Times, 7/29/2022

making it nearly impossible for people to work through their intense feelings:

> Denial — Accompanying the body of the deceased helps loved ones to move past denial of their death, while taking away this step allows denial to linger.
>
> Anger — Feelings of anger are intensified when loved ones are unable to accompany the patient during the last days of their life. The inability to hold a ceremony can also intensify feelings of anger and guilt.
>
> Bargaining — Family members may blame themselves for their loved one's death and run over scenarios they feel they could have done differently to protect them. "This can cause negative thoughts and emotions, which complicates this period," the Iran University of Medical Sciences researchers explained.
>
> Depression — Government-imposed lack of social support and inability to hold conventional funeral ceremonies can intensify depression.
>
> Acceptance — Under normal circumstances, most people take six weeks to several months to accept the loss, but this, too, will take longer without social support.

Experts are predicting that these profound disruptions are going to lead to a wave of unresolved bereavement, depression and even post-traumatic stress disorder (PTSD) as humans are robbed of their ability to participate in age-old bereavement rituals. — Dr. Joseph Mercola[81]

Disunity within an historic denomination becomes public:
"Over 100 Florida Churches File Suit to Leave United Methodist Church"[82] The churches leaving are conservative... the most divisive issue has been the biblical view of homosexuality...the UMC was divided between theological conservatives who believed in traditional marriage and theological liberals who believed in an ever-expanding list of sexual orientations...Theological conservatives responded that they attempted compromise for decades before church authorities broke their trust.

Disunity exists within eastern Europe:
In Moscow, the leader of the Russian Orthodox Church... blessed Russian troops and proclaimed the war in Ukraine a metaphysical conflict between the faithful of God and a decadent West. That has sent officials from other denominations fleeing to the western reaches of the country to escape the fighting. The emigres include Ukraine's Catholics, Protestants and members of Ukraine's own Orthodox Church. Even some clergy

---

81. https://articles.mercola.com/sites/articles/archive/2020/12/24/prolonged-grief-disorder.aspx?ui=dfae14f24ea59caf52f084f3c1ba898e6aae4c9268cd26e52080d4a932f08e2a&cid_source=dnl&cid_medium=email&cid_content=art1ReadMore&cid=20201224_HL2&mid=DM756307&rid=1042517992
82. The Epoch Times, 7/27/2022; page A4

of the Ukrainian branch of the Orthodox Church long under Moscow's putative control fled as its leaders in Kyiv denounced the war and declared the church's independence.[83]

The few remaining Christians in Afghanistan live in constant fear — even of their own families:

Afghan Christians who failed to escape when their nation fell to the Taliban in August live in constant isolation and in fear that the fundamentalist Islamic government, and practically the entire society, is out to persecute them, according to the leader of an Afghan house church community. "The Taliban, their plan eventually is the elimination of Christianity, and they have been very open about that," the head of the Afghan House Church Network, identified only as Luke, said during a recent episode of "USCIRF Spotlight," the weekly podcast of the U.S. Commission on International Religious Freedom. And that makes the ramifications of their conversion even more serious, he explained. "The moment an Afghan decides to follow Christianity, they know there are a lot of consequences. You can lose your job. University students can get kicked out of school, even from private universities. Some have lost the custody of their children, and they can lose their possessions. They can even lose their lives."[84]

---

83. "Invasion Widens Rifts Among Christian Groups" by Alan Cullison: The Wall Street Journal, 8/2/2022, page A7
84. Jeff Brumley, February 1, 2022: https://baptistnews.com/article/the-few-remaining-christians-in-afghanistan-live-in-constant-fear-even-of-their-own-families/#.YuPcynbMK70

The left has cleverly established race as America's new religion of choice, replacing Christianity. Black is the highest denomination of the left's race religion. Their doctrine argues that bowing to blackness is a righteous and responsible response to America's history of racism. Anything framed as black cannot be chastised, criticized, or shunned. To do so would be blasphemous and racist. Through hip-hop, pornography has been wrapped in black packaging. Through hip-hop, a self-destructive culture has been wrapped in black packaging. Music that promotes the degradation and exploitation of black people has been framed as the salvation and glorification of black people. That's the power of the race religion. Dr. Dre is black. His history of violence toward women is irrelevant. The race religion is killing America. The Alphabet Mafia — BLM-LGBTQ-CRT — has wrapped every issue in black packaging. Earlier this week, Playboy magazine promoted a bunny outfit using a young black man as the model. The gay and transgender issues have been framed as a black issue. We're being used to promote causes that defy God and the principles taught in the Bible.[85]

Defenders of the faith are deemed ineligible to critique the content of public education:

Parents of public school students, "shocked by X-rated reading lists, race-based indoctrination, and anti-Christian instruction"[86] are designated domestic

---

85. Jason Whitlock Blaze Media / Op-ed 10/01/2021
86. F. James Sensenbrenner, "The Patriot Act Wasn't Meant to Target Parents", The Wall Street Journal Op-ed 10/13/2021

terrorists by the DOJ and FBI when exercising their right of free speech by addressing these concerns to their school boards.

You may have heard that Harvest USA will be excluded from participation in the Lancaster County Community Foundation's "ExtraGive" fundraising event...A letter we received from the Foundation in July notified us that we no longer qualify to participate, and several of our supporters recently received emails from the Foundation indicating that an organization had been disqualified. That was Harvest USA! The Foundation told us that this decision was an extension of their new "equity" values and "anti-hate" policy, inferring that Harvest USA is a hate organization. This is a sad turn of events, but not surprising. In a Lancaster newspaper letter to the editor that I saw last spring, the writer implored the Foundation to drop organizations that did not comply with LGBTQ+ values. This has now happened to Harvest USA because of our commitment to the authority of Scripture regarding human sexuality. Recently, several other Christian organizations that formerly participated in ExtraGive have voluntarily withdrawn from it, realizing that they are now required to subscribe to new anti-discrimination policies that may be contrary to their faith. (September 16, 2022 Letter from the founder of Harvest USA to its donors) I also received a call from a pastor telling me that disapproving and hurtful words were spoken about Harvest USA at a gathering of conservative pastors. They spoke of Harvest USA as a harsh and mean-spirited ministry because of our biblical views of sexuality and our unwillingness to buy into the "gay Christian" identity position. Frankly, I'm not sure which is more disheartening—hostility from a cancel-culture world or wounding words from brothers in Christ. (September 19, 2022 Letter from the founder of Harvest USA to its donors)

Intolerant secularism is on the march. In a blatant campaign of cultural imperialism, secularists and their leftist allies aim to shrivel the "free exercise" of religion to mere "freedom of worship." Freedom of religion and freedom of worship aren't the same concepts. Indeed free exercise was ably described by the late Supreme Court justice as having "a double aspect – freedom of thought and action." In other words, we aren't merely free to believe, but (generally speaking) to also act in the public square according to our faith precepts...Both free exercise and freedom of worship are important to religious freedom. We might even say, they're mutually dependent to freely living a life of faith. Unfortunately, outside of explicitly worshipping contexts, federal and state laws and legislation are increasingly bent on forcing religious believers to act consistently with the values of reigning secular morality when outside the home, church, synagogue, temple, or mosque. The message is clear: Those with traditional religious views of morality had better keep their beliefs behind closed doors – or suffer the consequences...In 1990, the Supreme Court significantly weakened the Constitution's free exercise clause in Employment Division v. Smith... This ruling opened the door to oppressing faithful people by simply enacting laws of general applicability that are consistent with contemporary secular beliefs but also known to be offensive to certain religions. A perfect example of this suppression is ongoing in California. When the administrators of a Catholic hospital in the Dignity Health chain were informed that a patient's planned hysterectomy was a gender transition, the surgery was cancelled as a violation of Catholic moral teaching. Dignity Health was sued for violating California law requiring facilities to provide full and equal access to medical procedures without regard to gender {which was} allowed to remain in effect by the U.S. Supreme Court. Thus a catholic hospital may soon be forced to pay considerable damages for adhering to Catholic dogma because the law being enforced wasn't specifically aimed at suppressing Catholic institutions... Jack Phillips - the Colorado Wedding Cake Baker -... has been repeatedly attacked in Colorado courts for refusing to create cakes containing messages that violate his faith beliefs...{he was later} sued in again in state court for refusing to design a cake celebrating a gender transition and found liable for violating the Colorado Anti-Discrimination Act... Phillip's legal goose may truly be cooked for remaining true to his religious beliefs in the conduct of his business. The private sector may pose an even more potent threat to religious liberty by blackballing religious organizations and institutions... Today, social progressives, including some who manage many of the country's most powerful corporations, scorn religious freedom because they see it as an excuse to discriminate against LGBT individuals – which may explain why Chase closed all NCRF {National Committee for Religious Freedom} accounts last year...Thus, it's reasonable to suspect that Chase "de-banked" the NCRF because it defends religious freedom, including in LGBT controversies such as the Phillips cases. Private acts of discrimination such a debanking open a new front in the religious freedom wars...if the right to free exercise of religion is effectively suppressed, freedom of worship will be the next religious liberty on the chopping block.[87]

In addition to the suppression of Christianity the disenchanted, ungodly US citizens today are seeking to 'improve' what He had ordained to exist some 250 years ago by means of:

1] SOCIAL ENGINEERING

Voddie Baucham, an American who is currently Dean of Theology at African Christian University in Lusaka, Zambia, says that there's more to the social justice movement than what Christians typically think of justice. "Social justice is about redistributing resources and opportunities...Social justice is not the same as the biblical idea and the biblical concept of justice. You also need to understand that social justice is built on the back of critical theory. Which is all about the idea of, you know, hegemony and power structures.... 'Equal' essentially means that everyone will be given the same amount or opportunity whereas 'equitable' is a way of dividing things more fairly."[88]

---

87. "Freedom Of Religion On The Chopping Block" by Wesley J. Smith, The Epoch Times, 2/8/23; page A13
88. Social Justice Is Not the Same as Biblical Justice: Professor Issues Warning Issues Warning to Christians by Dan Andros; cbn.com, 6/22/2020

At the same time lockdowns came into vogue by treating the images of God as livestock. Dr. Scott Atlas, a Coronavirus Advisor in the Trump administration said on "Tucker Carlson Tonight" {July 29, 2020, Fox News network} that 2006 scientific literature said that a lockdown should not be employed because "it doesn't work and is extremely destructive...Severe economic downturns kill people," as the Covid-19 pandemic lockdown proved.

To understand the Great Reset, we must recognize that the project represents the completion of a centuries-long and ongoing attempt to destroy classical liberalism, American constitutionalism, and national sovereignty.[89]

> ...just last year, Klaus Schwab, founder and executive chairman of the World Economic Forum (WEF) – a famous organization made up of the world's political, economic, and cultural elites that meet annually in Davos, Switzerland – and Thierry Malleret, co-founder and main author of the *Monthly Barometer*, published a book called *COVID-19: The Great Reset*. In the book, they define the Great Reset as a means of addressing the "weaknesses of capitalism" that were purportedly exposed by the COVID pandemic. In May 2018 the WEF...collaborate with Johns Hopkins Center for Health Security...to conduct "CLADE X" simulation...and in October, 2019 again with Johns Hopkins {but this time also with} the Bill and Melinda Gates Foundation on another exercise, "Event 201," which simulated an inter-

---

89. "The Backstory of the Great Reset..." by Michael Rectenwald, The Epoch Times, 6/8/2022

national response to the outbreak of a novel coronavirus. This was two months before the COVID outbreak in China became news and five months before the World Health Organization declared it a pandemic, and it closely resembled the future COVD scenario, including incorporating the idea of asymptomatic spread. The CLADE X and Event 201 simulations anticipated almost every eventuality of the actual COVID crisis, most notably the responses by governments, health agencies, the media, tech companies, and elements of the public. The responses and their effects included worldwide lockdowns, the collapse of businesses and industries, the adoption of biometric surveillance technologies, an emphasis on social media censorship to combat "misinformation,", the flooding of social and legacy media with "authoritative sources," widespread riots, and mass unemployment. In addition to being promoted as a response to COVID, the Great Reset is promoted as a response to climate change... stakeholder capitalism involves the behavioral modification of corporations to benefit not shareholders but stakeholders – individuals and groups that stand to benefit or lose from corporate behavior. Stakeholder capitalism requires not only corporate responses to pandemics and ecological issues such as climate change, but also rethinking [corporations'] commitments to already-vulnerable communities within their ecosystems." This is the "social justice" aspect of the Great Reset. To comply with that, governments, banks, and asset managers use the Environmental, Social, and Governance (ESG) index to squeeze non-woke corporations and businesses out of the market... Other developments that advance the Great Reset agenda have included unfettered immigration, travel restrictions for otherwise legal border crossing, the Federal Reserve's unrestrained printing of money and the subsequent inflation, increased taxation, increased dependence on the state, broken supply chains, the restrictions and job loses due to vaccine mandates, and the prospect of personal carbon allowances. Such policies reflect the "fairness" aspect of the Great Reset – fairness requires lowering the economic status of people in wealthier nations like the U.S. relative to that of people in poorer regions of the world... Governance is not only increasingly privatized, but also and more importantly, corporations are deputized as major additions to governments and intergovernmental bodies. The state is thereby extended, enhanced, and augmented by the addition of enormous corporate assets...the goals of the Great Reset depend on the obliteration not only of free markets, but of individual liberty and free will. Like earlier attempts at totalitarianism, the Great Reset is doomed to failure. That doesn't mean, however, that it won't... leave a lot of destruction in its wake..."[90]

"Ideologically, the Great Reset and the Great Leap Forward are...both totalitarian assaults on the human race."[91]

When a group of engineers and researchers gathered in a warehouse in Mukilteo, Wash., 10 years ago, they knew they were onto something big. They scrounged up

---

90. What Is the Great Reset?" by Michael Rectenwald, Imprimis, 12/1/2021, Hillsdale College.
91. "Do US Business Elites Really Believe 'Woke' Ideology?" by Lee Smith, The Epoch Times, 9/28/2022; page A17

tables and chairs, cleared out space in the parking lot for experiments and got to work. They were building a battery — a vanadium redox flow battery — based on a design created by two dozen U.S. scientists at a government lab. The batteries were about the size of a refrigerator, held enough energy to power a house, and could be used for decades. The engineers pictured people plunking them down next to their air conditioners, attaching solar panels to them, and everyone living happily ever after off the grid. "It was beyond promise," said Chris Howard, one of the engineers who worked there for a U.S. company called UniEnergy. "We were seeing it functioning as designed, as expected." But that's not what happened. Instead of the batteries becoming the next great American success story, the warehouse is now shuttered and empty. All the employees who worked there were laid off. And more than 5,200 miles away, a Chinese company is hard at work making the batteries in Dalian, China. The Chinese company didn't steal this technology. It was given to them — by the U.S. Department of Energy. First in 2017, as part of a sublicense, and later, in 2021, as part of a license transfer. An investigation by NPR and the Northwest News Network found the federal agency allowed the technology and jobs to move overseas, violating its own licensing rules while failing to intervene on behalf of U.S. workers in multiple instances. Now, China has forged ahead, investing millions into the cutting-edge green technology that was supposed to help keep the U.S. and its economy out front.

Department of Energy officials declined NPR's request for an interview to explain how the technology that cost U.S. taxpayers millions of dollars ended up in China. After NPR sent department officials written questions outlining the timeline of events, the federal agency terminated the license with the Chinese company, Dalian Rongke Power Co. Ltd... Several U.S. companies have tried to get a license to make the batteries. The department is now conducting an internal review of the licensing of vanadium battery technology and whether this license — and others — have violated U.S. manufacturing requirements, the statement said. Forever Energy, a Bellevue, Wash., based company, is one of several U.S. companies that have been trying to get a license from the Department of Energy to make the batteries. Joanne Skievaski, Forever Energy's chief financial officer, has been trying to get hold of a license for more than a year and called the department's decision to allow foreign manufacturing "mind boggling. This is technology made from taxpayer {15 million} dollars," Skievaski said. "It was invented in a national lab. (Now) it's deployed in China, and it's held in China. To say it's frustrating is an understatement." Now that the Department of Energy has revoked the license, Skievaski said she hopes Forever Energy will be able to acquire it or obtain a similar license. The company plans to open a factory in Louisiana next year and begin manufacturing. Still, she says it will be difficult for any American company at this point to catch up. Industry trade reports currently list Dalian Rongke Power Co. Ltd. as the top manufacturer of vanadium redox flow batteries worldwide. Skievaski also worries about whether China will stop making the batteries once an American company is granted the right to start making them. That may be unlikely. Chinese news reports say the country is about to bring online one of the largest battery farms the world has ever seen. The reports say the entire farm is made up of vanadium redox flow batteries.[92]

The escalating regulatory attack on agricultural producers from Holland and the United States to Sri Lanka and beyond is closely tied to the United Nation's "Agenda 2030" Sustainable Development Goals and the U.N.'s partners at the World Economic Forum (WEF)...If left unchecked, multiple experts said, the U.N.-backed sustainability policies on agriculture and food production would lead to economic devastation, shortages of critical goods, widespread famine, and a dramatic loss of individual freedoms...Even private land ownership is in the crosshairs, a global food production and the world economy are transformed to meet the global sustainable goals...The {Vancouver Declaration} stated that "land cannot be treated as an ordinary asset controlled by individuals" and that private land ownership is "a principal instrument of accumulation and concentration of wealth, therefore contributes to social injustice." "Public control of land use is therefore indispensable," the U.N. declaration said, a prelude to the World Economic Forum's now infamous "prediction" that by 2030 "you'll own nothing." Experts...say that

---

92. "The U.S. made a breakthrough battery discovery — then gave the technology to China," aired 8/3/2022 on NPR's "All Things Considered" with Courtney Flatt and Laura Sullivan: https://www.npr.org/2022/08/03/1114964240/new-battery-technology-china-vanadium

some of the world's wealthiest and most powerful corporate leaders are working with the communists in China and elsewhere in an effort to centralize control over food production and crush independent farmers and ranchers...Dutch farmers, already at the breaking point, have responded...with massive nationwide protests. That followed violent unrest in Sri Lanka tied to food shortages caused by government policy...According to critics of the policies...the goal isn't to preserve the environment or fight climate change at all. Instead, the experts warn that the "sustainability" narrative and the other justifications are a tool to gain control over food, agriculture, and people...the U.N. plan {Goal 10} calls for national and international wealth redistribution... as well as "fundamental changes in the way that our societies produce and consume goods and services."... Alongside the U.N. are various "stake-holders' that are critical to implementing sustainable development policies through "public-private partnerships." At the heart of that effort is the WEF, which since 2020 has been pushing a total transformation of society known as the "Great Reset." In 2019, the WEF signed a "strategic partnership" with the U.N. to advance Agenda 2030 within the global business community.[93]

The American Prairie (AP), a conservation project in Montana, has quietly scooped up more than 450,000 acres of land with the help of its billionaire donors and

---

93. [In this same issue, on page A11 appears this article: "Canada and Ireland Issue Restrictions for Farmers, Similar to Netherlands.] "Behind The Global War On Farming" by Alex Newman, The Epoch Times, 7/26/2022

the federal government. The little-known project aims to create the largest "fully functioning ecosystem" in the continental U.S. by stitching together about 3.2 million acres of private and public lands, according to the American Prairie Foundation, which founded the reserve more than 20 years ago. The group has recorded 34 transactions spanning roughly 453,188 acres of land throughout central Montana — much of which were once used for farming and grazing — since 2004 and continues to aggressively expand." Our mission is to assemble the largest complex of public and private lands devoted to wildlife in the lower 48," Pete Geddes, AP's vice president and chief external relations officer, told Fox News Digital in an interview. "For comparison, about 25% larger than Yellowstone. We're not asking the federal government to create anything, we're not asking the federal government for any money," he added. "Instead, we're engaged in private philanthropy and voluntary exchange by buying ranches from people who would like to sell that to us."

The American Prairie Foundation has raised tens of millions of dollars in recent years, according to recent tax filings, thanks in large part to its donors, which include well-known Wall Street and Silicon Valley magnates. Hansjoerg Wyss, a Swiss financier and mega-donor of liberal causes, deceased German retail mogul Erivan Haub, John Mars, the heir to the Mars candy fortune, and Susan Packard Orr, daughter of the Hewlett-Packard Co. co-founder, have all donated to AP, Bloomberg previously reported. The AP said about 3% of its contributions have come from international donors. "It's an area that doesn't have a lot of people in it and has been depopulating for a long, long time," Geddes said. "So, the thinking was, perhaps there's greater potential for less conflict over conservation in this part of the world." However, AP's plans have faced increasing pushback from top state officials and local ranchers who argue such a nature reserve would remove key land from production and negatively impact surrounding privately-owned lands. Using its donor funds, the group has purchased about 118,000 acres of private land and leased another 334,000 acres of public land owned primarily by the federal government. "Those donors are able to write those contributions off as a charitable donation, so they don't have to live with the consequences of what they're doing to these communities," said Chuck Denowh, the policy director at the United Property Owners of Montana (UPOM), a group made up of local ranchers opposed to AP's plans. "It's really concerning that we have such an amount of foreign money coming into AP to buy up our ag land," he told Fox News Digital. "For the future of food security of this country, we need to take a close look at that."

Denowh said the vast majority of locals throughout the surrounding counties who have looked after and conserved the land for decades are opposed to the AP's plans. The region is almost entirely dependent on the agriculture industry. Opponents of AP have focused their ire in particular on one of the group's chief proposals to release wild bison onto the property, giving visitors "a chance to witness the majestic species." UPOM has expressed concern that free-roaming bison may infect surrounding livestock with brucellosis, an infectious disease commonly found in bison and elk populations, which could be extremely costly for ranchers if spread to their cattle. The foundation requested permission from the Bureau of Land Management (BLM), the federal agency responsible for managing 245 million acres of public lands, to allow bison grazing on portions of the leased property in 2017 and again in 2019. The agency announced Thursday that it had approved the AP's request for bison grazing across 63,500 acres of federal property. Gov. Greg Gianforte and a series of state agency heads penned letters to BLM late last year urging the agency not to approve the request. Montana Department of Agriculture Director Christy Clark said the plan would remove "large chunks of land from production agriculture," likely decrease agricultural production revenue and harm support industries in the area like machinery sales and ranch laborers. "It's just flatly illegal," Montana Attorney General Austin Knudsen told Fox News Digital in an interview. "This is federal land that is specifically — by the Taylor Grazing Act, by federal law — set aside for livestock grazing. Bison are not livestock, even under federal law. That's the part that everyone just seems to be ignoring here," he continued. "AP doesn't want to admit that, certainly the Bureau of Land Management and the Department of Interior don't want to admit that. But that's just the fact." Knudsen slammed AP for what he called its surreptitious plan to create an "American Serengeti" where "liberal coastal elites can come and hang out and look at the pretty animals." The attorney general added that his office is closely reviewing the Biden administration's decision Thursday to determine its next steps to protect ranchers and the state's interests. The Taylor Grazing Act, which Congress passed in 1934, is designed to prevent overgrazing by allowing local ranchers to lease public land for livestock grazing and raising forage crops. The bill was approved to increase food and livestock production on land that had, for years, been severely mismanaged. While AP has argued the law allows for bison grazing, the group has also acknowledged its plans are primarily centered on conservation, not production. For example, the group boasts on its website that its land acquisitions have already led to the retirement of 63,777 acres of cattle grazing leases in the Charles M. Russell National Wildlife Refuge, allowing federal authorities to "restore the habitat primarily for wildlife use. We don't think of it as non-productive use," Geddes told Fox News Digital. "Those bison are playing very productive roles. It's absolutely true they're not a commercial livestock production, but they're productive in the sense of what they do for that prairie ecosystem." An estimated 800 bison currently roam on some of AP's property, a number the group hopes will swell to "several thousand" as part of its wildlife restoration plan. AP currently leases out some of the land it oversees to cattle ranchers, who, amid a major regional drought, are desperate for grasslands available for livestock grazing. Geddes said those ranchers have been made well aware of AP's plans to eventually push them off reserve property once bison are allowed to roam on that leased land. "Let's say in a couple of years, we have 1,200 head of bison. In the seven counties in which we work, there are probably half a million head of cattle," he added. "This critique that we're somehow dropping the neutron bomb and wiping out agriculture in this area — it's just nonsensical." Montana's $4.72 billion agriculture industry is among the state's largest sectors and supplies the U.S. with a large supply of wheat, hay, lentils, corn and meat, according to the Montana Department of Agriculture. As of January, Montana ranchers operated an inventory of 2.2 million cattle, making it one of the few states with more cattle than people. Overall, cattle inventories have declined in Montana and across the country over the last several years, a recent report from the U.S. Department of Agriculture's National Agricultural Statistics Service showed. "AP is working to buy up as much land as they can to take as many cattle off the landscape as they can and, ultimately, drive those folks out of there," Denowh told Fox News Digital. "Those lands were created in the first place to ensure an adequate and consistent supply of protein for the country. That's probably one of the bigger dangers from AP," he said. "If they can set this new precedent with BLM, we think that [non-governmental organizations] throughout the West are going to be buying up land to take control of these grazing leases and take them out of production. This is really bigger than AP."[94]

---

94. "Billionaire-funded group quietly taking farmland out of production in rural" by Thomas Catenacci, Fox News, 7/29/2022

A recent purchase of 2,100 acres of prime North Dakota farmland by a group tied to billionaire Bill Gates {the largest private owner of farmland in the country} has some in the state concerned that they are being exploited by the ultra-wealthy. Gates owns some 269,000 acres across dozens of states, according to last year's edition of the Land Report 100, an annual survey of the nation's largest landowners. The Microsoft co-founder is considered to be the largest private owner of farmland in U.S. He owns less than 1% of the nation's total farmland. In question is a Depression-era law meant to protect family farms. North Dakota's attorney general has asked the trust involved in the purchase to explain how it plans to use the land in order to meet rules outlined in the state's anti-corporate farming law. The law prohibits all corporations or limited liability companies from owning or leasing farmland or ranchland, with some exceptions. "I don't know that it's quite as volatile a situation as some have depicted," North Dakota Republican Attorney General Drew Wrigley told The Associated Press Thursday. "It's taken off, it's all over the planet, but it's not me sticking a finger in the eye of Bill Gates. That's not what this is." The state's Agriculture Commissioner, Republican Doug Goehring, told a North Dakota TV station that some residents feel they are being exploited by the ultra-rich who buy land but do not necessarily share the state's values.[95]

---

95. "Purchase of prime North Dakota farmland tied to Bill Gates sparks outrage" by Ken Martin, FOX Business, 6/24/2022

It appears we're in a phase where global systems of food and energy production are being intentionally dismantled in an effort to force into effect what the World Economic Forum (WEF) calls The Great Reset and the Rockefeller Foundation calls Reset the Table. Controlling food and shifting us away from a natural diet is an important part of The Great Reset. While the destruction of food production is being justified by the Green Agenda, the real goal is to eliminate naturally-grown foods and replace them with patented foodstuffs, frequently synthetic...In addition to restrictions imposed by the Green Agenda, nearly 100 food production facilities in the U.S. alone have also mysteriously burned down since 2021. The U.K. has even issued an "urgent warning" that gardening can cause heart disease by exposing you to harmful soil pollutants. So, now they're trying to convince you that growing your own food is harmful too. Prepare for unavoidable food inflation, shortages and famine by stocking up on nutritious shelf-stable foods.[96]

Dr. Joseph Mercola's September 18, 2021 interview with Dr. Peter Breggin, known as "the conscience of psychiatry"[97] for his instrumental role in preventing the return of lobotomy as a psychiatric treatment in the

---

96. Dr. Joseph Mercola, 7/11/2022; https://articles.mercola.com/sites/articles/archive/2022/ 07/11/ shelf-stable-food.aspx?ui=dfae14f24ea59caf52f 084f3c1ba898e6aae4c9268cd26e52080d4a932f 08e2a&sd=20110604&cid_source=dnl&cid_medium=email&cid_content=art1ReadMore&cid=20220711_HL2&mid=DM12 10584&rid=1545009735

97. https://www.listennotes.com/podcasts/dr-joseph-mercola/the-conscience-of-psychiatry-Iv4gnq8becd/ Viewed: 3/2023

early 1970s, regarding his book, "COVID-19 and the Global Predators: We Are the Prey." Highlights:

1. We are in the middle of the biggest, most effective propaganda war in the history of the world, designed to make us helpless, obedient and docile. The end goal is to create a totalitarian world regime;
2. In psychotherapy, people who've been abused often cannot identify the abuse as evil. They can't bear to think there are people who take pleasure from injury and domination. Citizens across the world are currently being abused, and must face the fact that there are evil people intentionally trying to hurt them;
3. In 2015, a scientific paper announced they had the means to create a pandemic. The research was funded by the National Institute of Allergy and Infectious Diseases and carried out at the Wuhan Institute of Virology; 4] The Communist Chinese Party has been working with SARS-CoV-type viruses since at least 2003, and there have been four different leaks of SARS viruses since then; 5] In 2016, Bill Gates created a business plan for the World Economic Forum that details everything we're experiencing now. In videos dating back to 2017, Gates discusses the development of RNA vaccines. Fast-forward to 2020, and mRNA injections were the immediate choice for the fast-tracked COVID shots. And, as detailed in Gates' business plan, Pfizer and Moderna were

both given billions of dollars from the U.S. federal government through BARDA and the NIH/NIAID... Dr. Breggin: "Now we have a vaccine that has more deaths than all the other vaccines put together. How can we ignore that? On the other hand, we get all these huge [falsely inflated] numbers of deaths from COVID-19...you take this relatively benign epidemic and make it into a horror show by exaggerating everything...what is the goal? We can determine the goal by looking at what we know: 1] health leaders are ignoring COVID jab injuries and deaths; 2] They do not want anyone to use early treatment. They've done everything in their power to dismiss and vilify any and all potential treatments, from vitamin D to hydroxychloroquine and ivermectin; 3] Western countries that have been icons of freedom and liberty are being hit the hardest by the pandemic and put under the harshest countermeasures; 4] The risk of dying from COVID-19 is less than 0.5% for all but the very old who have multiple comorbidities; 5] Vaccine makers have no financial liability for vaccine injuries and deaths; 6] Government started out enticing people to get the experimental shot using a variety of bribes, then moved on to forcing the shots using threats such as loss of employment, higher health insurance rates, loss of travel privileges, loss of right to health care in general and more. The Chinese have been sinking their teeth into us for a long time, because we are the seat of liberty in this world... The forces are most locked into those of us who are now free, and they're aiming to destroy us...the spike protein is the spearhead of an assault on humanity. That has nothing to do with COVID-19 whatsoever, but is planned through COVID-19 in order to vastly increase the wealth of numerous institutions and individuals... many of them unfortunately originating from America, who are working in collaboration with the communist, Chinese Communist Party, to increase this vast exploitation of the world. In 2010, Bill Gates announced "the decade of vaccines." A partner in that declaration was Dr. Anthony Fauci, director of the National Institute of Allergy and Infectious Diseases (NIAID), as well as a number of other globalists, including the United Nations. In 2015, a scientific paper[3] assured that gain-of-function researchers had the means to create a pandemic. This research was funded by the NIAID and carried out by two top Chinese researchers at the Wuhan Institute of Virology (WIV) and all scientists in China work on behalf of the Chinese Communist Party (CCP). It's called military civil fusion. They all work together. That's the nature of the totalitarian state. People don't realize that, but Fauci had to know he was funding a potential pandemic virus. In fact, in the last few days, it's come out from his emails obtained through a Freedom of Information Act (FOIA) request...that he actually gave them instructions for how to combine...several SARS-Cov-type virus systems to make an actual source code...So, it's systematic, and public health people have always been totalitarian in nature. It's all about public health people telling the communities what they must do come the next public health threat. They don't say preserve the Bill of Rights. They don't say, 'make sure we check this out in the courts or a body supervising us for our ethics to protect the folks.'...the end goal is complete totalitarian control of all nations, very similar to the kind of societal control already in place in China...It's not going to be easy, because the globalist predators have infiltrated government, NGOs, academia, entertainment, business and every other major aspect of American life...We can also see that COVID-19 was nothing more than a means to an end because the same globalist elite are now calling for sanctions on the world to combat the health threat of global warming... So here we have China and America making what are essentially biological weapons, the excuse being, 'We're going to make vaccines.' But...the vaccines aren't going to work and they know it, because the coronavirus mutates all the time." Dr. Mercola: "In the days just after this interview, President Biden made clear his intention to force vaccinate Americans by mandating corporations with 100 employees or more to require COVID vaccination or face fines. It's as unconstitutional as you can get, but he's doing it anyway because, again, the end goal is totalitarianism and the means is medical tyranny."

"All over the world we are seeing those datasets that, unfortunately, the people that are dying and being hospitalized are overwhelmingly the highly vaccinated, not those that have natural immunity," said Dr. Robert Malone…"Another paper published in Nature shows that the evolution of the virus is not coming from the general population, but rather from immunocompromised people who have received multiple vaccine doses, and about 30 percent of the highly vaccinated population are having repeated infections. The paradox is that most of the countries with emerging economies and low vaccination rates also have the lowest COVID-19 mortality rates in the world," he said. "The RNA from the vaccine produces more spike protein than the natural infection does…Now that makes sense about why we see more adverse events with the vaccines than we see with the infection itself, because spike is a toxin." Malone, president and co-founder of the International Alliance of Physicians and Medical Scientists, said over 17,000 doctors and scientists have signed a declaration stating unequivocally that genetic vaccines need to be withdrawn. "These genetic vaccines are not working," he said.[98]

With the exception of Pearl Harbor and Sept. 11, 2001, Americans have not been attacked by an enemy on our own soil. Unlike countries in Europe during World War II, America has never been occupied by a military force or locked down under martial law. We have never seen

---

98. "COVID-19 Vaccines Hinder the Immune System, Lead to More Severe Illness: Dr. Robert Malone" by Ella Kietlinska and Joshua Philipp, The Epoch Times, 8/2/2022

soldiers in armored vehicles patrolling the streets, warning us to stay in our homes or face arrest – or worse. Beginning in 1776, when our freedom seeking founders wrote the Declaration of Independence and stood their ground from Lexington and Concord to Saratoga and Valley Forge, and then came together to create a constitutional Republic dedicated to protecting individual and minority rights, the United States of America has defined and served as a beacon for liberty for people around the world. This summer, we watched soldiers patrolling the streets of Sydney, Australia with helicopters overhead blaring warnings to a stunned, locked down people to stay in their homes in the name of the public health. We have watched hundreds of thousands of people, young and old, gather together again and again in the streets of Paris, London, Rome, Athens, and Berlin. They are marching against authoritarianism, the kind of Orwellian authoritarianism embodied in government issued vaccine passports that punish citizens for simply defending the right to make a voluntary medical decision for themselves and their minor children, a decision about whether to be injected with a biological pharmaceutical product that can cause serious reactions, injure, kill or fail to work. In what has become a prophetic primal scream for liberty, governments are ordering the police to break up the largely peaceful demonstrators flooding the big cities and small villages of western Europe, the first populations to organize massive public protests against old fashioned tyranny dressed up in 21st century clothes. The people of Europe were the first to stand up for freedom during this government declared public health emergency because they know how tyranny begins. They know what it looks like and they remember what it feels like. They remember and are declaring, "Never again." Most Americans living today do not remember World War II or, if they do, it is through what their parents or grandparents told them about it. World War II was not fought on American soil. Americans went to war in Europe to stop the slaughter of millions at the hands of an authoritarian fascist government commanding the Army of the Third Reich that killed in the name of the public health and safety, even an authoritarian communist government slaughtered many more millions during a "Reign of Terror" in the Soviet Union. Most American children today are not taught what happened in China after World War II, when the Chinese Communist Party (CCP) implemented the Great Leap Forward and the Great Proletarian Cultural Revolution. Those militant ideological cleansing campaigns imprisoned and killed tens of millions of citizens because they criticized or opposed authoritarian government policies. In America, we have taken our freedom for granted because, while we have been willing to fight to defend the freedom of others, we have never been called upon to defend it in our own backyard. Most Americans have never imagined we would experience a serious threat to autonomy and freedom of thought, speech, conscience and assembly. So deep has been our trust in the laws and cultural values which have, for the most part, ensured fundamental freedoms in our country, that we never believed it could happen here. But the last 20 months have changed everything. Many Americans have begun to understand that tyranny can be disguised to look like safety, even as many others still cannot bring themselves to believe it. Striking fear into the hearts and minds of the people, the move toward authoritarianism in America began with government officials suddenly telling us – even children as young as two years old – that we could not breathe fresh air or enter public spaces without a mask covering our face. Millions of American workers judged to be "non-essential" lost the ability to earn a living so they could eat and pay rent during "flatten the curve" lockdowns we were told would only last a few weeks but, instead, went on for months. Anyone who criticized government narratives about the origin of SARS-CoV-2 virus or questioned social distancing restrictions was immediately publicly shamed and censored. Any doctor, who tried to provide early treatment to COVID-19 patients by repurposing safe and effective licensed drugs and nutritional supplements to help their patients survive the infection, were also publicly shamed and censored. After the FDA granted Pfizer and Moderna an Emergency Use Authorization (EUA) in December 2020 to distribute their liability free experimental mRNA COVID-19 vaccines in the U.S., public health officials enlisted big corporations to launch a hard-sell national vaccine advertising campaign targeting all Americans over the age of 12. Anyone who asked questions or challenged the hard sell was immediately censored on social media. State governments and employers were encouraged to threaten workers, especially health care workers and emergency responders, with loss of their jobs for refusing the vaccine. Private businesses were encouraged to deny unvaccinated citizens entry to restaurants, stores and other public venues. By the end of July 2021, the Department of Veteran Affairs directed all VA health care workers to be fully vaccinated or lose their jobs. In early August, the Department of Defense announced that all military service members must be fully vaccinated when the FDA officially licenses a COVID-19 vaccine or lose their jobs. Suddenly, on Aug. 23, the Pfizer mRNA vaccine was licensed without a public meeting of the FDA Vaccines and Related Biological Products Advisory Committee (VRPBAC) and full disclosure of the scientific data supporting licensure. By the end of August, about 176 million Americans had been "fully" vaccinated, representing 53.6 percent of our population of 333 million people, which is the third largest in the world. And studies had confirmed that the SARS-CoV-2 infection mortality ratio (IFR) in the U.S. remains at less than one percent. But the Executive Branch of the US government was not happy. Federal health officials had publicly set the goal of persuading 90 percent of Americans to get the COVID vaccine, although it is clear now that the real goal all along was a 100 percent vaccination rate: no exceptions and no questions asked. At the beginning of September, the politics of persuasion gave way to an iron fisted approach using the heel of the boot of the State to try to club 100 million unvaccinated Americans into submission. On Sept. 9, 2021, the President of the United States followed the advice of top public health officials and, in effect, declared war on unvaccinated Americans. He scapegoated and placed all the blame for the ongoing COVID-19 pandemic on the unvaccinated, even though federal health officials admit that fully vaccinated people can still get infected and transmit the virus to others; and even though breakthrough COVID infections, hospitalizations and deaths in fully vaccinated people re on the rise; and even though evidence shows individuals who have recovered from the infection have stronger natural immunity than those who have been vaccinated; and even though officials at the World Health Organization now say that the SARS-COV-2 virus is mutating like influenza and is likely to become prevalent in every county - no matter how high the vaccination rate. The President told 100 million unvaccinated Americans that "our patience is running thin" and issued an Executive Order that every person working for the Executive Branch of the federal government – more than two million people - must get fully vaccinated or lose their jobs. That order also applied to about 17 million health care professionals working in medical facilities that accept Medicare and Medicaid. There is no option for Executive Branch employees to get tested - the rule is get vaccinated or be fired. It is interesting that the order does not apply to workers in the Judicial Branch or Legislative Branch, which includes members and staffers in Congress. The President also ordered the Department of Labor to issue a rule that carries penalties of $14,000 per violation to force private companies with more than 100 employees to get their workers fully vaccinated or be tested weekly.

He also called for all teachers and school staff in all schools to be fully vaccinated. The next day, the Director of the National Institute of Allergy and Infectious Diseases, Dr. Anthony Fauci, criticized the President for not going far enough.[105] Fauci said the government should give Americans no option but to get injected with the biological product that some describe as a vaccine, others characterize as a genetic therapy or cell disrupter biological, and others allege is a bioweapon made in a lab in China with U.S. funding. Then Fauci said all children must be vaccinated or denied a school education and all unvaccinated people must be banned from getting on an airplane. At the same time, a Virginia congressman introduced the Safety Travel Act that would require travelers getting on a plane or Amtrak train in the U.S. to show proof of COVID vaccination or a negative COVID test within 72 hours of boarding. Today, people in some cities are being denied entrance to restaurants and stores if they can't prove they have been "fully" vaccinated. Doctors are refusing to provide medical care to the unvaccinated. Hollywood entertainers are celebrating the deaths of unvaccinated people, saying they deserved to die, and are calling for the unvaccinated who get COVID to be denied admission to hospitals for treatment. Judges are separating children from mothers who have not gotten a COVID shot. Influential scientists are insisting lawmakers make it a hate crime for anyone to publicly criticize scientists and government health officials. Dissenters are told they are "selfish" and characterized as an enemy of the state for simply defending the human right to informed consent to medical risk taking. The normalizing of the ritualistic persecution of Americans who are refusing to give up the right to autonomy - which is the first and most fundamental human right - is underway. The Orwellian message is: the life of any person who dissents from government policy must be systematically destroyed. Demanding obedience, government health officials characterize public health policies that segregate, discriminate and turn people against each other as "the good." Yet, a lot of Americans instinctively know segregation and discrimination is not good. They know that persuading a majority of citizens to scapegoat a minority of citizens to cover up the failures of government is allowing evil to triumph. Dissenting Americans, both vaccinated and unvaccinated, fill the ranks of every socio-economic class, every political party and every faith-based community. They understand the meaning of the warning that, "The only thing necessary for triumph of evil is for good men to do nothing," and they are not going to stand by and do nothing. When government threatens to take away an individual's right to employment, education, health care and the ability to enter a store to buy food, enter a hospital or travel on public transportation, there is no other word for it but tyranny. This virus, which has a 99 percent survival rate, and this leaky vaccine, which fails to reliably prevent infection and transmission in the fully vaccinated, has racked up a record breaking more than half a million vaccine adverse event reports in the U.S. alone. It will not be the last virus and vaccine to be weaponized against the people in the name of the greater good. That is because forced vaccination is the tip of the spear in a culture war that has been going on for much longer than the 40 years that I have been a vaccine safety and human rights activist publicly warning that this day would come. It is a war that will cause more suffering until enough of us refuse to be siloed and, instead, join together to change dangerous laws that abuse the trust and good will of the people. Every single American, whether you have been vaccinated or not, should stop to reflect upon what is happening in our country. Think about what liberty means. Imagine what life will be like in the future if you cannot leave your home without being harnessed to a government issued digital ID, which contains personal information about your body and your life, and is hooked up to an electronic surveillance system that records and controls every move you make. Imagine if you are a health care worker and your medical license is taken from you for refusing to get a government mandated vaccine, which is a public health policy being implemented in Washington, DC, a city where doctors can now vaccinate children as young as 11 years old without the knowledge or consent of their parents. Imagine if you cannot hold any type of job or enter a grocery store to buy food to feed your family, or enter a drug store, cafe, gym, school, cinema, museum, park or beach without showing proof you've been vaccinated. Imagine if you are denied entrance to a doctor's office or lose your Medicare and social security benefits because you don't have the vaccine passport, a suggestion made recently on national television. Imagine if you cannot get on a plane or bus to visit your children or elderly parents because federal government officials have exercised authority over inter-state commerce and banned the unvaccinated from crossing state borders, an action that some proponents of forced vaccination are urging the current administration to invoke. Imagine if you cannot get a driver's license, file your taxes, open or access your bank account or use a credit card to make a purchase if you fail to produce the required vaccine paperwork stamped by the government. Imagine if you or your child have already suffered a previous serious vaccine reaction or have an underlying inflammatory immune disorder that increases your risk for being harmed by vaccination, but doctors refuse to see you because you are unvaccinated - which is already happening in America – and you are denied admission to a hospital for a life saving operation. If you think that that the vaccine passport is only about this virus and this vaccine, think again. Forced vaccination was always the end game both before and during this pandemic and the proof of that lies in the decades of federal legislation and federal agency rule making paving the way for what we are experiencing today. Right now, forced vaccination is the quickest means to what the World Economic Forum transparently describes on its website as "The Great Reset." You, your children and grandchildren are the commodity, and in the name of the greater good, you are expected to obediently allow others to "reset" your lives in all kinds of ways without making a sound. The government issued passport allowing you to function in society, is just the first step on the slippery slope to what will be many more requirements and restrictions on your freedom in the days, months and years to come. The question is, will you allow yourself to be used and abused by those currently holding the power to do what they want to do to you, or will you defend your God-given right to life, liberty and the pursuit of happiness? This pandemic of deception and incompetence has stolen from our daily lives the peace and joy we deserve to have, leaving too many of us confused and paralyzed by fear, divided from our family and friends, crippled with anxiety and despair, allowing hopelessness to rule our days. It doesn't have to be like this. We can refuse to be psychologically manipulated so we are unable to engage in rational thinking and are crippled by fear. We can push back against the authoritarians taking away our freedom and trying to divide us. We can do it the way that all successful social reform movements before us have done it: through actively participating in local, state and federal government and by engaging in non-violent civil disobedience, if that becomes necessary.[99]

Dr. Ben Carson told Newsmax TV on Monday that the COVID-19 pandemic has been the "best mechanism government has had for controlling the people ever" and that it's contrary to the founding principles of America. "Interestingly enough, when

---

99. "Forced Vaccination Was Always the End Game" by Barbara Loe Fisher, 9/22/2021; https://www.nvic.org/NVIC-Vaccine-News/September-2021/end-game-forced-vaccination.aspx

you think about the beginnings of our country, people came here so that they could be free, so that they wouldn't have the government's foot on their neck, mandating what they could and could not do," Carson, a retired neurosurgeon, said during an appearance on Newsmax's "National Report." "This COVID situation has been the best mechanism government has had for controlling the people ever and they're very reluctant to let it go." Politico reported Saturday that the Biden administration is expected to extend the COVID-19 public health emergency again, potentially continuing the emergency declaration past the November midterm elections and into next year. "So they're going to continue trying to extend it just as far as people will tolerate, quite frankly, and they're not looking at science at all," Carson said. "Science tells us that viruses tend to attenuate so each iteration of it becomes a little weaker, but it also is more transmittable." Carson added that viral weakening is the reason the U.S. is currently experiencing an uptick in COVID-19 cases but a low number of deaths. "It's a very different disease than what we had in the beginning, and they're not talking about natural immunity," Carson said. "People with natural immunity are doing just fine. They're doing extremely well, better than those who have been vaccinated." The Trump-era Housing and Urban Development secretary said that federal health officials don't want to hear about natural immunity.

"Because if you acknowledge natural immunity, then you can't insistent that everybody be injected," Carson said, referring to COVID-19 vaccine mandates.

When asked about the Biden administration's recent declaration of monkeypox as a health emergency, Carson said the focus of the federal response should be on preventing transmission. "As far as monkeypox is concerned, what we know is that it is mostly transmitted by sexual activity, and 95% of the cases have been in the homosexual community," he said. "Why are we not looking at the way that it's transmitted now and coming up with ways to deal with that?"[100]

The World Health Organization (WHO) is responding to a string of monkeypox outbreaks, and will be convening an emergency meeting on the virus and its global spread. In terms of government power, the timing of this outbreak couldn't be better for the WHO—which may soon be granted powers to manage laws on global health outbreaks, and which is oddly well-positioned for a monkeypox outbreak following a recent "germ-games" call, and recent incidents tied to figures who include Microsoft billionaire Bill Gates. The New York Post declared, "The World Health Organization is reportedly convening an emergency meeting into the alarming spread of monkeypox around the world—including a possible case in the Big Apple." The Telegraph reports that the United Nations health authority will be bringing together "a group of leading experts" in the meeting, which is believed to be focused on how the virus is suddenly spreading so widely. It also allegedly will look into

---

100. "Dr. Ben Carson to Newsmax: COVID 'Best Mechanism' for Govt Control" By Nicole Wells; 8/8/2022

the virus's prevalence among homosexual men and on the "vaccination situation." The numbers of infections are by no means high. By May 23, the University of Oxford and Harvard Medical School recorded 245 either confirmed or suspected cases in the entire world. Sajid Javid, the UK health secretary, wrote on Twitter: "Most cases are mild ..." The timing of all of this is important. It gives the WHO a chance to show its worth, since it's in the process of trying to get new and expansive powers—under the banner of governing global health emergencies. The United Nations is considering various amendments to the WHO at its 75th World Health Assembly in Geneva, that could give its director-general, Tedros Adhanom Ghebreyesus, the unilateral authority to declare a public health emergency with far-reaching powers over the laws of sovereign nations. Not only would this give Tedros the ability to declare a public health emergency in any nation he wants—using whatever evidence he wants— but it would also allow him to dictate policies that the target country should adopt to respond to the U.N.'s declared emergency. If a country refuses, a proposed amendment could give the WHO the ability to sanction that country. If you're wondering whether giving such powers to a U.N. agency that couldn't demonstrate its independence from the Chinese Communist Party (CCP) could fly in the face of U.S. law, it seems that President Joe Biden has the answer. Not only is the Biden administration allowing this shift in power to the WHO, but it's also helping advance it. The United States proposed amendments to the WHO in January, which will be considered at the U.N. meeting in Geneva, The Epoch Times reports. These included an amendment that would allow the WHO to make public declarations on a health crisis without needing to consult with the target country, and without needing to get verification from local officials. The Biden administration's proposals would also give $2.47 billion in funding to the Centers for Disease Control and Prevention (CDC) for things including "enhancements to domestic sentinel surveillance programs," "investments in global genomic surveillance approaches," and other systems. ("Monkeypox 'Games' Could Lay Groundwork for WHO Pandemic Response Takeover" by Joshua Philipp; The Epoch Times, May 24, 2022)

Two retired U.S. generals, MG Paul Vallely, U.S. Army, and Thomas McInerney, USAF, raised concerns over the World Health Organization's recent declaration of monkeypox as a global health emergency, alleging potential ulterior motives. "Each of us should not be alarmed by this alert as the credibility of WHO is in great question based on their actions and notices on COVID-19," Vallely told The Epoch Times. "The rare designation means the WHO now views the outbreak as a significant enough threat to global health that a coordinated international response is needed to prevent the virus from spreading further and potentially escalating into a pandemic," Vallely said. "Beware of this politically driven global organization that is funded by the global elite...WHO Director Tedros is not a medical doctor, he is a Marxist from Ethiopia, totally supported by the Chinese Communist Party. He lied about C-19 from the beginning to cover for China," Vallely added.[101]

The United States has declared monkeypox a public health emergency, the health secretary said Thursday, a move expected to free up additional funding and tools to fight the disease. The declaration comes as the tally of cases crossed 6,600 in the United States on Wednesday, almost all of them among men who have sex with men. "We're prepared to take our response to the next level in addressing this virus, and we urge every American to take monkeypox seriously," Health and Human Services Secretary Xavier Becerra said at a briefing. The declaration will also help improve the availability of monkeypox data, U.S. Centers for Disease Control and Prevention Director Rochelle Walensky said, speaking alongside Bacerra. The World Health Organization has also dubbed monkeypox a "public health emergency of international concern," its highest alert level. The WHO declaration last month was designed to trigger a coordinated international response and could unlock funding to collaborate on vaccines and treatments... Anthony Fauci, Biden's chief medical adviser, told Reuters on Thursday that it was critical to engage leaders from the gay community as part of efforts to rein in the outbreak, but cautioned against stigmatizing the lifestyle...The first U.S. case of

---

101. "'They Are Right on Our Predicted Schedule': Retired US Generals Issue Warning About New Pandemic Declaration" by Enrico Trigoso; The Epoch Times, 7/28/2022

monkeypox was confirmed in Massachusetts in May, followed by another case in California five days later.[102]

Harvey Risch, Emeritus Professor of Epidemiology at Yale University, said that monkeypox is not a risk to the wider population, since it is largely confined within particular communities. "It is spreading globally, but... it's not a risk to people as a whole," he explained. "Just like COVID was really only a risk for elderly people or people with high-risk comorbidities like obesity, diabetes, cardiovascular disease, chronic kidney disease, and so on. But for everybody else, it was a discomfort and could be really unpleasant, but not life-threatening."...Monkeypox is related to smallpox, a disease with a 30% case fatality rate. However, Risch said that monkeypox is a much milder illness. "Monkeypox is similar to smallpox," he explained. "However, it is a much milder, less aggressive form of infection than smallpox, although there is some overlap. That is why smallpox vaccines even have some benefit against monkeypox." The current strain of monkeypox, which is believed to have originated from West Africa, has a case fatality rate of 1%, which is like that of COVID. However, monkeypox is far less infectious than coronaviruses.

[Monkeypox] is not spread through casual contact, it's not spread through the air generally," said Risch. "[The CDC] says it takes prolonged face-to-face contact

---

102. "Biden WH Declares Monkeypox Outbreak a Public Health Emergency", 8/4/2022 - https://www.newsmax.com/health/health-news/monkeypox-public-health-emergency-us/2022/08/04/id/1081782/

in order to spread it, which means casual conversation is not enough... [What is needed] is contact with infected materials." Although a vaccine exists for monkeypox, Risch said that it should not be made mandatory. "First of all, the smallpox vaccine has overlapping effectiveness against monkeypox...Second, most people of older ages were vaccinated against smallpox, at least in North America. And thirdly, there are medications like TPoxx that treat monkeypox pretty effectively. There are two or three others as well." When asked whether he thought lockdowns for monkeypox would come, Risch responded, "I would hope not. I think it would be disruptive and foolish and against scientific evidence to do things like that. Those measures were counterproductive in the first place with COVID, and they will be doubly so with monkeypox."[103]

In an effort to fight monkeypox, the Centers for Disease Control and Prevention updated its guidelines on Friday, recommending people limit their sexual partners.

The agency excluded any specific direction toward same-sex partners despite nearly 98% of cases occurring in homosexual men, according to CDC data from last month. "Spaces like back rooms, saunas, sex clubs, or private and public sex parties, where intimate, often anonymous sexual contact with multiple partners occurs — are more likely to spread monkeypox," the

---

103. Risch spoke with David Lin, Anchor and Producer at Kitco News on 8/4/2020: https://www.kitco.com/news/2022-08-04/Monkeypox-is-not-a-general-risk-to-people-Lockdowns-to-contain-the-virus-would-be-foolish-and-disruptive-Harvey-Risch.html

agency wrote.[104] Note this from Wikipedia: "The global pandemic of HIV/AIDS that began in 1981 <u>is still an ongoing worldwide public health issue</u>. According to the World Health Organization, as of 2021, HIV/AIDS has killed approximately 40.1 million people, and approximately 38.4 million people are infected with HIV globally."

The *National Biotechnology and Biomanufacturing Initiative* was created by President Biden's Executive Order on September 12, 2022. It virtually guarantees that transhumanism and genetic manipulation of citizens will be the main topic of the 2024 election cycle.

The EO is tectonic in that it aligns and mandates all agencies "to coordinate a whole-of-government approach to advance biotechnology and biomanufacturing… to help us achieve our societal goals."…The real goal is in the introduction to the EO…: "We need to develop genetic engineering technologies and techniques to be able to write circuitry for cells and predictably program biology in the same way in which we write software and program computers; unlock the power of biological data, including through computing tools and artificial intelligence; and advance the science of scale-up production while reducing the obstacles for commercialization so that innovative technologies and products can reach markets faster."…Federal investment is specified to flood into "key research and development areas of biotechnology and biomanufacturing."…In sum,

---

104. "CDC Recommends Limiting Sex Partners to Avoid Monkeypox" by Luca Cacciatore; 8/5/2022 (newsmax.com/newsfront/cdc-monkeypox-virus/2022/08/05/id/ 1081988/)

Biden's *National Biotechnology and Biomanufacturing Initiative* is a complete capitulation of our government to Big Pharma, the biotechnology industry and the entire transhuman cabal that wants to create Humanity 2.0 by changing our genetic structure. Unfortunately, this is nothing more than a continuation and expansion of the eugenics movement from the 1930s and it should be recognized as such before tossing it back into the flames of hades where it belongs.[105]

2] MARXISM

"Communism sentences morality to death and attempts to have the communist New Man establish a fake revolutionary morality... Traditional laws come from morality and are intended to uphold it. Communism tries to separate morality from the law, then destroy morality by concocting malicious new laws...THE DIVINE CALLS UPON MAN TO BE KIND; COMMUNISM INCITES CLASS STRUGGLE AND ADVOCATES VIOLENCE AND KILLING."[106]

Can the communist elites be trusted?

China's carbon emissions are vast and growing, dwarfing those of other countries. Experts agree that without big reductions in China's emissions, the world cannot win the fight against climate change. In 2020, China's President Xi Jinping said his country would aim for its

---

105. Posted by Patrick Wood 9/14/2022; Technocracy News
106. The Epoch Times, 2/2/2022; page A19

emissions to reach their highest point before 2030 and for carbon neutrality before 2060. His statement has now been confirmed as China's official position ahead of the COP26 global climate summit in Glasgow. But China has not said exactly how these goals will be achieved.[107]

In the 1944 film "Gaslight" the husband attempts to convince his wife and others that she is insane by manipulating small elements of their environment and insisting that she is mistaken, remembering things incorrectly, or delusional when she points out these changes. The film's title alludes to the abusive husband's incrementally over time dimming the gas lights in their home while pretending that nothing had been changing, a cruel effort to make his wife doubt her own perceptions; the wife repeatedly asks her husband to confirm her perceptions about the dimming lights but he keeps insisting that the lights are the same, leading her into thinking she is going insane.

Today's US culture has become bombarded by satanic techniques: _deception_, which seeks to alter one's cognizance; _propagandizing_, comprised of a thought, phrase or dictum expressed so continuously enough orally or by written word that the audience accepts it without resistance; and _gaslighting_, the psychological abuse aimed at controlling a person by altering reality to the point where that person will doubt his/her own sanity. Unfortunately, we have become so subjected to the media's perpetual employment of gaslighting in

---

107. "Why China's climate policy matters to us all" by David Brown, 10/29/2021; https://www.bbc.com/news/world-asia-china-57483492

order to mentally reorient us into accepting 'what was once good is now bad and what was once illegal is now legal.' The reality we are being told by the media is at complete odds with what we are seeing with our own eyes. When we question the false reality to which we are being subjected or we claim that what we see is an actual reality, we become vilified and called racists or bigots or just plain crazy. Though in reality we know we are not racists or insane, we have become abusively subjected to gaslighting. A perfect example is the demonizing of 2020 election deniers executed by those who had actually rigged that event.

New York State has twice as many deaths from Covid-19 than any other state, and New York has accounted for one fifth of all Covid-19 deaths, but we are told that New York Governor Andrew Cuomo has handled the pandemic better than any other governor. But if we support policies of Governors whose states had only a fraction of the infections and deaths as New York, we're called anti-science and want people to die. So, we ask ourselves, am I crazy? No, we are being gaslighted.

We see mobs of people looting stores, smashing windows, setting cars on fire and burning down buildings, but we are told that these demonstrations are peaceful So, we ask ourselves, are we crazy? No, we are being gaslighted.

We see the major problem destroying many inner-cities is crime; murder, gang violence, drug dealing, drive-by shootings, armed robbery, but we are told that it is not crime, but the police that are the problem in the inner-cities. We are told we must defund the police and remove law enforcement from crime-riddled cities to make them safer but if we advocate for more policing in cities overrun by crime, we are accused of being white supremacists and racists. So, we ask ourselves, are we crazy? No, we are being gaslighted.

The United States of America accepts more immigrants than any other country in the world. The vast majority of the immigrants are "people of color", and these immigrants are enjoying freedom and economic opportunity not available to them in their country of origin, but we are told that the United States is the most racist and oppressive country on the planet, and if we disagree, we are called racist and xenophobic. So, we ask ourselves, are we crazy? No, we are being gaslighted.

Capitalist countries are the most prosperous countries in the world. The standard of living is the highest in capitalist countries. We see more poor people move up the economic ladder to the middle and even the wealthy class through their effort and ability in capitalist countries than any other economic system in the world, but we are told capitalism is an oppressive system designed to keep people down. So, we ask ourselves, are we crazy? No, we're being gaslighted.

Communist countries killed over 100 million people in the 20th century. Communist countries strip their citizens of basic human rights, dictate every aspect of their lives, treat their citizens as slaves, and drive their economies into the ground, but we are told that Communism is the fairest, most equitable, freest, and most prosperous economic system in the world. So, we ask ourselves, are we crazy? No, we are being gaslighted.

The most egregious example of gaslighting is the concept of 'white fragility.' You have spent your life trying to be a good person, trying to treat people fairly and with respect, disavowing racism and bigotry in all its forms, judging people solely on the content of their character and not by the color of their skin, not discriminating based on race or ethnicity. But you are told you are a racist, not because of something you did or said but solely because of the color of your skin. You know instinctively that charging someone with racism because of their skin color is itself racist. While you know that you are not a racist and try to defend yourself as such, you are informed that your self-defense is proof of your racism. In exasperation you ask yourself, am I crazy? No, you're being gaslighted.

Gaslighting has become one of the most pervasive and destructive tactics in American politics. It is the exact opposite of what our political system was meant to be. It deals in lies and psychological coercion, and not the truth and intellectual discourse. Should you ever ask yourself if you're crazy, you are not inasmuch as insane people are not mentally enabled to ask themselves if they're crazy. So, trust yourself, believe what's in your heart. Trust your eyes over what you are told. Never listen to the people who tell you that you are crazy, because you are not, you're being gaslighted. And that's what the media are trying to exploit. (https://conventionofstates.com/news/gaslighting)

Here are a few examples:
After the jury had voted 12-1 that Kyle Rittenhouse had acted in self-defence and thus was innocent of fatally

shooting two rioters in the 2020 Kinosha, Wisconsin riot, cable network MSNBC host Joy Reid on November 19, 2021 warned her audience to watch out for "male white tears," referring to the defendant's emotional collapse in court when learning of his innocence. She then seriously added: "You who support Black Lives Matter should be afraid." Her racist tirade presupposed that Kyle's two victims were black even though in court they were certified by videos to be white. To pour gasoline on the fire, presidential candidate Joe Biden had publicly called Kyle a "white supremacist" in 2020 and then on November 19, 2021 said he was angry and concerned but would abide by the jury's verdict. Racism is the progressive radicals' rallying cry in seeking to revolutionize the citizenry and transform the Constitutional democracy which historically had erected the foundation for the United States of America. The gaslighting in both instances was misrepresenting implicitly the victims' skin color.

"...in August 2019...the New York Times...published its 1619 Project, a revisionist history that argues that the nation's true founding was when the first enslaved Africans were brought to the country in 1619. {The project's founder} asserted without evidence that the Revolutionary War was actually fought to preserve slavery...The New York Times stood by the error-riddled, and even pushed out a curriculum for schools based on it. The 1619 Project won a Pulitzer Prize in 2020."[108]

---

108. Rigged, Mollie Hemmingway, Regnery Publishing, 2021, pages 117-118

Leaders of the {NYC's} Black Lives Movement... threatened "riots" and "bloodshed" in the streets if Mayor-elect Eric Adams reverses the abolition of the NYPD's controversial anti-crime units..."There will be riots, there will be fire and there will be bloodshed because we believe in defending our people," said Hawk Newsome, co-founder of a group known as Black Lives of Greater New York, after a heated meeting with Adams. (Chris Sommerfeldt, New York Daily News, November 10, 2021)

FBI director Christopher Wray had...told Congress in September {2020} that Antifa is "not a group or organization. It's a movement or an ideology."...There are regional chapters of Antifa and Antifa organizations that have websites. Antifa's political, moral, and legal claims to violence define it as a terrorist group...its "leaderless resistance" tactics, this...phantom cell structure makes it similar to how more commonly understood terrorist groups, such as al-Qaeda, commonly operate...During protests, members of Antifa carry weapons and coordinate their actions in order to evade law enforcement...Antifa spent much of {2020} sharing tactical intelligence to help rioters do maximum damage.[109]

"When George Floyd was killed resisting arrest {on May 25, 2022}, extremist groups such as Black Lives Matter sprang into action to help coordinate more than 10,330 demonstrations across more than 2,730 locations in all 50 states, plus the District of Columbia, through the latter part of 2020...At least twenty-five Americans

---

109. Rigged, Mollie Hemmingway, Regnery Publishing, 2021, page 136

were killed in the riots, which cost insurers more than $2 billion, but the media relentlessly referred to them as 'peaceful' or 'mostly peaceful...Most major media did not care about or cover those killed in the violence. It was at odds with their 'mostly peaceful' narrative. It was part of a plan."[110]

New York Times op-eds headlined, "Yes, We Mean literally Abolish the Police," demanding readers text their family members and tell them they wouldn't visit or speak to them until they make financial contributions to support "black lives"...[111]

While the media openly supported the mass BLM protests that were being held across the nation, they strongly opposed Trump's plan {to hold a massive rally in Tulsa, Oklahoma} and said it would be bad for public health.[112]

On October 14 {2020}, a raft of information about Biden family business dealings with China and Ukraine became public, albeit heavily suppressed by media and tech companies.[113]

More than 50 former intelligence officials signed a letter casting doubt on the provenance of a New York Post story on the former vice president's son. More than 50 former senior intelligence officials have signed on to a letter outlining their belief that the recent disclosure of emails allegedly belonging to Joe Biden's son "has all the

---

110. Rigged, Mollie Hemmingway, Regnery Publishing, 2021, pages 118-119
111. Rigged, Mollie Hemmingway, Regnery Publishing, 2021, page 135
112. Rigged, Mollie Hemmingway, Regnery Publishing, 2021, page 143
113. Rigged, Mollie Hemmingway, Regnery Publishing, 2021, page 188

classic earmarks of a Russian information operation." The letter, signed on Monday, centers around a batch of documents released by the New York Post last week that purport to tie the Democratic nominee to his son Hunter's business dealings. Under the banner headline "Biden Secret E-mails," the Post reported it was given a copy of Hunter Biden's laptop hard drive by President Donald Trump's personal lawyer Rudy Giuliani, who said he got it from a Mac shop owner in Delaware who also alerted the FBI.[114]

But then:

House Republicans on the Judiciary Committee sent out letters Wednesday demanding answers from the 51 former intelligence officials who claimed reports of emails from Hunter Biden's laptop detailing influence-peddling before the 2020 presidential election were Russian disinformation. Republicans are looking for responses from the former intel officials who dismissed the contents of a laptop belonging to Hunter Biden almost two years ago. More media outlets, including *The Washington Post* and *The New York Times*, have authenticated the younger Biden's emails, prompting the GOP to prepare for hearings if they capture the majority in November. In their letter to the former intel officials, the GOP lawmakers write, "The concerted effort to suppress public dissemination of the serious allegations about Hunter Biden and the Biden family, as first reported

---

114. Hunter Biden Story is Russian Disinfo, Dozens of Former Intel Officials Say" by Natasha Bertrand; https://www.politico.com/news/2020/10/19/hunter-biden-story-russian-disinfo-430276

in October 2020 by the New York Post, was a grave disservice to American citizens' informed participation in our democracy." They add, "We are investigating the role that the public statement played in this effort." All letter signers are asked to provide the names of all people they communicated with about the inception, drafting, editing, signing, publishing, or promotion of the "Public Statement on the Hunter Biden Emails."[115]

And yet the censoring continues:[116]

Over the past year, I've been researching and writing as much as I can to help you take control of your health, as fearmongering media and corrupt politicians have destroyed lives and livelihoods to establish global control of the world's population, using the COVID-19 pandemic as their justification.

Through it all, I have refused to succumb to these relentless attacks. I have been confident and willing to defend myself in the court of law.

Unfortunately, threats have now become very personal and have intensified to the point I can no longer preserve much of the information and research I've provided to you thus far. So, effective immediately, much of the information on my website will be permanently removed.

I've also kept you informed about billionaire-backed front groups like the Center for Science in the Public

---

115. "GOP seeks answers from 51 former intel officials who discredited Hunter Biden's laptop" by Kerry Picket; The Washington Times - 4/6/2022

116. Why I'm Removing {from my website} All Articles Related to Vitamins D, C, Zinc and COVID-19 by Dr. Joseph Mercola

Interest (CSPI), a partner of Bill Gates' Alliance for Science, both of whom have led campaigns aimed at destroying my reputation and censoring the information I share. Well-Organized Attack Partnerships Have Formed.

Other attackers include HealthGuard, which ranks health sites based on a certain set of "credibility criteria." It has sought to discredit my website by ensuring warnings appear whenever you search for my articles or enter my website in an internet browser. HealthGuard, a niche service of NewsGuard, is funded by the pharma-funded public relations company Publicis Groupe. Publicis, in turn, is a partner of the World Economic Forum, which is leading the call for a "Great Reset" of the global economy and a complete overhaul of our way of life.

HealthGuard is also partnered with Gates' Microsoft company, and drug advertising websites like WebMD and Medscape, as well as the Center for Countering Digital Hate (CCDH) — the progressive cancel-culture leader with extensive ties to government and global think tanks that recently labeled people questioning the COVID-19 vaccine as a national security threat.

The CCDH has published a hit list naming me as one of the top 12 individuals responsible for 65% of vaccine "disinformation" on social media, and who therefore must be deplatformed and silenced for the public good. In a March 24, 2021, letter to the CEO's of Twitter and Facebook, 12 state attorneys general called for the removal of our accounts from these platforms, based on the CCDH's report.

Two of those state attorneys general also published an April 8, 2021, op-ed in The Washington Post, calling on Facebook and Twitter to ban the "anti-vaxxers" identified by the CCDH. The lack of acceptance of novel gene therapy technology, they claim, is all because a small group of individuals with a social media presence — myself included — are successfully misleading the public with lies about nonexistent vaccine risks.

"The solution is not complicated. It's time for Facebook CEO Mark Zuckerberg and Twitter CEO Jack Dorsey to turn off this toxic tap and completely remove the small handful of individuals spreading this fraudulent misinformation," they wrote.

Pharma-funded politicians and pharma-captured health agencies have also relentlessly attacked me and pressured tech monopolies to censor and deplatform me, removing my ability to express my opinions and speak freely over the past year.

The CCDH also somehow has been allowed to publish in the journal Nature Medicine, calling for the "dismantling" of the "anti-vaccine" industry. In the article, CCDH founder Imran Ahmed repeats the lie that he "attended and recorded a private, three-day meeting of the world's most prominent anti-vaxxers," when, in fact, what he's referring to was a public online conference open to an international audience, all of whom had access to the recordings as part of their attendance fee.

The CCDH is also partnered with another obscure group called Anti-Vax Watch. The picture below is from an Anti-Vax Watch demonstration outside the halls of Congress. Ironically, while the CCDH claims to be anti-extremism, you'd be hard-pressed to find a clearer example of actual extremism than this bizarre duo.

Saul D. Alinsky, a community activist since 1939, wrote Rules for Radicals: A Pragmatic Primer for Realistic Radicals in 1971 to instruct current and new generations of radicals how to unite and transform low-income communities into social, political, legal and economic entities. His ten chapters include issues that range from ethics, education, communication and political philosophy. Though published for the new generation of counterculture-era organizers in 1971, Alinsky's principles have been applied by numerous government, labor, community, and congregation-based organizations, and the main themes of his organizational methods have been recurring elements in political campaigns in recent years.

In 1966, Columbia University sociologists Richard Cloward and his wife Frances Piven wrote an article about the need for "cadres of aggressive organizers" to spark "demonstrations to create a climate of militancy" in cities throughout the country. The plan was to disrupt law and order so thoroughly that America's politicians would impose a socialist economic system to quell the violence. (They) were explicit about exploiting racial tension to incite mass protests.[117]

The 'brainwashing' process communists had practiced prior to WW2 has now been benignly rebranded as 're-education':

> Russia has unveiled plans to retrain thousands of teachers from areas of Ukraine that have fallen

---

117. Rigged, Mollie Hemmingway, Regnery Publishing, 2021, pages 137-138

under its control...some 20,000 teachers from the Kherson and Zaporizhizhia regions in southern Ukraine would undergo retraining...so as to start the new school year in September {2022} under the Russian education system... Ukraine's ombudsman for human rights...said Russia aims to use education to implement a policy of destroying Ukrainians' national identity.[118]

Sayragul Sauytbay, a Chinese doctor, elementary school administrator and teacher in Kazakhstan and a very brave Muslim whistleblower for the Kazakh Chinese people, has modernized the name for this cruel process. She knew well about that system because she had escaped China's internment/reeducation system in 2018 and thereby became one of the first victims in the world to speak publicly about the Chinese repressive campaign against Muslims. She received political asylum from Sweden and emigrated there because Kazakhstan, her native country in which she is still hailed as a heroine, refused her asylum because of China's repressive strangle-hold on it:

> "Even more frightening than the coronavirus itself is the fascist Chinese 'virus of the mind' that has developed in the laboratory of East Turkestan and spread to all corners of the globe. Those infected do not realize that freedom, peace, and human rights are under threat all across the world. And that Beijing wants to use the much propagandized 'Chinese model' to prove the superiority of dictatorship over

---

118. The Wall Street Journal, 5/28-29/2022

> democracy...China's 'virus of the mind will never stop attacking the free world...the CCP and the government in Beijing threaten not just the Chinese but every citizen on Earth. This 'virus' is far more dangerous tha(n) COVID-19. It is hell."[119]

Ms. Sauytbay's two-year incarceration also has provided her insights into what the world's future might come to:

> Beijing is stealthily gaining a foothold in many parts of the world, overwhelming the market with cheap products and offering generous loans. The long-term goal of the government is to gain monopolies and establish a new world order. Once they've done so, the CCP – and only the CCP – will dictate the rules...The mass internments in East Turkestan are proof that the government in Beijing has no qualms about brutally destroying those who stand in {its} way. (pgs. 204,296-297)

Is *Bolshevism* gaining a foothold within the US culture?

> **Former President Donald J. Trump:**
> "These are dark times for our Nation, as my beautiful home, Mar-A-Lago in Palm Beach, Florida, is currently under siege, raided, and occupied by a large group of FBI agents. Nothing like this has ever happened to a President of the United States before. After working and cooperating with the relevant Government agencies, this unannounced raid on my home was not necessary or appropriate. It is prosecutorial misconduct, the weaponization of the Justice System, and an attack

---

119. The Chief Witness, Sayragul Sauytbay and Aleaxndra Cavlius, Scribe Publications, Minnneapolis, MN; 2021, page 289

by Radical Left Democrats who desperately don't want me to run for President in 2024, especially based on recent polls, and who will likewise do anything to stop Republicans and Conservatives in the upcoming Midterm Elections. Such an assault could only take place in broken, Third-World Countries. Sadly, America has now become one of those Countries, corrupt at a level not seen before. They even broke into my safe! What is the difference between this and Watergate, where operatives broke into the Democrat National Committee? Here, in reverse, Democrats broke into the home of the 45th President of the United States. The political persecution of President Donald J. Trump has been going on for years, with the now fully debunked Russia, Russia, Russia Scam, Impeachment Hoax #1, Impeachment Hoax #2, and so much more, it just never ends. It is political targeting at the highest level! Hillary Clinton was allowed to delete and acid wash 33,000 E-mails AFTER they were subpoenaed by Congress. Absolutely nothing has happened to hold her accountable. She even took antique furniture, and other items from the White House. I stood up to America's bureaucratic corruption, I restored power to the people, and truly delivered for our Country, like we have never seen before. The establishment hated it. Now, as they watch my endorsed candidates win big victories, and see my dominance in all polls, they are trying to stop me, and the Republican Party, once more. The lawlessness, political persecution, and Witch Hunt must be exposed and stopped. I will continue to fight for the Great American People!" The U.S. Justice Department decline to comment...One such strongly worded criticism came from Florida Gov. Ron DeSantis: "The raid of MAL is another escalation in the weaponization of federal agencies against the Regime's political opponents, while people like Hunter Biden get treated with kid gloves. Now the Regime is getting another 87k IRS agents to wield against its adversaries? Banana Republic." "I've seen enough," House Minority Leader Kevin McCarthy said in a statement. "The Department of Justice has reached an intolerable state of weaponized politicization." [120]

"The FBI is beyond redemption.[121]

The Justice Department is unleashing political furies it can't control and may not understand...the political and media pressure is intense on Attorney General Merrick Garland to indict Mr. Trump. The FBI search may be a fishing expedition to find evidence related to Jan. 6...The FBI search on Mr. Trump suggests that Mr. Garland may be committed to pursuing and indicting Mr. Trump. If so, he is taking the country on a perilous road. There is much ruin in a nation, but no one should want to test the limits of that ruin in America.[122]

Another trait of Marxism is the official denial of an actual event's significance: the Biden administration declared that the first half of the 2022 US economy was not in a recession, historically defined as the fall in

---

120. "'Dark Times': Trump Slams FBI Raid at His Mar-a-Lago Home as a Political Assault" by Jack Gournell, 8/8/2022; newsmax.com
121. Victor Davis Hansen on Fox News' "Tucker Carlson Tonight" 8/9/2022 edition
122. "The FBI's Dangerous Trump Search", The Wall Street Journal, 8/10/2022 editorial; page A16

GDP (the official formulation of economic activity) in two or more successive quarters, in spite of the published government data indicating the economy had contracted for a second consecutive quarter. And then here is this trait:

> At every point, the media and their Big Tech allies deliberately controlled the information the surrounding a major political corruption story {about Hunter Biden's and his family's dealings with China, Ukraine, Russian oligarchs, etc.} They withheld information on this corruption by any means necessary, eventually resorting to censorship and publishing disinformation in order to help Joe Biden win an election...Twitter's approach was even more draconian – the site simply made it impossible to post a link to the New York Post story {on Hunter and Joe Biden.}[123]
>
> Now comes hard evidence that Twitter booted blogger Alex Berenson after White House officials privately complained about him to Twitter employees. Mr. Berenson has been a vocal critic of government lockdowns, masks mandates and mRNA vaccine benefits... Twitter's censors and Biden Administration officials...have sought to silence public discussion about Covid vaccines and masks. Last July President Biden publicly blamed social media companies for "killing people" by not removing content that encouraged vaccine hesitancy. Hours after Mr. Biden's comment, Twitter locked Mr. Berenson's account. The

---

123. Rigged, Mollie Hemmingway, Regnery Publishing, 2021, pages 227, 243-247

next month Twitter permanently banned Mr. Berenson after he tweeted that mRNA vaccines don't "stop infection. Think of it – at best -- as a therapeutic with a limited window of efficacy and terrible side effect profile... Twitter acknowledged it erred in banning Mr. Berenson and agreed to restore his account... conversations from an internal Twitter Slack channel show that White House officials...met with its employees in April 2021 and targeted Mr. Berenson...[White House Covid adviser] Andy Slavitt suggested they had seen data viz that had showed he was the epicenter of disinfo that radiated outwards to the persuadable public. Twitter didn't ban Mr. Berenson until August, but its employees were clearly under White House pressure to do so.[124]

The Rev. Franklin Graham, president of Samaritan's Purse, {said} the United States is entering a "very frightening" time after recent events and needs to find God again... the FBI search of former President Donald Trump's Mar-a-Lago residence and a proposal by congressional Democrats to double the IRS' staff...the FBI and Department of Justice leaders were to blame for the search of Trump's Palm Beach home on Monday...During the Obama administration, because I was not supportive of their policies, we got audited at the Billy Graham Evangelistic Association...the next day Samaritan's Purse was notified, and we were audited...They will use the IRS to go after people that don't support {our} agenda...I think you see when they're going to be armed and

---

124. "Biden and Twitter Censorship", The Wall Street Journal, 8/13-14/2022, page A14

things like this. This is very frightening — and we're really going to turn into what we saw in communist countries...If we're willing to repent and turn from our sins and put our faith in Christ, God will forgive our sins..." But we as a nation are in trouble, and we're getting probably what we deserve."[125]

3] WOKISM

Moderate voices on the left, fearful that the current cultural revolution has/will devolve into tyranny where opposing voices are forcibly silenced... express concern that "{t}he free exchange of information and ideas, the lifeblood of a liberal society, is daily becoming more constricted...cancel culture {is} the term which bigots, having been called out due to their hate and plain ignorance, usually use as their defense in order to frame themselves as victims of "political correctness"... {moderates fear their woke} cultural revolutionaries} are giving the right ammunition to criticize the central tenets of the revolution with which they agree: "The way to defeat bad ideas is by exposure, argument, and persuasion, not by trying to silence or wish them away." [126]

Wokeness/wokeism, i.e., the state of being woke {the respective adjective}, "is one of the greatest threats to

---

125. "Rev. Graham to Newsmax: US in Trouble After Trump Search, Proposed IRS Growth" By Luca Cacciatore, https://www.newsmax.com/newsmax-tv/newsmaxtv-franklingraham-irs/2022/08/11/id/1082785/

126. "Moderates on the Left try to thwart a new 'reign of terror' of its own making" by William Watkins, 7/13/2020, catalyst.independent.org

modern civilization...it is humorless, condescending, hateful, divisive, exclusionary...it gives a mean person a shield to be mean and cruel armored in false virtue... Do we want a humorless civilization that is at its best divisive, exclusionary and hateful?...(it's) rife with condemnation and hate basically..."[127]

Meritocracy historically came into existence as the opposite of hereditary aristocracy, in which one's social position is determined by the lottery of birth. It is a social system in which advancement in society is based on the individual's capabilities and merits {quality of being particularly good or worthy} rather than on the basis of family, wealth, or social. But in recent years evolving Marxism has sought to replace meritocracy with DEI, the universally imposed 'non-racial' practice of diversity, equity, inclusion to be employed when every society member is considered for an income pursuit. Unfortunately, the adjective "non-racial" presupposes inclusion of only those white people who first publicly apologize for being white. In good faith I refuse to ask anyone to forgive me because God has made my skin color white. That is both absurd as well an affront to Him for in doing so I would be directly convicting Him of having made an error when He had formed my soul and body within my birthing mother's womb!

The medical profession has succumbed to the notion that it is plagued by "systemic racism." Those pushing this idea are making a large bet with potentially lethal consequences. Public and private research funding is

---

127. Elon Musk on "Tucker Carlson Tonight"; 4/4/2022

being redirected from basic science to political projects aimed at "dismantling white supremacy" in medicine. The result will be declining quality of medical care and slowing scientific progress. Virtually every medical organization...has embraced the idea that medicine is shot through with racism and inequality. The AMA's 2021 Organizational Strategic Plan to Embed Racial Justice and Advance Health Equity is a thicket of social-justice nostrums: {"}Physicians must confront inequities and dismantle white supremacy, racism, and other forms of exclusion and structured oppression, as well as embed racial justice and advance within and across all aspects of health systems."...The AMA strategic plan calls for the "just representation of Black, Indigenous and Latinx people in medical school admissions as well as...leadership ranks." The lack of "just representation," according to the AMA, is the result of deliberate "exclusion," which will end only when "we... prioritize and integrate the voices and ideas of people and communities experiencing great injustice and historically excluded, exploited, and deprived of needed resources such as people of color, women, people with disabilities, LG-BTQ+, and those in rural and urban communities alike."...Courses on racial justice and advocacy are flooding into medical school curricula; students are learning more about white privilege and less about cell pathology...A physician-scientist reports that his best lab technician...was a recent Yale graduate with a bachelor's degree in molecular biology and biochemistry. The former student was intellectually involved and an expert in cloning. His college grade-point advantage and Medical College Admissions Test scores were high. The physician-scientist recommended the student to the then-dean of Northwestern's medical school at the time but the student didn't get an interview. This "white, clean-cut Catholic," in the words of his former employer, was admitted to only one medical school...The scientific method is a natural corrective {but}...when it comes to the dubious hypothesis that racism is the defining trait of the medical profession and the source of health disparities, opposing views have been rules out of bounds. Political neutrality, essential to the scientific method, is a racist dodge that risks "reinforcing existing power structures," according to the editor of Health Affairs. The guardians of science have turned on science itself.[128]

The woke culture seeks to demonize all white people:
The "woke" revolution in the west was supposed to teach us that the "white male"-dominated Western world is toxic. Its origins, ascendence, and current leisure and affluence were supposedly due only to systemic exploitation, racism, and sexism. Elites introduced cancel culture, doxing, deplatforming, and social ostracism to shame these supposed exploiters and to destroy their lives and careers.[129]

Stakeholder capitalism requires not only corporate responses to pandemics and ecological issues such as

---

128. "Woke Medical Organizations Are Hazardous to Your Health" by Heather MacDonald; The Wall Street Journal, 8/6-7/2022, page A15
129. "The 'Real Reset' Is Coming" by Victor Davis Hanson; The Epoch Times, 3/30/2022, page A13

climate change, but also rethinking [corporations'] commitments to already-vulnerable communities within their ecosystems." This is the "social justice" aspect of the Great Reset. To comply with that, governments, banks, and asset managers use the Environmental, Social, and Governance (ESG) index to squeeze non-woke corporations and businesses out of the market...One of the functions of woke ideology is to make the majority in developed countries feel guilty about their wealth, which the elites aim to reset downwards – except, one notices, for the elites themselves, who need to be rich in order to fly in their private jets to Davos each year. (What Is the Great Reset?" by Michael Rectenwald; *Imprimis*, December, 2021, Hillsdale College.)

Woke ideology undermines military readiness in various ways. It undermines cohesiveness by emphasizing differences based on race, ethnicity, and sex. It undermines leadership authority by introducing questions about whether promotion is based on merit or quota requirements. It leads to military personnel serving in specialties and areas for which they are not qualified or ready. And it takes time and resources away from training activities and weapons development that contribute to readiness...Our fighting men and women are required to sit through indoctrination programs, often with roots in Marxist tenets of critical race theory... These indoctrination programs differentiate service members along racial and gender lines, which runs completely counter to the military imperative to build cohesiveness based on common loyalties, training, and standards. Traditional training and education programs...have been supplanted by programs that *promote* discrimination by replacing the American ideal of equality with the progressive ideal of equity – which in practice means unequal treatment based on group identity...all this detracts from the purpose of our military preserving the security and freedom of the American people and nation.[130]

A report released {yesterday} by two Republicans in Congress alleged the Biden administration's injection of liberal ideologies like Critical Race Theory into the Pentagon is harming military readiness and the safety of troops. "President Joe Biden and his administration are weakening America's warfighters through a sustained assault fueled by woke virtue signaling," Sen. Marco Rubio, of Florida, and Rep. Chip Roy, of Texas, wrote in the new report, titled "WOKE WARFIGHTERS: How Political Ideology is Weakening America's Military." "Our military's singular purpose is to provide for the common defense of our nation," they also wrote. "It cannot be turned into a left-wing social experiment. It cannot be used as a cudgel against America itself. And it cannot be paralyzed by fear of offending the sensibilities of Ivy League faculty lounges or progressive pundits." The two conservative lawmakers stated that liberal ideology and emphasis on diversity and inclusion over war fighting is affecting every aspect of Pentagon readiness and capability, including the operations of America's elite special forces... forcing our military

---

130. "The Rise of Wokeness in the Military" by Thomas Spoehr; Imprimis, 6-7/2022. Hillsdale College

to engage in DEI trainings encourages supporting and advancing people on criteria other than competence and ability to carry out a mission"... The report also argues the injection of Critical Race Theory into military academies has signaled a desire to "indoctrinate a new generation of military leadership" but its focus on race was actually harming military cohesion.[131]

The Marxist tide is subtly steering Congress to respect in practice wokism's establishment as a religion with the freedom to exercise itself in all walks of life:

> "...the Biden administration is proselytizing for woke ideology. The foreign-policy implications could be catastrophic. In an effort to 'promote diversity and inclusion,' the State Department is funding 'drag theater performances' in Ecuador through cultural grants....The moment of diplomatic idiocy pairs nicely with the Biden administration's request earlier this year for $2.6 billion to export woke ideology in the form of 'gender equity and equality' around the world... the Biden administration ridicules {Hungarian} officials for being justifiably repulsed by the woke ideology of American universities...Woke ideology frustrates and confuses allies and undermines our strength by attacking the very values on which America is built."[132]

---

131. "Woke ideology eroding war-fighting capability inside Pentagon, new congressional report warns", by John Solomon; Just The News. 11/21/22
132. "How Do Drag Shows Advance U.S. National Security?" by John Ratcliffe and Cliff Sims; Wall Street Journal, 10/28/22, page A19

In its same edition on p. A18 this letter appeared:

A Secular Religion Is Being Established in American Law I agree...that federal and state governments are blatantly discriminating against those who don't share their woke beliefs ...Merriam-Webster's definition of religion includes: 'a personal set or institutionalized system of religious attitudes, beliefs, and practices' and 'a cause, principle or system of beliefs held to with ardor and faith.' Can the woke agenda and its moral relativism be anything but a newly established government religion? It is slowly but assuredly being instituted into law via legislation and bureaucratic regulation, and it is occurring despite our First Amendment.

John M. Crosse Oceanside, Calif.

4] Cancel Culture

A Facebook group of Rhodes College alums with a focus on abortion and reproductive healthcare access are lobbying the school to remove Supreme Court Associate Justice Amy Coney Barrett from the Rhodes Hall of Fame.

The group's reasoning is stated in a posted online petition that analyzes Barrett's answers to questions posed during her Senate confirmation hearing in October of 2020. In short, the petition states, Barrett lied about her position regarding the recently overturned Roe v. Wade legal precedent. Her dishonesty, the petition contends, is in direct conflict with the Rhodes Honor Code. "She did testify that she had no agenda for overturning precedent such as Roe or

Casey. This statement seems not only disingenuous in retrospect after the Dobbs decision, but at the time it would have been at odds with her scholarly writings. It was, at the very least, misleading," the petition read.

Fox News contributor Jonathan Turley debunked the Rhodes College alumni petition for the removal of Supreme Court justice Amy Coney Barrett from the school's hall of fame because of her vote to overturn Roe v Wade by asserting it as "slanderous and false."[133]

Margaret Court, whose record {24 grand slams} still stands over Williams' 23 titles, noted that her wins were earned in a shorter length of time – despite critics who discredit it in comparison because she earned most of them during the amateur era..."Serena has played seven years more than I did," she said. "I finished in my early 30s. People forget that I took two years out. I first retired, like Ash Barty, when I was 25, thinking I would never return to tennis. I got married, had a baby, but then had one of my best years, winning 24 out of 25 tournaments."..."I would love to have played in this era – I think it's so much easier," she told The Telegraph. "How I would love to have taken family or friends along with me. But I couldn't, I had to go on my own or with the national team. People don't see all that. As amateurs, we had to play every week, because we didn't have any money. Now, they can take off whenever they want, fly back whenever they want."...Court, who became a Pentecostal Christian minister in 1990s, said

---

133. Fox News, 8/8/2022 "America Reports"

she believes she has been essentially shunned from the tennis community because of her beliefs, including her opposition to same-sex marriage in Australia... "In 2020, I was meant to be coming to Wimbledon for the 50th anniversary of my calendar grand slam. But then COVID hit, so the honor never happened. The French Open didn't invite me, the U.S. Open didn't invite me. Rod Laver had won the slam, and I was going to be honored in the same way, but no. I didn't lose any sleep over it. But the honor has not been there for what I did do. In my own nation, I have been given titles, but they would still rather not mention me."[134]

5] CRT

"Critical Race Theory...is a philosophy thoroughly grounded in Marxist ideology that asserts that America is 'systemically racist.' Its advocates say that American culture is a conspiracy to perpetuate 'white supremacy.' It divides all Americans along lines of race and gender, and between 'oppressors' and 'victims'...While CRT advocates have been pushing CRT for many years on college and university campuses, their impact on other levels of education through public school systems across the country, extending from first-grade through high school {and} has also reached into government bureaucracies, including the U.S. military, as well as

---

134. Margaret Court takes aim at Serena Williams, tennis community, Paulina Dedaj, 9/6/2002, https://www.foxnews.com/sports/margaret-court-takes-aim-serena-williams-tennis-community-dont-think-she-has-ever-admired-me Viewed: 3/2023

into corporations...In true Marxist fashion {the following} words are turned upside down by CRT proponents: Diversity means giving one racial (or gender) group preference over others; Equity...a Marxist concept {which} does not mean equality (equal treatment of all Americans under the law); it means that government (including public schools, the military and the bureaucracy) must treat individuals unequally according to skin color in order to force 'equal outcomes.'"[135]

Paul Kengor in his book The Devil and Karl Marx writes that the communists' goal parallels that of Satanists: replace God with man and rid society of the family concept and structure. "Critical theory" {the origination of CRT} in effect "is Marxism operating on the cultural front." (p.358) From this 'school' Critical {Race} Theory fulminated "against everything from 'the patriarchy' to 'white imperialism' to 'transphobia'... even biological sex {which is} no longer considered a settled issue."

> "...in the 1960's, left-wing radicals began their long march to undermine the ideas that had driven racial progress in this country for more than a century...the most extreme version of identity politics, what Marxist academics would label critical race theory, had gained purchase in the national conversation... identity politics teaches people to look at themselves through the lens of race, sex, sexual orientation, and gender identity."[136]

---

135. Critical Race Theory: A Citizen's Handbook, Judicial Watch, Inc., 2022
136. Rigged, Mollie Hemingway, Regnery Publishing, 2021, pages 116-7

Xi Van Fleet, a Virginia parent who had lived in China as a young child in the 1960s, spoke at a Loudoun County school board meeting about her experience under Chinese Communist revolutionary Mao Zedong's successful campaign to divide her society by means of cultural Marxism and likened that method to today's critical race theory. Van Fleet added that the left's intent on "cancel culture" and "canceling" everything from public statuary to references to uncomfortable historic events, to historic figures they deem flawed is the same thing that Mao sought when he essentially erased thousands of years of Chinese cultural history.[137]

A retired Michigan school teacher stated that CRT is "an exceedingly inhumane program (that) scares children by teaching them that their accomplishments are vicious relics of white supremacy...Students are indoctrinated to hate their country, hate their gender, hate their parents...{Critical race theorists} use the same ideology, the same methodology, even the same vocabulary. The ideology is cultural Marxism."[138]

Many of the country's most prestigious medical programs have implemented Critical Race Theory (CRT) as part of the core curriculum, according to the Critical Race Training in Education database. Fifty-eight of the top 100 medical schools ranked by the U.S. News & World Report include CRT in coursework and student training.

---

137. June 11, 2021, https://meaww.com/virginia-mom-xi-van-fleet-chinese-immigrant-mao-culural-revolution-like-school-critical-race-theory Viewed: 3/2023
138. Battle Over Critical Race Theory, Steven Kovac, Epoch Times, 10/2021

Of the top schools, 46 provide students and staff with work by Robin DiAngelo, author of "Nice Racism" and "White Fragility," two books that harbor anti-white racism and "woke" ideologies. Other authors include Ibram X. Kendi, director of the Center of Antiracist Research and author of several antiracist books, including "Stamped." This line of thinking with CRT portrays America to be fundamentally racist, teaching every social interaction and individual in terms of race. Adherents use words such as "antiracism" to reach their race-based means to an end. "As with our higher education database, some have embraced CRT explicitly, while others have a continuum of programming, such as 'antiracism,' 'equity,' and 'Diversity, Equity and Inclusion' that does not easily fit into a Yes/No construct," the Critical Race Training in Education database stated. "We provide information from which you can make the most informed decision possible." Harvard Medical School, ranked No. 1 by the U.S. News & World Report, is developing a more nuanced way of teaching its masters and Ph.D. programs that will guide students to "acknowledge the ways in which racism is embedded in science and scientific culture and work to redress these longstanding issues," according to the Harvard Medical School's website. Harvard's Global Surgery and Social Change program requires students to "participate in and lead informed discussions about antiracism through a dedicated antiracism curriculum" to educate students on the "history of racism and colonialism in health." Ranked third on the report, the University of California, San Francisco School of Medicine, has racial affinity caucusing groups for students to undergo "antiracist work and process the impact of racism on ourselves and our community," the school's webpage reads. In September, the University of California announced its "Differences Matter Initiative" to "accelerate the achievement of equity and inclusion across the medical profession." Ranked sixth, Duke University School of Medicine implemented an antiracism committee to "incorporate teaching racism and racial inequities" through "teaching, research and clinical missions," according to the school's webpage. Resources offered include Kendi's "antiracist reading list" to help further the school's goal as "an educational and research leader and agent of change towards an antiracist culture." Ranked third on the report, the University of California, San Francisco School of Medicine, has racial affinity caucusing groups for students to undergo "antiracist work and process the impact of racism on ourselves and our community," the school's webpage reads. In September, the University of California announced its "Differences Matter Initiative" to "accelerate the achievement of equity and inclusion across the medical profession." Ranked sixth, Duke University School of Medicine implemented an antiracism committee to "incorporate teaching racism and racial inequities" through "teaching, research and clinical missions," according to the school's webpage. Resources offered include Kendi's "antiracist reading list" to help further the school's goal as "an educational and research leader and agent of change towards an antiracist culture." Academia has always been known to push the boundaries, but the antiracism push in the medical education field grows steadily; 35.6% of medical schools already offer incentives to departments that reach diversity goals set by the university or college. In July, the Association of American Medical Colleges released new guidelines on diversity, equity and inclusion initiatives for medical schools considering "privilege" and patients' "intersectionality" when providing treatment.[139]

> Woe to those who call evil good and good evil, who substitute darkness for light and light for darkness, who substitute bitter for sweet and sweet for bitter…who justify the wicked for a bribe and take away the rights of the ones who are in the right!
> —Isaiah 5:20,23

6] THE SUBTLETIES OF CHEMICAL AND BIOLOGICAL WARFARE

Satan's quietly expanding influence manifests itself in the driving force of politics, primarily to rewrite as well as to flip the history and morality of our cultural heritage. One glaring example is the world's pharmaceutical industry and its dynamic:

- recognition of a newly discovered disease makes the 'market' anxious in demanding a drug to fight it;

---

139. Over Half of Top Medical Schools Teach Critical Race Theory, Brian Pfail, 11/28/22, https://www.newsmax.com/newsfront/crt-critical-race-theory-academia/2022/11/28/ id/1098231/ Viewed: 3/2023

- after extensive research, production and government approval, the expectant 'market' is wooed and bombarded by written, broadcast and digital advertisements;
- physicians are inadequately informed about the product but their -clientele are hounding them to get a prescription for it in order to acquire it at a pharmacy. Such drugs, though legally purchased, often get into the wrong hands and cause all manners of harm.

As mentioned before, the major threat in the opioid crisis the world faces today are natural poppy plants refined/processed to yield morphine and heroin as well as synthetic substances, particularly deadly fentanyl, which is exported by China to Mexican cartels for refining and delivering across the southern US border with the goal to murder thousands of unsuspecting, drug-addicted American users.

And now the systematic legalization of marijuana (cannabis) is jeopardizing the health of the world's population mostly for economic (profiting and taxing) reasons. Addicts are treated not as accountable for their abusing drugs but as victims of those substances. Then there's the plethora of vaccines that have gained control over citizens' health 'for their greater good,' even though the drugs' effectiveness and safety remain questionable enough for the U. S. government to maintain a trust fund in order to underwrite court-awarded damages caused by specified vaccines.

I harp on this subject because I believe it represents one of the means Satan will employ to amass his control over all the world: φαρμακεία, the use of drugs, medicines, potions or spells for any purpose; it also can be translated as poisoning, witchcraft, sorcery, magic or enchantment. The word 'pharmacy' comes "from Middle English *pharmacy*, borrowed from Middle French *pharmacie*, from Old French *farmacie*, from Medieval Latin pharmacia, from Ancient Greek φαρμακεία (employment of drugs, medicines, potions or spells for any purpose; poisoning; witchcraft; sorcery; magic; enchantment), from φάρμακον (drug, poison, philter {love potion}, charm)..."[140]

> "You shall not allow כָּשַׁף (practice of sorcery, witchcraft)/*LXX*: φαρμακεία (sorceress) to live..."
> —Exodus 22:18

> Moses to all Israel:
> "There shall not be found among you anyone who makes his son or his daughter pass through the fire, one who uses divination, one who practices witchcraft, or one who interprets omens, or a sorcerer, or one who casts a spell, or a medium, or a spiritist, or one who calls up the dead... whoever does these things is detestable to Yaweh..."
> —Deuteronomy 18:10-12

I apologize for filling this chapter with other peoples' views but I wanted to impress upon the reader what and why Franklin Graham had said, "This is very

---

140. https://en.wiktionary.org/wiki/pharmacy Viewed 3/2023

frightening...If we're willing to repent and turn from our sins and put our faith in Christ, God will forgive our sins..." Yes indeed, the days are evil:

> The words of the Preacher, the son of David, king in Jerusalem..."I have seen under the sun {that} in the place of justice there is wickedness and in the place of righteousness there is wickedness."
> —Ecclesiastes 1:1,3:16

> Yaweh to Solomon:
> "If...My people who are called by My name humble themselves and pray, and seek My face and turn from their wicked ways, then I will hear from heaven, will forgive their sin and will heal their land."
> —2 Chronicles 7:14

> Hezekiah, king of Judah:
> "Be strong and courageous, do not fear or be dismayed...for with us is Yaweh our God to help us and to fight our battles."
> —2 Chronicles 32:7-8

BOOK OF LIFE'S FINAL CHAPTER

> Turning and turning in the widening gyre
> The falcon cannot hear the falconer
> Things fall apart; the centre cannot hold,
> Mere anarchy is loosed upon the world,
> The blood-dimmed tide is loosed, and everywhere
> The ceremony of innocence is drowned;
> The best lack all conviction, while the worst
> Are full of passionate intensity.
> —*William Butler Keats, "The Second Coming"*

Fraught with symbols and mysteries, the only known narrative concerning the closing phase of Yaweh's plan for life is the book of Revelation itself:

> Voice in heaven:
> "Now the salvation and the power and the kingdom of our God and the authority of His Christ have come, for the accuser {cf. Job 1:11,2:5; Zechariah 3:1; Luke 22:31} of our brothers has been thrown down (v. 9)...(the brothers) overcame him because...they {cf. 6:9} did not love their life even to death... Woe to the earth and the sea because ὁ διάβολος [the devil] has come down {v. 9} to you, having great wrath, knowing that he has only a short time {angel: "there shall be delay no longer" (10:6).
> —Revelation 12:10-12

> The twenty-four elders to Yaweh:
> "....the nations ὠργίσθησαν [were enraged] and Your wrath came {as did} the time for the dead to be judged...διαφθεῖραι [to destroy {cf. Revelation 8:9}] those διαφθείροντας τὴν γῆν [destroying the earth.]"
> —Revelation 11:18

Whenever I ponder the essential theme of my prior chapter this fills my mind: will Yaweh adjudicate once again that "the wickedness of man {is} great on the earth and that every intent of the thoughts of his heart is only evil continually" (Genesis 6:5)? To me the clue

resides in the covenantal (Genesis 9:9-17) promise He had made to Noah and his family:

> I will never again destroy every living thing as I have done. While the earth remains, seedtime and harvest, and cold and heat, and summer and winter and day and night will not cease.
> —Genesis 8:21-22

His qualifying phrase "while the earth remains" implies that sometime in the future the earth will cease remaining, that Yaweh will destroy all living things but not by water. The varying degrees of awareness concerning that historic *diluvial*, or its variant *diluvian*, should stir a segment of humanity into pondering when the earth and life itself will cease to be. This Jesus knew and said so:

> Jesus:
> "Heaven and earth will pass away, but My words will not pass away. But of that day or hour no one knows...but the Father. Take heed, be awake, be vigilant, for you do not know when the time is...therefore be on guard..."
> —Mark 13:31-33,35

Here Yaweh's Son is humbly confessing that even He does not know when this cataclysmic event will occur – nor do all those listening to Him. The earth's existence is not eternal; its demise is to be expected. But most humans today tend to live either desperately or leisurely 'in/for the moment,' without any concern about the world's future. Now if someone you respect and trust would express an extraordinary statement about the world's disappearance, would you accept it without question or would you just ignore it?

To assist His disciples in assimilating what He had just predicted, Jesus bluntly revealed to them what His future would entail:

> "But who do you say I am?" And Peter answered and said, "The Christ of God." ...but He warned them... saying, "The Son of Man must...be killed and be raised up on the third day."
> —Luke 9:20-22

> Jesus:
> "so shall the Son of Man be three days and three nights ἐν τῇ καρδαί τῆς γῆς [in the inner part of the earth {a tomb "hewn out in the rock" (Matthew 27:60; Luke 23:53.)}]
> —Matthew 12:40

> Simon Peter said, "You are the Christ, the Son of the living God."...From that time Jesus Christ began to show His disciples that He must...be killed, and be raised up on the third day."
> —Matthew 16:16,21

> Jesus to His disciples:
> "Yaweh will strike down the Shepherd (Zechariah 13:7) "But after I have been raised I will go before you to Galilee."
> —Matthew 26:31-32; Mark 14:28

> Jesus to His disciples:
> "Are you deliberating together about this, that I said, 'A little while and you not behold Me and again a little while and you see Me.'? Truly, truly I say to you that you will weep and lament but the world will rejoice; you will be sorrowful but your sorrow will be turned into joy."
> —John 16:19-20

But did His apostles and disciples accept His revelation as truth and believe Him, as well as in Him, after He had made it? Well, many did:

> "In the temple at Jerusalem Jesus told antagonistic Jews, 'Destroy this temple and in three days I will raise it up',,,He was speaking of the temple of His body. When therefore He was raised from the dead, His disciples remembered that He said this and they believed the Scripture {Psalm 16:10} and the word which Jesus had spoken."
> —John 2:19,21-22

As did some of His adversaries:

> The chief priests and the Pharisees warned Pilate that "when He was still alive that deceiver said, 'after three days I rise again' {cf. Matthew 16:21, John 2:19-21}..."
> —Matthew 27:63

But some of His closest disciples did not:

> An "angel" (Matthew 28:5), a "young man" (Mark 16:5), "two men...in dazzling apparel" (Luke 24:4) informed Mary Magdalene and Mary that

Jesus has arisen and instructed them to inform His disciples. The women were astonished and afraid (Mark 16:8) but Mary Magdalene did so. "When (those who priorly had been with Him) heard that He was alive and had been seen by her, they refused to believe it."
—Mark 16:5-11

Two men {angels – v. 23} in dazzling apparel to the women bearing spices at the tomb: "'Remember how He spoke to you...saying that the Son of Man must be...crucified, and the third day rise again.' And {the women} remembered His words...and reported all these things to the eleven...{but their} words appeared to {the apostles – v. 10} as nonsense and they would not believe them."
—Luke 24:6-11

Simon Peter and "the other disciple whom Jesus loved" (v. 2) "came to the tomb and...saw the folded linen wrappings and believed Jesus' body had been "taken away" (v. 2) for as yet they did not understand the Scripture {Psalm 16:10; Acts 13:35} that He must rise again from the dead. So the disciples went away again to their homes."
—John 20:8-10

But sensitive to their doubting, Jesus gently chided his Apostles:

Jesus "reproached them for their unbelief and hardness of heart because they had not believed those who had seen Him after He had arisen. And He said to them,...'He who has believed and has been baptized σωθήσεται [shall be saved from final ruin (1 Timothy 1:15)], but he who has disbelieved shall be condemned.'"

—Mark 16:14-16

Doubting Thomas   (John 20:24-29)

The Synoptic Gospels independently relate the Son of Man making predictions of His resurrection in three identical settings:

1. Matthew 16:21 // Mark 8:31 // Luke 9:22
2. Matthew 17:23 // Mark 9:31
3. Matthew 20:19 // Mark 10:34 // Luke 18:33

The historic accounts of His resurrection are for the benefit of all believers because it profoundly attests to the Son of God's divine nature and character; it proves to the "many" {cf. Acts 13:48} that He has always been truthful about everything He had said during His earthly ministry. This irrefutable fact should encourage all professing Christians to believe Him, as well as in Him, that what He had prophesied He Himself had substantiated. A few years after His resurrection, one of His prophesies, separately recorded by Matthew (24:2), Mark (13:2) and Luke (21:6), became revealed as truth when in 70 AD the temple in Jerusalem had been totally levelled.

> Yaweh in Balaam's mouth... "God is not a man that he should lie..."
> —Numbers 23:16,19

Samuel:
"...the Glory of Israel will not lie..."
—1 Samuel 15:29

Yaweh:
Nor was there any deceit in {the} mouth {of the God of Israel's servant.}
—Isaiah 53:9

Paul: "....God...cannot lie..."
—Titus 1:2

...it is impossible for God to lie...
—Hebrews 6:18

All of God's words are absolutely true, including all that He conveys to His image bearers either directly or by His Breath or His Son. It is reasonable then to assert that Jesus's forthright warning about heaven and earth passing away {Mark 13:31; cf Genesis 8:22, 2 Peter 3:7} is definitely true as well and that all believers are called to practice what He prescribed in preparation for that event. So in order to prepare for what He had prescribed, we need first to recognize the personal relationship every individual should strive to enjoy with Yaweh. In order to achieve that, he or she needs the wisdom, knowledge and understanding of Yaweh Himself, which becomes available only as one endeavors to יְרָא [fear] Him:

יִרְאַת [the fear] of Yaweh is the beginning of knowledge; fools despise wisdom and instruction.
—Proverbs 1:7

יִרְאַת [the fear] of Yaweh is the beginning of wisdom and the knowledge of the Holy One is understanding.
—Proverbs 9:10

Yaweh to Moses: "you יָרֵאתָ מֵאֱלֹהֶיךָ [shall revere your God]"
—Leviticus 19:14,32; 25:17,36,43

Grammatically speaking, whenever Yaweh is the direct or implied object, the corresponding translation of the Hebrew verb יָרֵא and its noun variant יִרְאַת is determined by the context in which it is employed:

a. negative [to dread / be afraid of] –

...the word of Yaweh came to Abram in a vision, saying, " אַל־תִּירָא [fear not], Abram, I am a shield to you..."
—Genesis 15:1

...God called to Hagar from heaven and said to her, "...אַל־תִּירְאִי [fear not] for God has heard the voice of the lad where he is...I will make a great nation of him."
—Genesis 21:17-18

b. positive [to adore / idolize / revere / worship / be in awe of] –

Jacob:
"Surely Yaweh is in this place and I did not know it." וַיִּירָא [and he was in awe and said, "How מַה־ נוֹרָא [awesome] is this place! This is none other than the house of God and this is the gate of heaven."
—Genesis 28:16-17

c. simultaneously positive and negative, i.e., adore/ idolize/ revere / worship / be in awe of God while simultaneously on guard not to offend Him by being disobedient: Yaweh in "mighty power... instructed Isaiah, 'אֹתוֹ תַקְדִּישׁוּ; וְהוּא מוֹרַאֲכֶם, וְהוּא מַעֲרִצְכֶם [He {Yaweh} shall be your fear and He shall be your dread]'." (Isaiah 8:11,13)

Yaweh's angel to Abraham: "...I know כִּי-יְרֵא אֱלֹהִים [that you fear God] since you have not withheld your son, your only son, from Me."

—Genesis 22:12

Joseph in Egypt to his brothers:
"Do this and live for אֶת-הָאֱלֹהִים, אֲנִי יָרֵא [I fear the God.]"

—Genesis 42:18

Job:
"And to man {God} said, 'Behold, יִרְאַת [the fear] of the Lord, that is wisdom; and to depart from evil is understanding.'"

—Job 28:28

Surely {Yaweh's} salvation is near לִירֵאָיו [to those who fear Him.]

—Psalm 85:9

If You, Yaweh, should mark iniquities, O Yaweh, who could stand? But there is forgiveness with You, that תִּוָּרֵא [You may be feared.]

—Psalm 130:3-4

{Naïve ones – v. 22} hated knowledge and did not choose יִרְאַת [the fear] of Yaweh. (Proverbs 1:29) Do not be wise in your own eyes! יְרָא אֶת־יְהוָה [Fear Yaweh] and turn away from evil.

—Proverbs 3:7

בְּיִרְאַת יְהוָה [In the fear of Yaweh] there is strong confidence and his children will have refuge.

—Proverbs 14:26

יִרְאַת יְהוָה [Fear of Yaweh] is a fountain of life that one may avoid the snares of death.

—Proverbs 14:27

My son, יְרָא־אֶת־יְהוָה וָמֶלֶךְ [fear Yaweh and king]; do not associate with those who are given to change.

—Proverbs 24:21

...in many dreams and in many words there is emptiness. כִּי אֶת־הָאֱלֹהִים יְרָא [Rather fear the God.]

—Ecclesiastes 5:7{6}

The conclusion, when all has been heard is אֶת־הָאֱלֹהִים יְרָא [fear the God] and keep His commandments...

—Ecclesiastes 12:13

So the church..., going on in τῷ φόβῳ [the fear] of the Lord and in the comfort of the Holy Breath ...continued to increase.

—Acts 9:31

> We must all appear before the judgment seat of Christ, that each one may be recompensed for his deeds in the body...whether good or bad. Therefore, knowing τὸν φόβον [the awe] of the Lord, we endeavor to convince men...
> —2 Corinthians 5:10-11

> ...work out your salvation with φόβου [awe] and τρόμου [mental agitation {cf. Psalm 4:4}] for it is God in you, both to will and to work for {His} good pleasure.
> —Philippians 2:12-13

> ...if you address as Father the One who impartially judges according to each man's work, conduct yourselves ἐν φόβῳ [in fear] during the time of your stay {upon earth.}
> —I Peter 1:17

> After the second woe the twenty-four elders proclaimed, "Oh Lord God, the Almighty.... Your wrath came and the time {came} for the dead to be judged and to their reward to Your bond-servants the prophets and to the saints and φοβουμένοις [to those who fear] Your name, the small and the great, and to destroy those who destroy the earth."
> —Revelation 11:16-17

To fear Yaweh, then, is to give Him complete guidance and direction of your temporarily embodied soul, to let Him fully influence the goal of your existence as well as the strategies needed to achieve it. This commitment requires complete control of one's abilities as well as total responsibility and accountability for all of one's

thoughts and actions. The Old Testament's יִרְאַת יְהוָה complements the New Testament's ἐν Χριστῷ [in Christ, "the power of God and the wisdom of God" (1 Corinthians 1:24)] in that the former is revealed by one's walk and character based on Yaweh's ten commandments whereas the latter is bestowed by grace to facilitate the believers in becoming Christlike {cf. Romans 8:29, 1 Corinthians 11:1} through the working out of their salvation "with fear and trembling." (Philippians 2:12)

Vertical {spiritual} wisdom consists of the knowledge, fearing and understanding of Yaweh Himself whereas horizontal {social} wisdom is the sound application of experience and intelligence derived from the dynamic interaction between discernment, discretion, prudence and judgment. Yet Jesus's prophetic message informs those who fear Yaweh that there is something God has withheld from them concerning the end times: "Take heed, ἀγρυπνεῖτε [be vigilant], for you do not know when the time is... γρηγορεῖτε οὖν [therefore be on guard]..." (Mark 13:35) Alertness and vigilance in all aspects require critical thinking, an objective analysis and evaluation of an issue in order to form a judgment formed by the following process:

DISCERNMENT is perception /detection by one's sight or intellect:

> ...Yaweh has a day of vengeance, year of recompense for the cause of Zion . Its streams will be turned into pitch and its loose earth into brimstone and its land will become burning pitch. It will not be quenched night or day; its

smoke will go up forever. From generation to generation it will be desolate, none will pass through it forever and forever.
—Isaiah 34:8-10

And this is my prayer: that your love may abound more and more in real knowledge and discernment, so that you may be able to discern what is best and may be pure and blameless for the day of Christ...
—Philippians 1:9-10

...the day of the Lord will come like a thief, in which the heavens will pass away with a roar and the elements will be destroyed with intense heat; and the earth and its works will be burned up.
—2 Peter 3:10

JUDGEMENT is formation of an opinion or estimation of a subject after careful consideration:

...let him who thinks he stands take heed lest he fall. No temptation has overtaken you but such as is common; and God is faithful, who will not allow you to be tempted beyond what you are able but with the temptation will provide the way of escape also, that you may be able to endure it.
—1 Corinthians 10:12-13

DISCRIMINATION (a clear, sensible decision / distinction {i.e., right or wrong}):

Paul:
"I also do my best to maintain always a blameless conscience before God and before

man." (Acts 24:16) Paul: Take "every thought captive to the obedience of Christ."
—2 Corinthians 10:5

Human wisdom, then, consists of the knowledge about Yaweh as well as the fear of Him based on the intelligence derived from one's prudent processing of discernment, discretion, prudence and judgment:

> Paul:
> "if we brought to account [διεκρίνομεν] ourselves rightly, we should not be brought under question [ἐκρινόμεθα] {cf. Romans 14:22.}
> —1 Corinthians 11:31

> ...if any of you lacks wisdom, let him ask of God...and it will be given to him. But let him ask in faith without any doubting...
> —James 1:5-6

Jesus warned His disciples, "Βλέπετε μή τις ὑμᾶς πλανήσῃ", which in context translates, "discern, perceive, judge {that} no one would lead you astray... many false prophets will arise and will lead many astray." (Matthew 24:4,11)

When Jesus arrived at the Mount of Olives in Bethpage to teach in the temple, the Pharisees, hoping to seize Him {cf. John 7:32}, challenged Him with evil intent by bringing a woman they claimed ἐπὶ μοιχείᾳ κατειλημμένην [was detected in the act with a view to adultery] and publicly tested Him with this question: should we kill this woman according to Leviticus 20:10? He judiciously responded, "He who is without sin among you...be the first to throw

a stone at her." And then to the woman: "neither do I condemn you; go your way, from now on sin no more." (John 8:7,11) He continued His teaching, provoking the Pharisees to yell, "Your witness is not true!" (v. 14) Sternly He rebuked them: ὑμεῖς κατὰ τὴν σάρκα [after the likeness of flesh] κρίνετε [you form a judgment], ἐγὼ οὐ κρίνω οὐδένα [I do not form any judgment.] (v.15) The sense I take from this abrupt chastisement is that Jesus told them that as created image bearers of God they're incapable of dispensing true justice:

> "μὴ κρίνετε [do not form a judgment] κατ' ὄψιν [according to what you see] but τὴν δικαίαν κρίσιν κρίνετε [form a decision {as respects} justice].
> —John 7:24

Jesus added that while temporarily in human body He judges no one. He said that because His "hour has not yet come," (John 2:4), His "time is... at hand" (John 7:6) Upon His resurrection He indeed will adjudicate [διακρίνω] by examining, discerning and discriminating in the role of Son of Man (Matthew 16:27,25:31-33) and of Christ (John 5:22; Acts 10:42,17:31; 2 Corinthians 5:10; 2 Timothy 4:1.)

Now in the same setting that He had discussed the timing of the earth's end Jesus warned His disciples:

> ...nation will rise against nation, and kingdom against kingdom...they will deliver you up to tribulation and will kill you, and you will be hated by all nations on account of My name... many will fall away and will betray one another and hate one another...most people's love will grow cold...this gospel of the kingdom shall be

preached in the whole world for a witness to all nations and then the end will come.
—Matthew 24:7-12,14

This ominous message brings to my mind the promise Yaweh made to Abraham that He would make his son by Hagar a great גּוֹי [heathen people/nation] and that Ishmael's sons would be princes (Genesis 17:20.) This reflection perplexes because it's very possible the Son was including Ishmael's enduring kingdom-state in the hatred and battling against His "kingdom." (v. 14 above) However, the major takeaway in His warning is that in the near future believers will be despised and killed or will become disheartened in their faith to the extent that they hate and betray those who staunchly persevere with hope as well as this incentive:

> Jesus "But the one who ὑπομένω [to bear up under, stand firm, persevere] to the end...shall be saved... γρηγορέω [watch, be vigilant, attentive] for you do not know on which day your Lord will come...the Son of Man is coming at an hour when you do not think {He will.}.
> —Matthew 24:13,42,44

Traits to be practiced and mastered for enabling one to bear up under, stand firm, persevere [ὑπομένω] {cf. Romans 12:12} in the upcoming tribulations:

> Be agitated and do not sin; meditate in your heart on your bed and be still... Offer the sacrifices of righteousness and trust in Yaweh.
> —Psalm 4:4-5

How blessed is the man who יָרֵא [fears] Yaweh, who greatly delights in His commandments...He will not יִירָא [be afraid of] evil tidings; his heart is steadfast, <u>trusting</u> in Yaweh.
—Psalm 112:1,7

{Yaweh's} word is a lamp to my feet and a light to my path. I have sworn, and I will confirm it, that I will keep Your righteous ordinances.
—Psalm 119:105-106

Trust in Yaweh with all your heart and do not lean on your own understanding.
—Proverbs 3:5

Consider it all joy, my brethren, when you are involved in various πειρασμοῖς [trials / tests / temptations], knowing that the testing of your faith produces endurance. And let endurance have a perfect result, that you may be perfect and complete, lacking in nothing...and blessed is a man who bears up under πειρασμόν [trial / test / temptation]; for once he has been approved, he will receive the crown of life...
—James 1:2-4,12

"If any one is for captivity, to captivity he goes; if anyone kills with the sword, with the sword he must be killed. Here is ἡ ὑπομονὴ [the bearing up under, standing firm, perseverance] and the faith of the saints."
—Revelation 13:10

"Herein is ἡ ὑπομονὴ [the bearing up under, standing firm, perseverance] of the saints who keep the commandments of God and their

faith in Jesus. And I heard a voice from heaven saying, 'Write, "Blessed are the dead who die in the Lord from now on."' 'Yes,' says the Breath, 'that they may rest from their labors since their deeds follow with them.'"
—Revelation 14:12-13

For the benefit of all living and future believers Paul provides a 'personality profile' of courage, awareness, humility, love and peace in preparation for the trials and tribulations culminating in the earth's disappearance:

...present your bodies a living and holy sacrifice, acceptable to God, your spiritual service of worship. And do not be conformed to this world but be transformed by the renewing of your mind, that you may prove what the will of God is, that which is good and acceptable and perfect...Abhor what is evil; cling to what is good...Bless those who persecute you; bless and curse not... Never pay back evil for evil to anyone. Respect what is right in the sight of all men. If possible, so far as it depends on you, be at peace with all men.
—Romans 12:1-2,9,14,17-18

...those of Christ [Jesus] make the(ir) flesh a sacrifice with the passions and desires. If we are alive by {His} Breath, we also ought to walk by {His} Breath. We ought not become boastful, challenging one another, envying one another.
—Galatians 5:24-26

...do not {merely} look out for your own personal interests but also for the interests of others.
—Philippians 2:4

In the Romans and Philippians passages above "others" always include your enemies (Matthew 5:44, Luke 6:27,25) as well. The Believer's goal leading up to the end of time is to bear up under, stand firm, persevere in all future adversities by being "renewed by the animating force of your mind {and continue to mature your} new self which in the likeness of God has been created in righteousness and holiness of the truth." (Ephesians 4:23-24) This mental, physical and sanctifying exercise needs to be 'practiced, practiced, practiced' for one's enduring to the end. Take to heart as well these two humanistic observations: "Courage is resistance to fear, mastery of fear – not absence of fear" {Mark Twain} and "Fear is a reaction, courage is a decision" {Winston Churchill.}

> Apostle John ἐν πνεύματι: "ὁ νικῶν [the one who conquers / overcomes / prevails] shall thus be clothed in white garments and I {the Son of God (v. 2:18)} will not erase his name from the book of life and I will confess his name before My Father and before His angels... ὁ νικῶν [the one who conquers / overcomes / prevails], I will make him a pillar in the temple of My God..."
> —Revelation 3:5,12

John here is confirming what Jesus in the fifth chapter of Matthew had preached: for those who persevere "is the kingdom of heaven... {i.e. those who} are "poor in spirit,...mourn,...gentle,...hunger and thirst for righteousness,...merciful, pure in heart,...peacemakers..."(Matthew 5:3-9)

Many tribulations since Jesus's death have plagued mankind. Most recently there have been European programs, Hitler's holocaust of Abraham's descendants as well as Stalin's, Mao's, Kim Il-sung's and Islam's brutalities of Christians. In any tribulation the believer must remain inspired by the indwelling of Yaweh's Breath to focus on leading friends as well as hostile enemies "to be born again to a living hope through the resurrection of Jesus Christ from the dead." (1 Peter 1:3) Here Peter affirms that each rebirth is caused by the "God and Father of our Lord Jesus Christ" and that we believers, as planned by Him, are to serve as His 'conception' instrument for each new birth while we strive to "do nothing from selfishness or empty conceit, but with humility of mind let each of {us} regard one another as more important than himself. Do not look out for your own personal interests but also for the interests of others." (Philippians 2:3-4)

> Paul:
> "For God has not given us πνεῦμα {a disposition} of timidity but of power and love and discipline; therefore do not be ashamed of the testimony of our Lord…"
> —2 Timothy 1:7-8

TIME UNWINDS

> **Yaweh to the serpent:**
> "I will put hostility between you and the woman...and her seed...will crush you on the head and you shall bruise it on the heel {cf. Isaiah 53:10.}"
>
> —Genesis 3:15

Yaweh's choice for personifying evil is הַשָּׂטָן / Σατανᾶς [Satan, the adversary], διάβολος [the devil], a 'created-turned-unrighteous' (Ezekiel 28:15) supernatural force. In Genesis 3:1 Moses introduces it {neither he nor she and thus not made in His image} as "more crafty than any beast of the field." Disguised physically as a serpent it deceived Eve {"You surely shall not die!" (v. 4)}, the trait by which it is most associated {cf. Revelation 3:9 and 19:20.} Zechariah 3:2 describes it as an evil accuser; it "was a murderer from the beginning." (John 8:44) Jesus informed Peter that Satan's focus was always on man's interests, not on God's (Matthew 16:23), exemplified by its continual thwarting (1 Thessalonians 2:18) and preventing (Romans 1:13) His image-bearers.

Now there is a unique, hard-to-define function attributed to Satan – its luring capability:

> Paul decided to surrender [παραδοῦναι] a man who lay down with "his father's wife"…to Satan for the destruction of his flesh that his πνεῦμα [animating force] may be saved by the day of the Lord Jesus."
>
> —1 Corinthians 5:5

> Paul:
> "I have surrendered [παρέδωκα] {two who have lost their faith} over to Satan, so that they may be corrected [παιδευθῶσιν] {cf. 2 Samuel 7:14} not to blaspheme."
>
> —1 Timothy 1:20

The essence of this attribute is best understood in light of what Jesus had hinted to Simon Peter that one of His twelve disciples διάβολός ἐστιν [was the devil] (John 6:70-71) and later divulged to the twelve that one of them was going to betray Him {cf. Matthew 26:14-16.} In effect His excusing Judas from the table signified His surrendering him "to Satan," for after the betrayal the disciple "hanged himself" (Matthew 26:5) out of hopelessness. The idea of betraying his Master was caused by his voluntary submission to Satan by allowing it "εἰσέρχομαι [to enter]/ γίνομαι [to come into]" him (Luke 22:2; John 13:2) I aver 'voluntary' based on the restriction imposed by Yaweh on Satan: "all that {Job} has is in your power, only do not put your hand on him." (Job 1:12) In other words, it may

tempt His image-bearers but cannot physically or mentally force them into sinning inasmuch as God justly holds all mankind completely accountable to Him for every sin:

> **Yaweh to Cain:**
> "if you do not do well, sin is crouching at the door and its desire is for you, but you will rule it."
>
> —Genesis 4:7

Satan was crafty enough to be invited into Eve's heart and mind by means of its power of assertive persuasion (v. 4.) What, however, had emboldened it to tempt Jesus? Unrighteous {cf. Ezekiel 28:15}, conceit or wily interest in the human nature {cf. Matthew 16:23} of the Son of God? In my Prologue to Life chapter I had discussed Genesis 1:3, which indicated that God was the creative 'author' of the book of life, not God the Father but the triune God, which included His Son, Jesus. But to His disciples on the Mount of Olives Jesus professed that "of that day...no one knows...nor the Son but the Father alone" (Matthew 24:36), "of that day...no one knows, not even...the Son, but the Father." (Mark 13:32) The mystery here is whether that was His human nature exposing itself? Inasmuch as Jesus had been led out by His Breath "into the wilderness to be subjected to a trial [πειράζω] by the devil" (Matthew 4:1), I speculate that it was focusing on Jesus's Son of Man 'profile' {cf. Daniel 7:13}, to which He often alluded Himself to His disciples and followers

{Matthew 8:20;9:6;12:8,40;13:41; 17:9;19:28;24:27,30, 37, 39,44; 26:64}, culminating in:

> Jesus:
> "Who do people say that the Son of Man is?"...
> Simon Peter answered and said, "You are the Christ, the Son of the living God."
> —Matthew 16:13,16

In the same manner as in Job 2:1, Satan presented itself before Jesus, but this time with assertive demands against which He sternly admonished it with Deuteronomy 6:16 { "You shall not test [נָסָה / ἐκπειράζω - *LXX*]} and 6:13 { "you shall worship Yaweh your God and swear by His name."} The Son of Man ordered it to go away and it departed quietly "until an opportune time" (Luke 4:13) for the Son of God/Son of Man had proved Himself {cf. Numbers 20:13}, "under trial has been approved" (James 1:12) to be "the Lamb of God who takes away the sin of the world" (John 1:29), who "bore the sin of many and intercede for the transgressors." (Isaiah 53:12)

Jesus also provides us an understanding of the 'surrendering to Satan' Paul had practiced: it was his way of dealing with a sinner he believed he pastorally could no longer benefit, i.e., his way of shaking off the dust of his feet {cf. Matthew 11:14}:

> "Simon, Simon, behold Satan has demanded to sift you like wheat but I prayed for you that your faith may not fail and you, when once you have turned again, strengthen your brothers."
> —Luke 22:31-32

I have profiled Satan because of its prominent role in the last chapter of the book of life. The reason for why Yaweh chooses to suffer Satan's activities I believe is found in the response Jacob's favored son, Joseph, had made to his reunited brothers: "...you meant evil against me, but God meant it for good in order to bring about this present result." (Genesis 50:20) Consistent with and sourced in His divine nature, anything Yaweh purposes is forever good to Him. But His dealings with Satan will soon come to an end:

> Yaweh's "taunt {through Isaiah} against the king of Babylon: "You said in your heart, 'I will ascend to heaven...I will make myself like the Most High.' Never the less you will be thrust down to Sheol..."
> —Isaiah 14:4,12-15

> ...Yaweh has a day of vengeance, year of recompense for the cause of Zion. Its streams will be turned into pitch and its loose earth into brimstone. And its land will become burning pitch. It will not be quenched night or day; its smoke will go up forever. From generation to generation it will be desolate; none will pass through it forever and ever.
> —Isaiah 34:8-10

> The word of Yaweh to Ezekiel:
> "take up a lamentation over the King of Tyre and say to him...'You were in Eden, the garden of God...the abundance of your trade filled your midst with violence and sin. Therefore I have cast you as profane from the mountain of God and I have destroyed you."
> —Ezekiel 28:12-16

> Jesus to His 70 appointees: "I watched Satan fall from heaven like lightening {cf. Matthew 4:10.}
> —Luke 10:18

> ...the one whose coming {cf. Revelation 17:10} is in accord with the activity of Satan, with all power and signs and false wonders, and with all the deception of wickedness for those who perish because they did not receive the love of the truth so as to be saved.
> —2 Thessalonians 2:9-10

> ...the day of the Lord will come like a thief, in which the heavens will pass away with a roar and the elements will be destroyed with intense heat, and the earth and its works will be burned up.
> —2 Peter 3:9-10

I present this profile of Satan to help the reader comprehend the apostle John's narrative of the 'end time,' because it focuses on the devil in its various behemoth-like manifestations threatening all of God's image-bearers alive in the final minutes of time, even 'entering by invitation' {cf. Luke 22:2; John 13:2} many of them to the latter's eternal detriment. Even now fulfillment of Isaiah 5 has begun affecting the cultures of mankind, an example of which being what Ayatollah Ruhollah Khomenei, founder of the theocratic Islamic Republic, called the US: "The Great Satan":

> Woe to those who call evil good and good evil; who substitute darkness for light and light for darkness; who substitute bitter for sweet and sweet for bitter... Who justify the wicked for a bribe and take away the rights of the ones who are in the right.
> —Isaiah 5:20,23

TIME IS RUNNING OUT

> For our struggle is...against the rulers, against the powers, against the world forces of this darkness, against the spiritual of wickedness in the heavenly.
> —Ephesians 6:12

What now follows is the apostle John's account of "the things which must shortly take place" (Revelation 1:1), which he had acquired while ἐν πνεύματι on the Lord's day (1:10).

> ἐν πνεύματι (Matthew 22:43; Revelation 1:10,4:2,17:3,21:10) is a divinely established state of mind, as described by David: "The Breath of Yaweh spoke by me and His word was on my tongue."
> —2 Samuel 23:2

My focus will be on believers' increasing exposure to ἀνομία [wickedness, sin, lawlessness] about which Jesus had prophesized on the Mount of Olives (Matthew 24:12.) I caution the reader to prepare for the lack of consistent chronological succession throughout his recollection.

Revelation 12:9,12 - Heaven evicts evil:

> And the great dragon was thrown down, the serpent of old {cf. Genesis 3:1-5} who is called the devil and Satan...and deceives the whole world. He was thrown down to the earth and his angels were thrown down with him... {Heavenly voice:} "Woe to the earth and the sea because the devil has come down to {the earth and the sea}, having great wrath, knowing he has a short time" {cf. 20:2, 10.}

Revelation 13:1 - The Antichrist, a manifestation of Satan (cf. 11;20:2,10), rises up from the sea as a θηρίον [wild beast {cf. Mark 1:13}] with 10 horns {cf. 17:12,16} and 7 heads {cf. 17:9)} with a diadem on each horn and blasphemous names on his head {cf. 12:3,17:3}, hinting of the fulfillment of Daniel's dream:

> As for the ten horns, out of this kingdom ten kings will arise; and another will arise after them, and he will be different from the previous ones and will subdue three kings. He will speak out against the Most High and wear down the saints of the Highest One, and he will intend to make alterations in times and in law; and they will be given into his hand for a time, times, and half a time.
> —Daniel 7:24-25

Revelation 13:2 - The fallen dragon {serpent}, Satan {cf. 4:12;12:3,9; 13:2;20:2}, endows the beast from the sea with power as well as its throne and authority {cf. 2:13.}

Revelation 13:3-4 - The entire earth worships the fallen dragon and the Antichrist {cf. 12:10.}

<u>Revelation 13:5</u> - The duration of the Antichrist's authority is 42 months, (approximately 1,290 days):

> **Jesus:**
> "many will come in My name...and will mislead many."
> —Matthew 24:5

> **Man dressed in linen above waters:**
> "From the time that the regular sacrifice is abolished and the abomination causing desolation is set up {cf. Daniel 9:27} (is) 1,290 days..."
> —Daniel 12:11

> **Jesus:**
> "...leave out the court which is outside the temple and do not measure it, for it has been given to the nations; and they will tread under foot the holy city for forty-two months. And I will grant authority to my two witnesses, and they will prophesy for twelve hundred and sixty days (cf. 12:6) {1,260 divided by 30 days in a month equals 42 months }, clothed in sackcloth."
> —Revelation 11:2-3

<u>Revelation 13:6</u> - The Antichrist blasphemes God and His heavenly dwellers, i.e., angels {cf. Matthew 25:31.}

<u>Revelation 13:7</u> - The Antichrist receives power to overcome the saints in war as well as in global authority "over every tribe and people and tongue and nation."

> **Jesus:**
> "they will deliver you up to tribulation and will kill you and you will be hated by all nations on account of My name."
> —Matthew 24:9

Revelation 13:8 - All earthly dwellers whose names are not in the book of life will worship the Antichrist voluntarily, not caused by the book of life itself {cf. 13:16.}

Revelation 13:10 - The perseverance, i.e., "τηρέω [obeying] the commandments of God and maintaining faith in Jesus" (v. 14:12), of the saints becomes evident either by their resisting while in captivity or by dying by the sword while fighting the Antichrist.

> Jesus said to him, "Put your sword back into its place; for all those who take up the sword shall perish by the sword."
> —Matthew 26:52

> **Lord God:**
> "Since you have kept my command to endure patiently, I will also keep you from the hour of a trial that is going to come on the whole world to test the inhabitants of the earth.
> —Revelation 3:10

Revelation 13:11 - Then the false Prophet {cf. v. 19:20}, another manifestation, rises out of the earth bearing two sheep horns and spoke ὡς [naturally related to - i.e., sounded like] a dragon.

Revelation 13:12 - The false Prophet exercises all the Antichrist's authority in the presence of the latter, whose "fatal wound was healed..." and the false Prophet makes fire (possibly lightening?) descend "out of heaven to the earth in presence of men."

> Then the fire of the Lord fell and consumed the burnt offering and the wood and the stones and the dust, and licked up the water that was in the trench.
>
> —I Kings 18:38

Jesus:
> "For false (cf. John 8:24) Christs and false prophets will arise and will show great signs and wonders, so as to mislead, if possible, even the elect" {an allusion to Hebrews 6:4-6?}
>
> —Matthew 24:24

> And Jesus began to say to them, "See to it that no one misleads you. Many will come in My name, saying, 'I am He!' and will mislead many."
>
> —Mark 13:5-6

<u>Revelation 13:14</u> - The false Prophet deceives {cf. Matthew 24:24} the earth dwellers in the presence of the Antichrist and commands them to make an image of the Antichrist "who had the wound of the sword and has come to life."

<u>Revelation 13:15</u> - The false Prophet then "gives breath" to the Antichrist's image so that it can speak and cause "as many as do not worship (it)...to be killed."

> Then the satraps, the prefects and the governors, the counselors, the treasurers, the judges, the magistrates and all the rulers of the provinces were assembled for the dedication of the image that Nebuchadnezzar the king had set up; and

they stood before the image that Nebuchadnezzar had set up. Then the herald loudly proclaimed: "To you the command is given, O peoples, nations and men of every language, that at the moment you hear the sound of the horn, flute, lyre, trigon, psaltery, bagpipe and all kinds of music, you are to fall down and worship the golden image that Nebuchadnezzar the king has set up. But whoever does not fall down and worship shall immediately be cast into the midst of a furnace of blazing fire."
—Daniel 3:3-6

Revelation 13:13:17-18 - The image of the Antichrist ποιεῖ πάντας [prepares everyone]... ἵνα δῶσιν [in order that they would bestow] to themselves his mark {contrast Galatians 6:17 and Revelation 7:3} on their right hand or forehead. (13:16) [The false prophet had deceived them and those who worshipped his image into receiving the mark of the beast (v. 19:20)] The image of the Antichrist prohibits all commerce for all {cf. 3:10,13:12,15-16} who do not bear the mark either of the image's name or of its name's number, "of a human ...666." Thus commences "tribulation...a great tribulation, such as has not occurred since the beginning of the world until now, nor ever shall." (Matthew 24:9,21) Concerning this mark, will it be outwardly visible on the bearer or only visible in the bearer's 'fruits', i.e., his/her character and walk?

From now on let no one cause trouble for me, for I bear on my body the brand-marks of Jesus.
—Galatians 6:17

> Angel to the four angels:
> "Do not harm the earth or the sea or the trees until we have sealed the bond-servants of our God on their foreheads."
> —Revelation 7:3

Is it possible that the dragon, the beast {who received ruling authority from the dragon (v. 13:4)} and the false prophet (v. 16:13) together with the "spirits of demons" (v. 16:14 { cf. 12:9}) were all mirroring the heavenly angels to mock the triune God and His angels?

<u>Revelation 14:9-10</u> - The third angel said with a loud voice, "If anyone worships the beast and his image, and receives a mark on his forehead or on his hand (14:9), he also will drink of the wine of the wrath of God, which is mixed in full strength in the cup of His anger:

> For a cup is in the hand of the Lord, and the wine foams; It is well mixed, and He pours out of this; Surely all the wicked of the earth must drain and drink down its dregs.
> —Psalm 75:8

> Rouse yourself! Rouse yourself! Arise, O Jerusalem, You who have drunk from the Lord's hand the cup of His anger; The chalice of reeling you have drained to the dregs.
> —Isaiah 51;17

Word of the Lord:
"With pestilence and with blood I will enter into judgment with him; and I will rain on him and

> on his troops, and on the many peoples who are with him, a torrential rain, with hailstones, fire and brimstone.
> —Ezekiel 38:22

> Jesus:
> "For whoever is ashamed of Me and My words in this adulterous and sinful generation, the Son of Man will also be ashamed of him when He comes in the glory of His Father with the holy angels."
> —Mark 8:38

Revelation 14:10-11 ...and he, i.e., the worshipper, will be tormented with fire and brimstone...And the smoke of their torment goes up forever and ever; they have no rest day and night, those who worship the beast and his image, and whoever receives the mark of his name.

> For the Yaweh has a day of vengeance, A year of recompense for the cause of Zion. Its streams will be turned into pitch, And its loose earth into brimstone, And its land will become burning pitch. It will not be quenched night or day; its smoke will go up forever. From generation to generation it will be desolate; None will pass through it forever and ever.
> —Isaiah 34:8-10

Revelation 14:12,19:10 - Here is the perseverance of τῶν ἁγίων [the holy ones] who keep the commandments of God and their faith in Jesus, "who ἐχόντων [keep] the testimony/witness of Jesus ...the πνεῦμα ["professedly divine communication - 1 Corinthians 12:10; 2 Thessalonians 2:2; 1 John 4:1-3,"(The Analytical Greek Lexicon)] of prophecy."

> Jesus:
> "unless those days had been cut short, no life would have been saved, but for the sake of the elect those days shall be cut short."
> —Matthew 24:22

Revelation 16:2,8-11 - The first angel poured "into the earth" God's wrath "and it became a loathsome and malignant boil {cf. Exodus 9:11} upon the men who had the mark of the beast and...worshipped his image." ...Another angel affected the sun "to scorch men with fire...{who} were scorched with fierce heat; and they blasphemed the name of God...and...did not repent... Another angel poured his bowl of God's wrath on the beast's throne, darkening its kingdom, all of whom blasphemed Him "because of their pain and boils and did not repent of their deeds."

Revelation 17:1-18 - Angel to John: "The beast that you saw was (vs. 13:3,12,14} and is not, is about to come up (v. 13:1) out of the abyss {"the bottomless pit" (v. 9:1); Romans 10:7 implies the abyss is שְׁאוֹל/*LXX*: ὁ ᾅδης, the spaceless area where all human souls after death are sleeping temporarily}... and goes to destruction [ἀπώλειαν {"destined for Gehenna"-John 17:12, 2 Thessalonians 2:3.}

Revelation 19:20-21 - "And the beast was seized, and with him the false prophet who performed the signs in {the former's} presence, by which he deceived those who had received the mark of the beast and those who had worshipped his image; these two were thrown ζῶντες [**exercising the functions of life**] εἰς τὴν λίμνην τοῦ πυρὸς τῆς καιομένης ἐν θείῳ [**into the lake of fire which burns with brimstone {the acrid odor of sulfur dioxide given off by lightning strikes}**]... and all the birds were killed with their flesh (indicating a covenant fulfillment?)

Revelation 20:1-3,5 - The dragon/serpent of old/the devil/Satan becomes bound by a great chain and cast into the abyss {Romans 10:7 implies the abyss is שְׁאוֹל/ *LXX*: ὁ ᾅδης, the spaceless area where all human souls after death are sleeping temporarily} for a thousand years, "so that {it} should not deceive the nations any longer" after which to "be released (but) for a short time...The rest of the dead {those other than in verse 4} did not come to life until the thousand years were completed. This is the first resurrection."

> Those who "had not revered by prostration the beast or his image and had not received the mark on their forehead and upon their hand... became possessed of vitality {cf. I John 4:9} and reigned with Christ for a thousand years."
> —Revelation 20:4

Revelation 20:10,12-15 - "And the devil...was thrown into the lake of fire and brimstone, where the beast and the false prophet are also; and they will be tortured day and night forever and ever {as will any who "worships the beast and his image and receives a mark on his forehead or upon his hand" (Revelation 14:9-11)}... And I saw the dead, the great and the small, standing before the throne, and books were opened; another book was opened, which is of life; and the dead were judged from the things which were written in the books, according to their deeds. And the sea gave up the dead which were in it, and death and ἅ ὁδης were thrown into the lake of fire. This is the second death, the lake of fire. And if anyone's name was not found written in the book of life, he was thrown into the lake of fire. I interpret the lake of fire to be employed by Yaweh for three purposes:

1. As the means for destroying all disembodied souls of those who "will pay the penalty of ὄλεθρον αώίνιον [eternal destruction] away from the presence of the Lord"(2 Thessalonians 1:9), "Who is able to destroy [ἀπολέσαι] both soul and body in γεέννῃ {the metaphor Jesus used eight times to benefit His audience's comprehension.}" (Matthew 10:28) Comprehensively speaking, anyone whose "name was not found written in the book of life...was thrown into the lake of fire." (Revelation 20:15)
2. As the eternal fiery 'prison' for "those who had received the mark of the beast and those who had worshipped his image" (Revelation 19:20) as well as for all of Satan's manifestations.

3. Also thrown into this fire will be death and Hades {the *Septuagint's* translation for שְׁאוֹל [death], "Christ's last enemy that will be abolished" (1 Corinthians 15:26.) Therefore, without death there is no life and the book of life terminates.

Now Satan's unreal, behemoth-like {cf. Job 40:15-18} manifestations described by John transform some creatures Yaweh had originally created – possibly to shock even the Apostle. The challenge though is to understand what role these manifestations, animated by the devil's angels, play in the unfolding of the 'end times.' The key to that interpretation resides I believe in these key phrases: רוּחַ־רָעָה [evil, wicked spirit] and τὸ ἀκάθαρτον πνεῦμα [the unclean spirit.] "The Breath of Yaweh departed from Saul and רוּחַ־רָעָה מֵאֵת יְהוָה/ *LXX*: πνεῦμα πονηρὸν παρὰ κυρίου [evil, wicked spirit from, of Yaweh/Lord] terrorized him." (1 Samuel 16:14) "רוּחַ־ אֱלֹהִים רָעָה / *LXX*: πνεῦμα κυρίου πονηρὸν [evil, wicked spirit of God/ Lord]" (1 Samuel 16:15 {cf.23;18:10}) Two problems appearing here need to be addressed:

1. The appearance of the preposition מֵאֵת [from] / παρὰ [from] because it implies Yaweh as the conveyor of an evil, wicked spirit into the soon-to-be-deposed king Saul in order to terrorize him. But I think the preceding phrase in verse 14, "the Breath of Yaweh departed from Saul" indicates the immediate absence of His Breath drove {cf. 1 Peter 5:8} Saul to invite the evil, wicked spirit into his then morally depraved heart; in other words,

Yaweh did not put the devil's angel into the king's heart, rather Saul had invited it in {cf. 1 Timothy 4:1}and thus was accountable for whatever that spirit accomplished with his physical body:

Jesus:
"the things which proceed out of the man are what defile the man."
—Mark 7:15

2. **Regarding** רוּחַ־אֱלֹהִים רָעָה /**LXX**: πνεῦμα κυρίου πονηρὸν **[evil, wicked spirit of God/ Lord], the preposition '*of*' implies 'belonging to', thus the Creator is possessed with an evil, wicked spirit. But the dictionary also defines '*of*' as 'made from.' Thus we become aware of angels with opposing profiles: one which obeys the voice of Yaweh's word (Psalm 103:20) and the other whom tradition has dubbed as 'fallen angels':**

"God sent רוּחַ רָעָה /*LXX*: πνεῦμα πονηρὸν
—Judges 9:23

רוּחַ יְהוָה רָעָה / *LXX*: πνεῦμα θεοῦ πονηρὸν
[evil, wicked spirit made from Yaweh/God]
—I Samuel 19:9

...our struggle is against...the spiritual {forces} made from wickedness in the heavenly {places.}
—Ephesians 6:12

...God did not spare angels when they sinned but cast them into death and committed them to pits of darkness, reserved for judgment.
—2 Peter 2:4

> ...angels who did not keep their own domain but abandoned their proper abode, {the Lord} has kept in eternal bonds under darkness for the judgment of the great day.
> —Jude 1:6

Jesus:
> "Depart from Me, accursed ones, into the eternal fire which has been prepared for the devil and his angels."
> —Matthew 25:41

Disciples:
> "Lord even the demons are subject to us in Your name."
> —Luke 10:17

The New Testament labels רוּחַ רָעָה /*LXX*: πνεῦμα πονηρὸν as the unclean spirit [τὸ ἀκάθαρτον πνεῦμα], angels who also refuse to obey their Creator:

> Jesus cast demons from two blind men into a herd of swine.
> —Matthew 9:29-30

> Jesus gave His disciples authority to cast out unclean spirits, {saying}...Heal the sick, raise the dead, cleanse lepers, cast out demons.
> —Matthew 10:1,8

> When the unclean spirit has gone out of a person, it passes through waterless places seeking rest, but finds none.
> —Matthew 12:43

A man with an uncleaned spirit [ἀκάθαρτον πνεῦμα] cried out...and Jesus rebuked him, saying. 'Be quiet and come out of him!' and the unclean spirit [τὸ ἀκάθαρτον πνεῦμα] cried out with a loud voice and came out of him.
—Mark 1:23,26

"a man...with an uncleaned spirit" [ἀκάθαρτον πνεῦμα] which introduced himself to Jesus as "Legion, for we are many... about two thousand" and He permitted Legion and fellow unclean spirits [τά ὀκάθαρτον πνεῦμα] to enter a herd of swine.
—Mark 5:2,9,13; Luke 8:27-33

And He called the twelve and began to send them out two by two, and gave them authority over the unclean spirits.
—Mark 6:7

Jesus:
"When the unclean spirit [τά ὀκάθαρτον πνεῦμα] has gone out of a person, it passes through waterless places seeking rest, and finding none it says, 'I will return to my house from which I came.'
—Luke 11:24

Now the Breath expressly says that in later times some will depart from the faith by devoting themselves to deceitful spirits and teachings of demons...
—1 Timothy 4:1-16

By this you know the Breath of God: every spirit that confesses that Jesus Christ has come in the flesh is from God, and every spirit that does not

> confess Jesus is not from God. This is the spirit of the antichrist, which you heard was coming and now is in the world already.
> —1 John 4:2-3

> For they are demonic spirits, performing signs, who go abroad to the kings of the whole world, to assemble them for battle on the great day of God the Almighty.
> —Revelation 10:16:14

Now רוּחַ-רָעָה [evil, wicked spirit] of the Abrahamic culture is akin to τὸ ἀκάθαρτον πνεῦμα [the unclean spirit] of the early church culture: both identify as angels of the devil Satan (Revelation 12:9). Now the New Testament attributes human traits attributed to his angels when in reality:

- crying and talking (Mark 1:23,26;5:2,9,13; Luke8:27-33,11:24)
- deceiving and propagating (1 Timothy 4:1)
- performing signs and advising kings abroad (Revelation 16:14)

But the unclean spirits are limited in what they can do on earth:

- Jesus and His disciples are able to evict them from human hosts (Matthew 9:29-30,10:1,8; Mark 6:7)
- When cast-out, demons seek protective shelter in swine herds (Matthew 9:29-30, Mark 5:2,9,13; Luke 8:27-33)

Satan's angels are physically limited while on earth for they rely on the shelter, strength and motions of their human hosts:

- **demonic spirits perform...signs, (and) go abroad to the kings of the whole world, to assemble them for battle on the great day of God the Almighty. (Revelation 10:16:14)**

  (The second beast {the false Prophet}) performs great signs so that he even makes fire come down out of heaven to the earth in the presence of men. And he deceives those who dwell on the earth because of the signs which it was given him to perform in the presence of the {Antichrist}, telling those who dwell on the earth to make an image to the Antichrist...there was given to {the false Prophet} to give breath to the image of the {Antichrist}, that the image of the {Antichrist} might even speak {and the false Prophet will} cause as many as do not worship the image of the {Antichrist} to be killed. And he causes all {by deception (Revelation 19:20)}, the small and the great, and the rich and the poor, and the free men and the slaves, to be given a mark on their right hand or on their forehead.
  —Revelation 13:13-17

Thus my 'take' on John's unnatural descriptions of Satan's angels is that each satanic manifestation in Revelation 13 portrays the result of a human being having permitted a devil's angel into his/her heart in order to satiate that human's sinful nature. Each

'behemoth' described by John will be invisibly harboring by invitation within the heart of a descendant of Adam and Eve. So when Jesus had warned His disciples not to be misled by anyone, He literally meant by any human - and not by any creature. Thus all believers of Jesus Christ must be on guard to prevent any person from 'deleting' their faith in Him.

Because Jesus's Matthew 24:2 prophesy {cf. John's in Revelation 6}) stands irrefutably credible inasmuch as historians have verified as truth the Jerusalem temple's destruction in 70 AD, He has to be believed when warning His disciples about the events God's Breath had portrayed allegorically to John in chapters 9-12 in Revelation:

> Jesus:
> ...This gospel of the kingdom shall be preached in the whole world as a testimony to all nations, and then the end will come...For then there will be a great tribulation, such as has not occurred since the beginning of the world until now, nor ever will...Then if anyone says to you, 'Behold, here is the Christ,' or 'There He is,' do not believe him. For false Christs and false prophets will arise and will show great signs and wonders, so as to mislead, if possible, even the elect."
> —Matthew 24:14-15,21,23-24

His credibility extends as well to what He confessed to Mary's sister, Martha:

> "I am the resurrection and the life; he who believes in Me will live even if he dies, and everyone who lives and believes in Me will never die."
> —John 11:25-26

Christ died for others' souls whereas many believers have been, are being, and will be called upon to persevere/endure in their faith even unto death in order to eternally preserve their souls, mostly in the end times. Such is this beautiful, encouraging witness of Pastor Andrew Brunson, who had been unjustly incarcerated in various prisons for 735 days by Recep Tayyip Erdogan, President of Turkey, a Muslim-dominated 'democracy':

> I understand persecution, yet I was unprepared for what happened to me. In part this is because I counted the cost for some things, but never for prison... what really broke me was unmet expectations. I expected that God would intervene to carry me above my circumstances into joy, that even in grief I would feel strength and an infusion of grace, and most importantly, that I would have a sense of {H}is presence. Instead, I felt abandoned by God. The truth is, God's faithfulness and loyalty and love are never put to the test in our difficulties; it was my faithfulness, my loyalty, my love for {H}im that was being tested...not sensing {H}is presence was part of the test. I had to learn the lesson of Isaiah 50:10: "Let him who walks in darkness and has no light trust in the name of the Lord and lean on his God." God was teaching me to stand in the dark, to persevere apart from my feelings, perceptions, and circumstances. It is clear to me, especially as I remember my weakness and brokenness, that God's grace brought me through. Mostly it was an unfelt grace, but it was there. I had a part as well: I had to cooperate with God. At every point, every time I was broken, I had a choice to make, and I chose to turn my face toward

> God. I had doubts, questions, I complained and fought with God, but eventually I would once again embrace {H}im.[141]
>
> For we are a fragrance (i.e., a pleasing sacrifice) of Christ to God among those who are being saved and among those who are perishing {ἀπόλλυμι}; to the one an aroma from death to death, to the other an aroma from life to life.
> —2 Corinthians 2:15-16

> Blessed is a man who endures/perseveres under trial, for once he has been approved he will receive the crown of life, which {Jesus} has promised to those who love Him {cf. Matthew 24:13.}
> —James 1:12

Metaphoric 'hell' {cf. Revelation 13:15,17} will affect all believers during the tribulation cited by Jesus {cf. Matthew 24:9} because survival itself will be their challenge. During it believers will experience flogging, scrounging, family/friend betrayal, hatred, testing, murder or persecution, yet with this promise from "the Alpha and the Omega" (Revelation 1:8), whom Satan had unsuccessfully tested (Luke 4:2):

> Jesus:
> "These things I have spoken to you that in Me you may have peace. In the world you have tribulation, but take courage {for} I have overcome the world.
> —John 16:33

---

141. God's Hostage, Andrew Brunson with Craig Borlase, Baker Books, 2019; page 244

> The risen Christ, Jesus, to John:
> "Because you have kept the word of My perseverance, I also will keep you from the hour of testing, that hour which is about to come upon the whole world, to test those who dwell on the earth."
> —Revelation 3:10

This tribulation is going to pose a global, two-prong attack on all saints still living: by summary execution for any who do not worship the image of the Antichrist or by starvation and unprotected exposure to the elements. Satan's threat to all believers will be to trick them deceptively {cf. Matthew 24:24; Mark 13:5-6,22; Revelation 20:8} into disobeying God:

> And Jesus said to (His twelve disciples), "You will be caused to stumble [σκανδαλίζω] (The Analytical Greek Lexicon {cf. verse 29}) because it is written (Zechariah 13:7), 'I will strike down the shepherd, and the sheep shall be scattered.'"
> —Mark 14:27

And even to the extent of causing them to abandon their faith:

> But the Spirit explicitly says {cf. John 16:13; Acts 20:23} that in later times some will fall away (ἀφίστημι – leave, desert) from the faith, paying attention to deceitful spirits and doctrines of demons, by means of the hypocrisy of liars seared in their own conscience as with a branding iron...
> —1 Timothy 4:1-2

> ...made partakers (cf. Galatians 3:2; Hebrews 2:4) of the Holy Spirit and have tasted (γεύομαι – experience) the good word of God and the powers of the age to come, and then have fallen away (παραπίπτω; The Analytical Greek Lexicon: make defection from)...
>
> —Hebrews 6:4-6

In Matthew 24 Jesus prophetically details to His disciples specific events that will appear in their future:

Vs. 4-8: Do not be misled nor frightened by many pretenders of Him as well as by war rumored or real between nations and kingdoms, for such will take place, with some famines and earthquakes following.

Vs. 9-12: You will be thrust into a tribulation, killed and hated because of My authority; many will lose faith, hate and betray one another as well as practice wicked and immoral conduct.

> ...the people will be oppressed, each one by another, and each one by his neighbor; the youth will storm against the elder and the inferior against the honorable.
>
> —Isaiah 3:5

> ...bless those who curse you, pray for those who mistreat you."
>
> —Luke 6:28

> "not knowing what will happen to me...except that the holy Breath solemnly testifies to me in every city, saying that bonds and afflictions

await me. But I do not consider my life of any account as dear to myself, in order that I may finish my course..."

—Acts 20:22-24

"...we also exult in our tribulations, knowing that tribulation brings about perseverance/endurance..."

—Romans 5:3

V. 13: Those who endure to the tribulation's finality will be rescued from its horrors.

Jesus:
"...you will be hated on account of My name {i.e., authority}, but it is the one who has endured to the end who will be rescued. But whenever they persecute you in this city, flee to the next... you shall not finish {going through} the cities of Israel until the Son of Man comes."

—Matthew 10:22-23

Jesus:
"No one after putting his hand to the plow and looking back is fit for the kingdom of God."

—Luke 9:62

Paul:
"not knowing what will happen to me...except that the holy Breath solemnly testifies to me in every city, saying that bonds and afflictions await me. But I do not consider my life of any account as dear to myself, in order that I may finish my course..."

—Acts 20:22-24

"...we also exult in our tribulations, knowing that tribulation brings about perseverance/endurance..."
—Romans 5:3

"But we have this treasure in earthen vessels that the surpassing greatness of the power may be of God and not from ourselves, afflicted in every way but not crushed, perplexed but not despairing, persecuted but not forsaken, struck down but not destroyed, always carrying about in the body the dying of Jesus that the life of Jesus also may be manifested ἐν τῷ σώματι ἡμῶν [in our body {the church}]"
—2 Corinthians 4:7-10

"God has not given us an animating force of timidity but of power and love and discipline... Suffer evils together as good soldiers of Christ Jesus...do not be ashamed of the testimony of our Lord...but join with me in suffering for the gospel according to the power of God...I have fought the good fight, I have finished the course, I have kept the faith."
—2 Timothy 1:7;2:3,8;4:7

Consider it all joy...when you encounter various trials, knowing that the testing of your faith produces endurance. And let endurance have a perfect result, that you may be perfect and complete, standing in need of nothing.
—James 1:2-4

Here is the perseverance/endurance of τῶν ἁγίων [the holy ones] who keep the commandments of God and their faith in Jesus ...who ἐχόντων

> [keep] the testimony/witness of Jesus ...the πνεῦμα ["professedly divine communication - 1 Corinthians 12:10; 2 Thessalonians 2:2; 1 John 4:1-3," {The Analytical Greek Lexicon)}] of prophecy."
> —Revelation 14:12, 19:10

V. 14: "this gospel of the kingdom {cf. 4:23} will be preached in the whole world for a witness to all nations {cf. 28:19-20}, and then the end shall come." The universal spread of His gospel is struggling today because Satan's angels are actively attacking the church's evangelistic outreaches around the world:

> As for the ten horns, out of this kingdom ten kings will arise; and another will arise after them, and he will be different from the previous ones and will subdue three kings. He will speak out against the Most High and wear down the saints of the Highest One, and he will intend to make alterations in times and in law; and they will be given into his hand for a time, times, and half a time.
> —Daniel 7:24-25

> "...our gospel is veiled,,,to those who are perishing [ἀπόλλυμι], in whose case the god of this world has blinded the minds of the unbelieving..."
> —2 Corinthians 4:3-4

Vs. 15-22: Matthew editorially {cf. Mark 13:14; Revelation 1:3} alerts his readers that when they experience the desolation prophesied by Daniel to take very seriously Jesus's charge for them to flee away to remote shelters without delay, "because there will be a great tribulation

such as not occurred since the beginning of the world, nor ever will...but for the sake of the elect {cf. 22:14} those days shall be cut short."

> ...the anointed one/Messiah [מָשִׁיחַ] {Isaiah 9:6} will be cut off and have nothing and the people of the prince who is to come will destroy the city {Jerusalem} and the sanctuary. And his end (will come) with a flood {cf. Nahum 1:8}; even to the end there will be war, desolations are determined... and on the wing of abominations {v. 11:31 – what makes desolate, causes horror}, even until a complete destruction, one that is decreed, is poured out on the one who causes horror.
> —Daniel 9:26-27

Vs. 24-28: "False Christs and false prophets will arise and will show great signs and wonders so as to mislead if possible even the elect.

Vs. 29-31: "...immediately after the tribulation of those days the sun will be darkened and the moon will not give its light and the stars will fall from the sky and the powers of the heavens will be shaken...the sign of the Son of man will appear in the sky...the tribes of the earth will mourn...and He will gather together His elect..."

Vs. 32-35: "...when (the fig tree's) branch has already become tender and puts forth its leaves, you know that summer is near, so you too, when you see all these things, recognize the {the Lord} is near, right at the door...this generation will not pass away until all these things take place. Heaven and earth will pass away..."

Vs. 42-45: "...be on the alert...be ready {as} is the faithful and sensible slave whom his master put in charge of his household to give them their food at the proper time..." {cf. Mark 13:31-33,35}

The essence of Jesus's words here is threefold: a) count on a great tribulation happening because that is what Yaweh is willing; b) prepare both physically and mentally for it and c) wisely discern its occurrence.

> **And we know that God causes all things to work together for good to those who love God, according to πρόθεσιν κλητοῖς οὖσιν [{His predetermination for those who are invited]**
> **—Romans 8:28**

"...the wickedness of man was great...that every intent of the thoughts of his heart was only evil continually" (Gen. 6:5) compelled God "to blot out {i.e., to drown most life on the earth} ...from the face of the land, from man to animals to creeping things and the birds in the sky..." (Gen.6:7) Such is the same quality and intensity of evil Jesus had prophesized that will require again the elimination of all life in our future, but not by water on earth's surface; rather it will be by man's reckless destruction of the entire earth, the epitome of mankind's uncontrolled disobedience.

At least a dozen supervolcanos are known to exist today, the prominent one being the Yellowstone Caldera, a crater tightly nestled under Yellowstone Lake in northwestern Wyoming {a magma chamber measuring 37 miles long and 18 miles wide and extending 5 miles deep into the

earth's crust.} It is believed that the earth's center is closest to the world's surface under this lake and possesses an extraordinarily destructive force that is more than 4,000 times as powerful as that of Mt. St. Helens. Its eruption occurring 2.1 million years ago was so powerful that it left in the earth a hole larger in size than the state of Rhode Island. If it were to erupt at full force again, it would bury under lava {underground molten rock that has penetrated in liquid form the earth's surface} everything within 40 miles and its cloud of brimstone [sulfur {cf. Genesis 19:24; Isaiah 30:33; Revelation 9:17-18,14:10,19:20}] and ash would spread across the entire continent. Its ash, unlike that from a burning fire, would be composed of tiny bits of rock and glass, which when inhaled would carve up a victim's lungs and cause him to cough up blood. Its weight would collapse roofs as well as threaten electrical grids by taking down the transformers. It even would poison water and soil as well as keep airplanes from flying. Ultimately it would create a volcanic winter lasting as long as a decade and thereby affect the whole world's food supply {Isaiah 3:1?} It is estimated that such an eruption is twice as likely as a severe asteroid strike of the earth. A 2017 study by Oxford's Future of Humanity Institute warned that "supervolcanoes are possibly the natural existential risk that poses the highest probability of extinction."

> For the Lord has a day of vengeance, a year of recompense for the cause of Zion. Its streams will be turned into pitch, and its loose earth into brimstone, And its land will become burning pitch. It will not be quenched night or day; its

EPILOGUE

Fraught with symbols and mysteries, the only known narrative concerning the closing phase of Yaweh's plan for life is the book of Revelation. At its completion life will have been a gracious gift bestowed by the Creator on all creatures, including those in His image. His perfectly conceived and executed plan yields Him a predetermined group of those ἐν Χριστῷ Ἰησοῦ (Romans 8:1, 1 Peter 5:14) to complement His spiritual kingdom.

All the Power and the Glory to the Father and His Son and His Holy Breath forever! Amen.

www.ingramcontent.com/pod-product-compliance
Lightning Source LLC
Chambersburg PA
CBHW080329170426
43194CB00014B/2504